Presidential Temples

CULTUREAMERICA

Karal Ann Marling
Erika Doss
Series Editors

Presidential Temples

How Memorials
and Libraries
Shape Public
Memory

For
Gail + Elgim

Thanks for coming

**Benjamin
Hufbauer**

Best wishes,
B── Hufbauer

University Press
of Kansas

Published by the University

Press of Kansas (Lawrence,

Kansas 66045), which was

organized by the Kansas

Board of Regents and is

operated and funded by

Emporia State University,

Fort Hays State University,

Kansas State University,

Pittsburg State University,

the University of Kansas, and

Wichita State University

Library of Congress Cataloging-in-Publication Data

Hufbauer, Benjamin.
  Presidential temples : how memorials and libraries shape
    public memory / Benjamin Hufbauer.
    p.   cm. — (CultureAmerica)
Includes bibliographical references and index.
ISBN 0-7006-1422-2 (cloth : alk. paper)
1. Presidents—Monuments—United States. 2. Presidential
    libraries—United States. 3. Library architecture—United
    States. 4. Memorials—United States. 5. Memory—Social
    aspects—United States. I. Title. II. Culture America.
E176.1.H845 2006
  973.09′9—dc22   2005026802

British Library Cataloguing-in-Publication Data is available.

Printed in the United States of America
10 9 8 7 6 5 4 3 2 1

The paper used in this publication meets the minimum
requirements of the American National Standard for
Permanence of Paper for Printed Library Materials
z39.48-1984.

To my wife, Bess Reed, my parents, Sally and Karl Hufbauer,

and my children, Emory and Eleanor.

Ozymandias

I met a traveller from an antique land,

Who said—"two vast and trunkless legs of stone

Stand in the desert. . . . near them, on the sand,

Half sunk a shattered visage lies, whose frown,

And wrinkled lips, and sneer of cold command,

Tell that its sculptor well those passions read

Which yet survive, stamped on these lifeless things,

The hand that mocked them, and the heart that fed;

And on the pedestal these words appear:

My name is Ozymandias, King of Kings,

Look on my Works ye Mighty, and despair!

Nothing beside remains. Round the decay

Of that colossal Wreck, boundless and bare

The lone and level sands stretch far away."

—Percy Bysshe Shelley (1792–1822)

CONTENTS

ILLUSTRATIONS

ACKNOWLEDGMENTS

The genesis of this book lies in Africa. When I was in Nigeria assisting my wife, Dr. Bess Reed, with her dissertation research, we had discussions late into the night in our apartment in Enugu about African art. At that time I was preparing for my minor examination in African art and had compiled a long list of books to read, which included *African Arts of Leadership*, cowritten by our advisor, Herbert M. Cole of the University of California at Santa Barbara. I began to think about the arts of leadership in the United States, and suddenly, from a continent away, they seemed strange to me. And so my first thanks go to Skip Cole for his insightful lectures and writings on the arts of leadership in cross-cultural context. Ulrich Keller, my advisor, encouraged and supported my decision to undertake my somewhat unusual art historical study after we returned from Africa. Ulrich has always been a source of intellectual stimulation on a great variety of topics, and his inspiring and often humorous lectures greatly aided my own development as a teacher and scholar. Bruce Robertson, Ann Bermingham, Constance Penley, and the late David Gebhard all provided crucial intellectual stimulation and support over the years. This book grew out of my dissertation, but it is different enough in focus and approach to constitute almost a completely different work.

Since my arrival at the University of Louisville, Erika Doss has provided the most important touchstone for my career. Her many outstanding books, as well as her personal guidance, have inspired my professional studies. Carol Krinsky and Alice Friedman have also been rigorous editors and kind mentors. Will Morgan has offered keen architectural insights into these presidential shrines.

This study would not have been possible without the assistance of the professional staffs at the various presidential libraries where I conducted archival research. I would especially like to thank the following people, some of whom have retired, for helping me with my archival work, as well as for sharing their insights about presidential libraries: Larry Hackman, Raymond Geselbracht, Clay Bauske, Tom Heuertz, Judi O'Neill, and Liz Safly of the Truman Library; Martin Teasly and Dennis Medina of the Eisenhower Library; Mark Renovitch, Wendell "Tex" Parks, Verne Newton, John Ferris, and Herman Eberhardt of the Roosevelt Library; Susan Naulty of the

Nixon Library; and Richard Jacobs of the Office of Presidential Libraries in Washington, D.C. Claudia Anderson, of the Johnson Library, had an amazing ability to track down information hidden within the shelves of the millions of documents of the Johnson Library, and she also provided crucial insights into her institution and gave me an unforgettable architectural tour.

At the Smithsonian, Edith Mayo and Tracy Robinson offered essential help. Robinson was an indefatigable digger in the vast archives of that institution, while Mayo offered me her personal experience of what it was like to curate an exhibit in the 1990s on the first ladies.

At my academic home at the University of Louisville, I thank the chair of the Fine Arts Department, Professor James Grubola, for his unwavering support of my work, including teaching relief and support for grant applications. Over the years I have enjoyed many conversations with my colleagues in Fine Arts, and I appreciate their support. I would also like to thank Gail Gilbert, Nancy Alexander, and Janice Blair.

At the University Press of Kansas, I would particularly like to thank Nancy Scott Jackson for her support, superb editing, and sense of humor. I also appreciate the valuable anonymous reviews of the manuscript that the press commissioned. I also thank Susan Schott for her excellent marketing efforts, Larisa Martin for her outstanding work in preparing the manuscript for publication, Karl Janssen for the jacket design, and Ranjit Arab for his work on publicity.

My writing group—which consists of three insightful English professors at the University of Louisville, Susan Ryan, Karen Chandler, and Carol Mattingly—edited my work with sensitivity, precision, and dedication over many years. I will never forget their help.

I would also like to acknowledge three of my undergraduate teachers who gave me the foundation I needed to pursue a career in art history: Donna Hunter, Reyner Banham, and Virginia Janson of the University of California at Santa Cruz. I can still hear Banham's voice and see the twinkle in his eye when I read his books. Hunter was such a gifted teacher, that she convinced me to major in art history, and provided me with intellectual nurturance when I was an undergraduate.

I dedicate this book to my beloved wife, Bess Reed, and to my parents, Sally and Karl Hufbauer. For many years now, Bess has brainstormed with me, edited text, organized illustrations, solved computer problems, and found footnotes. My parents gave me essential and constant support, emotional, intellectual, and financial, and also assisted greatly with editing.

And my sisters, Ruthie and Sarah Beth, pulled me through when I was in doubt. Our son, Emory, and our daughter, Eleanor, always helped by giving me their tremendous love and by showing me how smart little people are. My book topic was born before they were, but they grew faster, which somehow made sense because I always loved them so much more.

INTRODUCTION The Transformation of Presidential Commemoration

Since 1940 the rise of the federal presidential library has transformed presidential commemoration. Its emergence marks the dramatic increase in presidential authority that has occurred during an era when the United States has become the most powerful nation in the world. A presidential library is a monument—but also a history museum and an archive. What is at stake in the transformation of presidential commemoration is how power is remembered and how these constructed memories of power shape contemporary and future presidential authority. Because federal presidential libraries are created and partially supported by private foundations created by a president and his supporters, but run by the National Archives and Records Administration, there is a tension in these institutions between authenticity and reproduction, between education and entertainment, and between history and "heritage."

As historian Michael Kammen has written, the heritage industry has advanced "an impulse to remember what is attractive or flattering and to ignore all the rest."[1] This is exactly what most presidents want at their presidential libraries, because most presidents, even if they would not phrase it this way, hope to find a place for themselves in what has been called the civil religion of the United States—that veneration that has existed since the country's founding for particular events, people, and things.

This study is primarily, but not exclusively, about presidential libraries and the transformation of presidential commemoration that they represent. As prologue to this transformation, it opens with a site dedicated to one of the most important "saints" in the American civil religion, the Lincoln Memorial, which marks the beginnings of the transition. Though such monuments remain compelling, there has been a profound transformation of presidential commemoration since the Lincoln Memorial was dedicated in 1922. The presidential monuments of the past—the obelisks and classical temples built by and for posterity—have largely been replaced by presidential libraries, built outside of Washington, D.C. Since Franklin Delano

Roosevelt's library was completed in 1940 in Hyde Park, New York, every president has had a hand in designing his own memorial.

These libraries enshrine not just national dreams but also national nightmares. The presidential nightmare, the flip side of the dream that any American can become president, is that a president will plunge the nation into crisis—as Lyndon Johnson did with the Vietnam War or as Richard Nixon did with Watergate. Although presidential libraries initially present a heroic view of their subjects, the Johnson Library in Austin, Texas, and the Nixon Library in Yorba Linda, California, reflect—whether consciously or unconsciously—these presidential nightmares.[2] Their museum displays, and even their architecture, speak eloquently of these presidents' personalities and the crises they engendered.

For instance, at the Nixon Library a dimly lit room with a computer display with headphones allows visitors access to the library's version of the Watergate scandal. Visitors listen to a short section of one of the Watergate tapes—one of the so-called smoking gun sections—with a word-for-word transcription appearing on the computer screen. The tape seems to show President Nixon trying to stop the investigation of the Watergate scandal—in other words, obstructing justice—but the voice-over interpretation provided alongside the transcription attempts to demonstrate that that is not what Nixon is saying at all. By the library's account, the entire scandal boils down to the misinterpretation of a few words. Visitors, if they believe this interpretation, see the smoking gun vanish and wonder how this misunderstanding about a few words could possibly have brought down Nixon's presidency.

If the Nixon Library reveals aspects of Nixon's stonewalling in its displays, the Johnson Library reveals aspects of President Johnson's overbearing personality in its architecture. The library, completed in 1971, was designed by architect Gordon Bunshaft. Its Italian travertine–clad form looms 85 feet in the air—compared to 80 feet for the Lincoln Memorial—and visually overwhelms approaching visitors. The building symbolizes Johnson himself, in Bunshaft's words, "an aggressive . . . big man,"[3] who forcefully used the federal government and his own personality to push his agenda, from the Great Society to Vietnam.[4]

Presidential Libraries as Expressions of Modern Presidential Power

The Johnson Library, like other presidential libraries, may lack the immediate emotional power of the Lincoln Memorial, but in other ways it surpasses its predecessor. The Johnson Library's museum has extensive exhibits, periodically redesigned and updated, covering Johnson's entire life. The library's massive archive includes more than thirty million documents relating to Johnson's political career, as well as hundreds of thousands of photographs, miles of film, and thousands of hours of audiotape and videotape.[5] Spread over eight floors, the Johnson Library has 119,000 square feet of floor space, compared to roughly 9,200 square feet for the central interior of the Lincoln Memorial.[6] Standing next to the Johnson Library, the Johnson School of Public Affairs, part of the University of Texas at Austin, turns out scores of graduates each year, many of whom go on to serve in the public sector.

But the presidential library as a commemorative form is even more than the sum of these practical functions. The presidential library reflects the extraordinary power of modern presidents—in domestic, foreign, and cultural affairs. This kind of federal commemoration is not given to chief justices of the Supreme Court or to leaders of Congress.[7] A central theme of this book is that the presidential library is a symptom of the striking expansion of presidential authority that has occurred during an era when the United States has become the most powerful country in the world. As historian Arthur M. Schlesinger, Jr., asserted in his classic 1973 book, *The Imperial Presidency*, the modern presidency is "the imperial presidency"—an office that has disrupted the balance of power among the branches of government by absorbing a seemingly ever-greater share for itself.[8] U.S. presidents, starting with Franklin Roosevelt, have become some of the most powerful people in history. Decisions that modern presidents make in the Oval Office at times affect the fate of a significant part of the world.

The idea that presidents since the 1930s are some of the most powerful people in history might seem remarkable. And in some ways American presidential power is constrained compared to, for example, the power wielded by Roman emperors or twentieth-century dictators. Ancient emperors and modern dictators may have approached absolute power within their domains, but their realms of power—even when as large as the Roman Empire—pale next to the power of modern American presidents to project massive force across the globe, from Korea to Iraq. And to state the obvious, this power is not theoretical but actual. Several American presidents since Franklin Roosevelt have, usually with little interference from the other branches of government, engaged in wars that have profoundly affected several nations around the world.

This is surprising, because the Constitution states that "the Congress shall have Power to declare War."[9] This power is not shared with the president, although he is "Commander in Chief of the Army and Navy . . . when called into the actual Service of the United States."[10] Especially since World War II, however, some lapses in strictly following the Constitution serve to illustrate the growing power of the presidency—a power commemorated in presidential libraries. For example, on 24 June 1950, as President Harry Truman vacationed at his home in Independence, Missouri—just a few blocks from where his presidential library would later be built—he received a call from Secretary of State Dean Acheson informing him that North Korea had launched an invasion of South Korea. "My father made it clear," Truman's daughter, Margaret, later wrote, "from the moment he first heard the news, that he feared this was the opening of World War III."[11] A few days later in Washington, D.C., Truman committed the United States to war in Korea, a conflict that would eventually cost 54,000 American lives. Truman never sought or obtained any approval from Congress, for he wanted to assert the president's authority to conduct military affairs without congressional consent.[12] The Truman Library depicts Truman's expansive authority in foreign affairs through coverage of the Korean War, as well as the Marshall Plan, the Berlin Airlift, and the founding of NATO.

When we think of presidential power in foreign affairs since 1945, beyond the president's ability to shape policy or even initiate wars, the power of presidents to authorize the use of nuclear weapons comes to mind. Truman is the only president ever to use nuclear weapons in war, and this is the action for which he is probably most remembered.[13] In the Oval Office on 14 August 1945, after the destruction of Hiroshima and Nagasaki, Truman announced Japan's surrender. No nuclear weapons have been used in combat since, but some presidents have considered their use.[14] The president's nuclear authority is part of the backdrop at most presidential libraries and, I believe, part of what underlies the spread of Oval Office displays in presidential libraries across the country, beginning with the Truman Library. These life-size Oval Office replicas provide a symbol-laden environment in which to think about the president's nuclear authority.

Although nothing can match the potentially world-altering power modern presidents have in foreign affairs, in domestic affairs the modern presidency has also had the potential to create sweeping changes. On 14 August 1935, for instance, Roosevelt signed into law the Social Security Act, the most far-reaching piece of New Deal legislation. Before Social Security, devastating poverty among a significant percentage of the elderly was an entrenched part of American life. After Social Security, destitution among the elderly was largely eliminated. Other presidential initiatives, such as Medicare, the Environmental Protection Agency, and the establishment of the Corporation for Public Broadcasting, have had substantial social, environmental, and cultural effects on the nation.

Just as importantly, beginning with FDR and the Great Depression, the president became responsible for the economy. Before Roosevelt, presidents were certainly blamed when the bottom dropped out of the economy, but before FDR not a single president did much about it. And so presidents such as Herbert Hoover were thrown out of office for not controlling a problem that they considered largely beyond their purview. Since Roosevelt, presidents have taken seriously their responsibility for maintaining the economy, especially during election years, by trying—not always successfully—to engineer prosperity. Thus the economy and domestic policy figure prominently in most presidential libraries.

Overall, the concentration of power in the president in both domestic and foreign affairs has meant that the spectacle offered by the presidency far overpowers those offered by the other branches of government. The president often has cinematically designed stage props to use in making dramatic pronouncements, sign legislation, commit troops to foreign wars, and visit them on the battlefield—all of which are magnified by the mass media. In contrast, the Supreme Court works behind closed doors, and Congress debates legislation. Since the beginning of the Republic, national identity and the presidency have been linked, and it is not surprising that, as one textbook puts it, "for most Americans the president is the focal point of public life."[15] The president has become for some the person who embodies the nation, and the presidential library is a material manifestation of this reality.

It is not a coincidence that Roosevelt, the first president to garner the kind of power—and celebrity—that we expect of a modern president, was also the first to have a federal presidential library.[16] In fact, FDR invented the presidential library as we know it by thinking of his life as a tourist attraction and heritage site. On viewing Egypt's pyramids during World War II, Roosevelt said that "man's desire to be remembered is colossal," and what he observed about the pharaohs was true of himself and his successors.[17]

Percy Bysshe Shelley's 1818 poem "Ozymandias" highlights the folly of political ambition for immortality when compared to the expanse of time.[18] Ozymandias was the Greek name for Ramses II (1304–1237 B.C.), Egypt's pharaoh during the time of Moses and one of the greatest builders in history. Ramses II left statues and temples dedicated to the glory of his reign— from the 65-foot-high statues carved into the sandstone cliffs at Abu Simbel to the engraved exploits of the pharaoh at Karnak. American presidential temples—such as Lyndon Johnson's, which looks like a cross between an ancient Egyptian pylon temple and a space-age bureaucracy—project a similar desire for immortality. We might prefer to think of our political commemoration as being altogether different from the pyramids of Egypt or the temples dedicated to the Caesars for the Roman imperial cult,[19] but there are similarities. On the most fundamental level, much presidential commemoration in the twentieth and twenty-first centuries is an assertion of ego and power—an attempt to claim immortality and induce political veneration—just as it was for Egyptian pharaohs and Roman emperors.

Presidential libraries are part of what has been called the civil religion of the United States. The term "civil religion" was first used by Jean-Jacques Rousseau at the end of The Social Contract, where he imagined an ideal society tied together by a rather abstract faith in a benevolent deity combined with veneration for "the sanctity of the social contract and of the laws."[20] In a 1967 article, sociologist Robert N. Bellah stated that civil religion, although largely unrecognized, was a reality in the United States:

> What we have, then, from the earliest years of the republic is a collection of beliefs, symbols, and rituals with respect to sacred things and institutionalized in a collectivity. . . . The Declaration of Independence and the Constitution were the sacred scriptures and Washington the divinely appointed Moses who led his people out of the hands of tyranny. The Civil War . . . was the second great event that involved the national self-understanding so deeply as to require expression in civil religion. . . . In this way, the civil religion was able to build up . . . powerful symbols of national solidarity and to mobilize deep levels of personal motivation for the attainment of national goals. . . . It is concerned that America be a society as perfectly in accord with the will of God as men can make it.[21]

American civil religion has at least four elements: "saints," such as Washington and Lincoln; sacred places, such as Mount Vernon and the Lincoln Memorial; sacred objects, such as the Declaration of Independence and the Constitution; and, finally, ritual practices, such as the Pledge of Allegiance, Fourth of July celebrations, and pilgrimages to sacred sites.[22] Bellah's thesis led to a wave of scholarship on civil religion in various periods in American history, as well as to attacks on the idea as merely an idealization of patriotism. Bellah denied that the idea of civil religion supported national self-idolization and argued instead that it was a tool for understanding aspects of American history and life and a means of guarding against uncritical patriotism.[23] More recently, Marcela Cristi has argued that the study of civil religion needs to take into account how it may be used to spread patriotic propaganda in order to "force group identity and to legitimize an existing political order by injecting a transcendental dimension or a religious gloss on the justification."[24]

Presidential libraries are an attempt to construct sites that have all four of the elements of civil religion. They are meant to be sacred national places where pilgrimages can be made to see relics and reconstructions of presidential history, all in order to elevate in the national consciousness presidents who, even if figures lesser than Washington or Lincoln, are represented as worthy of patriotic veneration. They certainly are part of the civil religion of the United States. But the more important question is, what is the nature of that religion—Bellah's more positive vision or Cristi's more critical one?—and what is the part that they play in it? At some times and places, such as during the Revolution, scholars have convincingly argued that there was a substantial voluntary and spontaneous component to civil religion—that is, although it was a strong pillar of the state, the state did not need to do much actively to support it because of the outpouring of feeling that made it part of popular political culture.[25] Presidential libraries, in contrast, at times fit better with a reading of civil religion that sees it as having ties to state propaganda. Presidential libraries are temples that promote the best possible place for their subjects within civil religion.

Inevitably, presidential commemoration is not merely about the power of presidents—white, male, and rich—but also about questions of race, gender, national identity, and even national destiny. Presidential memorials can be nodal points for the negotiation of who we are as a people and where we are going, politically and culturally. Each presidential monument not only represents that president but also projects an image of the nation, and an ideology, into the future. The obelisks, temples, and presidential libraries that commemorate presidents are ideologically charged spectacles of history and personality meant to inspire reverence for the presidency. Presidential monuments present narratives about the Union, whiteness, the cult of the presidency, the economy, the Cold War, and civil rights to their audiences. Audiences do not just passively receive these narratives, however, but sometimes actively reconstruct them.

The bigger picture that *Presidential Temples* paints is that increasing presidential power has led to a new kind of presidential commemoration: self-commemoration—a development simultaneously ominous and practical. It is ominous because only when the presidency broke out of its former boundaries of power did the presidential library become an accepted form of commemoration. The presidential library promotes the imperial presidency that it commemorates. But the presidential library is also practical because it provides a convenient means to preserve and display the vast collections and significant events that are part of the power of the modern presidency. Whether looked at as practical, ominous, or a combination of the two, however, the stakes are high. What is ultimately reflected in the transformation of presidential commemoration is the nature of our constitutional government and the balance of power among its branches.

Presidential Temples: How Memorials and Libraries Shape Public Memory is made up of a series of case studies, each focusing on a particular monument, or a specific part of a monument, showing how presidential commemoration has unfolded and what it means. It focuses almost exclusively on federal presidential commemoration, in other words, on sites that are run by and owe their existence to the national government. The subject of presidential commemoration—from stamps and coins, to preserved homes, to Mount Rushmore, is almost limitless. This book focuses much more narrowly on the presidential temples sponsored or run by the federal government, from the Lincoln Memorial constructed beginning in 1914 to the Clinton Presidential Center dedicated in Little Rock, Arkansas, in 2004.

Each commemorative example, it is important to note, is analyzed as a separate entity. Although overarching themes exist, such as the aggrandizement of presidential power, this study examines individually and on its own terms each monument that brought presidential commemoration to the next stage in its development. In the prologue, I examine the way that the Lincoln Memorial addressed the issue of equality in national identity and how it became the culmination of the traditional presidential memorial. The chapter on the Roosevelt Library, the first federal presidential library, examines the ways in which this monument pointed toward the future of presidential commemoration. The next chapter looks at the Truman Library's Oval Office replica. The Truman Library featured the first Oval Office replica found in a presidential library that, when paired with a painting by Thomas Hart Benton, created a combined narrative about Manifest Destiny and the Cold War. The architecture of the Johnson Library is examined as a reflection of LBJ's personality as well as of the imperial presidency. First ladies, usually neglected in presidential memorials before the presidential library, were first commemorated in the Smithsonian early in the twentieth century. This chapter in some ways stands apart from the other studies in the book, but the Smithsonian is an important cultural temple in the United States and one that pioneered, in its own contested ways, the commemoration of women in national political life. The exhibits on the first ladies at the Smithsonian also influenced the displays on first ladies at presidential libraries. Finally, the chapter on the new displays at the Truman Library reveals how, even within an institution that by its very existence elevates The Imperial Presidency, critical and thought-provoking museum displays are possible. The Truman Library is not merely a temple but also a forum where history is challenged by curators and historians, as well as by students and tourists, demonstrating how a mature library can evolve to become a place where cautionary and inquisitive approaches to history are practiced.

PROLOGUE The Words in the Lincoln Memorial

The Lincoln Memorial, dedicated to a Civil War president revered by many but reviled by others, is the most important presidential monument built thus far. Featuring a combination of words and sculpture, it anticipated the museum displays in presidential libraries. More importantly, the Lincoln Memorial holds a poignant place in our national memory and identity because it has come to symbolize equality.

The Lincoln Memorial consists of four elements—the temple itself, designed by architect Henry Bacon; the huge statue of Lincoln by sculptor Daniel Chester French; two murals by artist Jules Guérin; and, most importantly, Abraham Lincoln's Gettysburg Address and Second Inaugural Address, engraved in beautiful serif letters in tablets on the side walls. In most interpretations of the memorial, however, Lincoln's speeches are given little attention. For instance, Scott Sandage in his groundbreaking article, "A Marble House Divided," affirms Dixon Wector's 1940 comment that Lincoln's speeches have been "worn so smooth by a million tongues that we are not apt to feel the edge of Lincoln's words,"[1] and he leaves it at that. Kirk Savage, in his insightful article, states that "Lincoln's own speech carved on the right describes the war as divine retribution for slavery's offense,"[2] but he goes no further. And Christopher Thomas's outstanding book on the Lincoln Memorial devotes a very small percentage of its pages to Lincoln's words.[3]

There is a separate literature, however, not about the memorial, but about Lincoln's words—and specifically about the Gettysburg Address and the Second Inaugural. This literature analyzes the profound impact these two speeches have had on national identity. To give just one example, George Fletcher's recent book, *Our Secret Constitution: How Lincoln Redefined American Democracy*, analyzes what he sees as the legal revolution that Lincoln's words reflected and contributed to during the Civil War.[4]

I believe that Lincoln's words were and are central to the Lincoln Memorial's meaning. These words helped shift national identity before—but

The Lincoln Memorial. Architect: Henry Bacon; sculptor: Daniel Chester French; muralist: Jules Guerin. Photo, Benjamin Hufbauer.

more importantly after—they were placed in the monument, which became a focal point of the civil religion of the United States. They did so by appealing to the ideal of equality found in the Declaration of Independence, which Lincoln described as "an abstract truth, applicable to all men and all times."[5] Ultimately, our government is a government of words as well as one of people, and our national identity often hangs on the meanings of words. And perhaps no words are more important to our national identity— not even the words in the Constitution—than the words in the Lincoln Memorial. There is still conflict over the meaning of these words that is playing itself out, among other places in the U.S. Supreme Court. As Harry Jaffa has written, "The Confederacy is alive and well" in the legal thinking of the right wing of the Supreme Court. Jaffa concludes that "the Union victory at Appomattox has not been accompanied by . . . [an] ascendancy of the principles of the Gettysburg Address."[6]

The Lincoln Memorial

Before getting to the words in the Lincoln Memorial, however, we should look briefly at the building within which they are found. The me-

Statue of Abraham Lincoln in the Lincoln Memorial. Sculptor: Daniel Chester French. Photo courtesy Bess Reed.

morial's architect, Henry Bacon, designed a modified Greek temple, with the entryway on one of the longer sides (Greek temples, like the Parthenon, were entered from the shorter sides). The Greeks, as is commonly known, not only gave birth to democracy but were also slaveholders. Critics of the building have correctly pointed out that several of its features appeal to the idea of Union but attempt to blot out the issue of equality and the problem of slavery in U.S. history. Not only was the architecture tied to slavery's

... GIVES TO BOTH NORTH AND SOUTH THIS
TERRIBLE WAR AS THE WOE DUE TO THOSE BY
WHOM THE OFFENSE CAME SHALL WE DIS-
CERN THEREIN ANY DEPARTURE FROM
THOSE DIVINE ATTRIBUTES WHICH THE
BELIEVERS IN A LIVING GOD ALWAYS ASCRIBE
TO HIM. FONDLY DO WE HOPE — FERVENTLY
DO WE PRAY — THAT THIS MIGHTY SCOURGE
OF WAR MAY SPEEDILY PASS AWAY · YET IF
GOD WILLS THAT IT CONTINUE UNTIL ALL
THE WEALTH PILED BY THE BONDSMAN'S
TWO HUNDRED AND FIFTY YEARS OF UN-
REQUITED TOIL SHALL BE SUNK AND
UNTIL EVERY DROP OF BLOOD DRAWN WITH
THE LASH SHALL BE PAID BY ANOTHER
DRAWN WITH THE SWORD AS WAS SAID THREE
THOUSAND YEARS AGO SO STILL IT MUST
BE SAID "THE JUDGMENTS OF THE LORD
ARE TRUE AND RIGHTEOUS ALTOGETHER."
WITH MALICE TOWARD NONE WITH CHARITY
FOR ALL WITH FIRMNESS IN THE RIGHT AS ...

Portion of Lincoln's Second Inaugural Address inside the Lincoln Memorial. Photo courtesy Bess Reed.

history, but the temple's thirty-six columns refer to the thirty-six states re-united through the Civil War,[7] implying that the preservation of the Union rather than the elimination of slavery was the primary reason Lincoln was considered worthy of commemoration by the white Americans responsible for the monument's design. Finally, the inscription over French's sculpture refers exclusively to the Union. It reads, "IN THIS TEMPLE / AS IN THE HEARTS OF THE PEOPLE / FOR WHOM HE SAVED THE UNION / THE MEMORY OF ABRAHAM LINCOLN / IS ENSHRINED FOREVER." Royal Cortissoz, the author of the inscription, explained what he intended his words to do: "The memorial must make a common ground for the meeting of the north and the south. By emphasizing his saving the union you appeal to both sections. By saying nothing about slavery you avoid the rubbing of old sores."[8]

Lincoln himself, however, rubs the sores of those nostalgic for the Confederacy in his speeches engraved on the side walls of the monument. The first words on the south wall—"Four score and seven years ago"—are words so familiar that we might neglect their political meaning. The eighty-seven years Lincoln refers to point not to the Constitution of 1787 but in-stead to the Declaration of Independence of 1776, and specifically to five words in that document that Lincoln repeats verbatim: "All men are created equal." Abraham Lincoln spent much of his life thinking about the meaning of these five words. In fact, in studying Lincoln's papers it becomes clear that he was obsessed with them. Nothing else in the Declaration or the Constitution—aside from the idea of the Union itself—was of comparable importance to him, and in fact Lincoln trampled a good deal on the other parts of the Constitution when he was president.

To understand the Gettysburg Address and the Second Inaugural, which were the culmination of a lifetime of political thought, it is helpful to illuminate their meaning with some of Lincoln's earlier words. Shortly after Lincoln was elected president, and during the time that some states in the South were in the process of seceding, Lincoln wrote a fragment of text for his own reflection:

> All this is not the result of accident. It has a philosophical cause . . .
> entwining itself . . . closely around the human heart. That something is the
> principle of "Liberty to All." . . . The expression of that principle, in our
> Declaration of Independence . . . has proved an "apple of gold" to us. The
> Union and the Constitution are the picture of silver subsequently framed
> around it. The picture was made not to conceal or destroy the apple, but to
> adorn and preserve it. The picture was made for the apple—not the apple
> for the picture.[9]

Lincoln was a creative constitutional thinker, because for him the most important part of the Constitution was not even in the Constitution at all—it was in those five words about equality in the Declaration. As Lincoln himself said, "I have never had a feeling politically that did not spring from the sentiments embodied in the Declaration of Independence."[10] When Lincoln referred to the Declaration with the sentence, "Four score and seven years ago our fathers brought forth on this continent a new nation, conceived in Liberty, and dedicated to the proposition that all men are created equal," it was to define the meaning not just of the Civil War, but of the entire nation and its foundation.

But was Lincoln reading this foundation correctly? The words Lincoln was preoccupied by were written by slaveholder Thomas Jefferson. Jefferson criticized slavery, but aside from his words in the Declaration and in his Notes on Virginia he did nothing about it.[11] In any case, it is fair to say that Lincoln overestimated the founders' actual desire for equality. Lincoln felt that the nation's essential core was this ideal of equality, obviously not immediately realized, but an equality that would eventually include more and more people. For example, at the age of twenty-eight Lincoln wrote in favor of woman's suffrage, eighty-four years before this right was achieved.[12] Ultimately, it can be argued that Jefferson never believed in his most famous words, whereas Lincoln—at least more than Jefferson—did.

However, the progress toward equality that Lincoln felt the Declaration of Independence promised was not being fulfilled as Lincoln became more politically active during the 1850s. Slavery was not the only issue. There was also the rising power of the nativist Know-Nothing Party. Lincoln wrote in 1855,

> As a nation, we began by declaring that "all men are created equal." We now practically read it "all men are created equal, except negroes." When the Know-Nothings get control, it will read "all men are created equal, except negroes, and foreigners, and catholics." When it comes to this I should prefer emigrating to some country where they make no pretense of loving liberty—to Russia, for instance, where despotism can be taken pure, and without the base alloy of hypocracy [sic].[13]

On the north wall of the Lincoln Memorial is the Second Inaugural Address, written as the Civil War neared conclusion. Its most famous words are in the long last sentence that begins, "With malice toward none; with charity for all," but Frederick Douglass, who heard Lincoln deliver the speech, believed that the most important words are actually those that come just before. Douglass recited these words from memory at Lincoln's funeral six weeks after the speech was given:

> Fondly do we hope—fervently do we pray—that this mighty scourge of war may speedily pass away. Yet, if God wills that it continue, until all the wealth piled by the bond-man's two hundred and fifty years of unrequited toil shall be sunk, and until every drop of blood drawn with the lash, shall be paid by another drawn with the sword, as was said three thousand years ago, so still it must be said, "the judgments of the Lord, are true and righteous altogether."

Perhaps most important in the Second Inaugural was Lincoln's reference to divine justice. The Second Inaugural, however, was not initially well received, and most newspapers criticized it, including even the normally supportive *New York Herald*, which said it was full of "glittering generalities."[14] Lincoln himself explained the poor reception of the speech as a negative reaction to his theme. Lincoln wrote, "I believe it is not immediately popular.

Men are not flattered by being shown that there has been a difference of purpose between the Almighty and them. To deny it, however, in this case, is to deny that there is a God governing the world."[15] Both before and after his election, Lincoln repeatedly said that slavery was incompatible not only with the nation's principles but also with reason and with God. Slavery conflicted with reason because it was a self-evident truth that a person was a person, no matter what the color. As Harry Jaffa has noted, in terms of logic and rationality, saying that all men are created equal is like saying that all chairs are chairs. It is not just a truth, it is a truism.[16] And this self-evident truth was for Lincoln divinely sanctioned.

Southern supporters of slavery and secession believed that no distinction could or should ever be made between the protections given in the Constitution to various liberties and the protections in the Constitution given to slavery.[17] Lincoln, on the other hand, felt that distinctions must be made between the Constitution's principles and its compromises—between the apple of equality that the nation promised and some parts of the frame that had been made to preserve the Union at its foundation. Before the Civil War began, Lincoln felt bound to reluctantly support the protections given to slavery—and Lincoln's position, not surprisingly, disgusted abolitionists, such as Frederick Douglass. But Lincoln also consistently denounced slavery as wrong. As Lincoln once said, "If slavery is not wrong, nothing is wrong."[18] The election of a man who believed in these words was the immediate reason that believers in slavery attempted to dissolve the Union, which brought about the Civil War.

If, for Lincoln, the most important part of the Constitution was not even included in its text, it became clear during the Civil War that Lincoln did not care as much about many parts of the Constitution that were actually stated there. Lincoln violated the letter and spirit of the Constitution several times during his term in order to prosecute the Civil War, by, for instance, censoring the press, suspending the writ of habeas corpus, and taking over many of the powers of Congress. As even admiring biographer David Herbert Donald writes, Lincoln's term in office saw "greater infringements on individual liberties than in any other period in American history."[19]

Lincoln's devaluation of many of the specific words in the Constitution during the Civil War and his elevation of the ideas of both a mystical perpetual Union,[20] and of those five words in the Declaration about equality, made the Gettysburg Address and Second Inaugural of overriding importance to national identity. As George Fletcher writes, Lincoln's speeches are in a sense the preamble of a second Constitution, made permanently part of the original Constitution through the Thirteenth, Fourteenth, and Fifteenth Amendments, which banned slavery, granted citizenship to all persons born or naturalized in the United States, and ensured the right to vote regardless of race. The problem was that in the late nineteenth century and for much of the twentieth century this new Constitution granting more complete citizenship to more people was largely overturned by segregation and disenfranchisement. Segregation, as many have noted, was found even at the Lincoln Memorial's dedication ceremony on 30 May 1922, where a separate and unequal area was set up for the African Americans who attended the ceremony.[21]

Several events since the memorial's dedication—analyzed by Sandage, Savage, and Thomas, among others—such as Marian Anderson's concert in 1939 and the "I Have a Dream" speech of Martin Luther King, Jr., in 1963, have transformed the monument from a racist temple about the Union into a symbol of equality. The most important of these events was, of course, King's address, which came at a crucial moment in the civil rights movement. It has been suggested that King overcame the racist conception that whites had when they designed the memorial. This is true, but it was crucial to the success of King's speech that it had textual support inside the monument. Indeed, King's speech and Lincoln's words have a strongly overlapping theme—that of human equality legitimated both by the Declaration and by religious values. King's speech begins, "Five score years ago, a great American, in whose symbolic shadow we stand signed the Emancipation Proclamation." The "five score" with which King begins is a deliberate reference to the beginning of the Gettysburg Address. King's speech continues:

> This momentous decree came as a beacon of light of hope to millions of Negro slaves who had been seared in the flames of withering injustice. . . . When the architects of our republic wrote the magnificent words of the Constitution and the Declaration of Independence, they were signing a promissory note to which every American was to fall heir. This note was a promise that all men would be guaranteed the inalienable rights of life, liberty, and the pursuit of happiness.[22]

In the second half of the speech, King said, "I have a dream that one day this nation will rise up and live out the true meaning of its creed: 'We hold these truths to be self-evident: that all men are created equal.'" The words that Lincoln was obsessed with, because of how grossly they were being violated, were quoted by King for the same reason a century later. King's words—which were in part influenced by Lincoln's words and Jefferson's words—pricked the nation's conscience, and especially the conscience of many white Americans who tried to ignore the institutionalized segregation, racism, and disenfranchisement in the country. King's words were powerful in part because, as King said, his dream was "deeply rooted in the American dream." And it was deeply rooted in the American dream precisely because of Lincoln's words in the Lincoln Memorial. King, like Lincoln, linked equality to religion, especially in his final passage:

> When we let it [freedom] ring from every village and every hamlet, from every state and every city, we will be able to speed up that day when all of God's children, black men and white men, Jews and Gentiles, Protestants and Catholics, will be able to join hands and sing in the words of the old Negro spiritual, "Free at last! Free at last! Thank God Almighty, we are free at last."

King's words were effective not only because of his astounding oratorical skills, but also because they resonated with Lincoln's words, which in turn resonated with Jefferson's words that "all men are created equal." And King, like Lincoln and Jefferson, said that this equality is divinely sanctioned.

King's speech resonated with what the Lincoln Memorial is all about: a religious experience of national identity. What is often sought but rarely achieved in national commemoration is the same thing that people in many societies seek in sacred ceremonies. This is what symbolic anthropologist Alessandro Falassi has called a "time out of time."[23] Falassi has noted in analyzing sacred festivals that they often involve a process "of valorization . . . that modifies the usual and daily function and meaning of time and space" so that "an area is reclaimed, cleared, delimited, blessed, adorned, [and] forbidden to normal activities." The Lincoln Memorial—especially as enframed by Martin Luther King, Jr., and the civil rights movement—is an extraordinary encounter with national identity that is not found in daily experience. Although it is not possible to ignore the temple within which Lincoln's words are found, the most important part of this temple is not the building and sculpture but Lincoln's words. Shortly after the memorial was completed, architectural critic Elbert Peets observed firsthand that the Lincoln Memorial's words—more than the temple and the sculpture—were what drew visitors. Peets was disappointed that French's statue of Lincoln did not hold them for long. . . . Before they had been in the hall twenty seconds, most of the crowd had turned and discovered the inscriptions. And the moment they saw [them], they moved toward the columns and took their stance where they could see the first panel. I could sense the relief with which they turned away from the statue . . . and began to read the familiar words of the inscriptions. . . . The result is that half a minute after a group of people enter the Memorial, they are all standing with their backs or shoulders toward Lincoln.[24]

But in turning their backs on the sculpture of Lincoln while simultaneously facing his words they have, in fact, embraced Lincoln's words as the most crucial embodiment of national identity found in the nation's capital.

The statue and the temple are important, but to a large degree only important as supporting and sacralizing elements for the words inside. As much as the builders of the monument tried to repress their meaning and "whiten" history, the civil rights movement and King's speech brought about what in psychological terms is called a "return of the repressed." As Pierre Nora has observed, commemorative memory increasingly relies upon "the materiality of the trace, the immediacy of the recording, the visibility of the image."[25] Lincoln's texts—supported by the rendering of Lincoln's careworn face taken from photographs[26]—are the trace elements that authenticate the monument. Without Lincoln's words, the monument risked collapsing into pomposity without content.

Some, however, might point out that in spite of Lincoln's words in the memorial, Lincoln himself, before he was president, said many things that were racist. For instance, in the 1850s, Lincoln stated that the African American "is not my equal in many respects—certainly not in color, perhaps not in moral or intellectual endowment. But in the right to eat the bread, without the leave of anyone else, which his own hand earns, he is my equal and the equal . . . of every living man."[27] However, in his two speeches engraved in the Lincoln Memorial, Lincoln finally got it right.

Frederick Douglass, after hearing Lincoln's Second Inaugural Address on 4 March 1865, was determined to go to the inaugural reception that evening at the White House. But as Douglass arrived, he was blocked at the door by two policemen. They informed Douglass that their "directions were to admit no one of color." Douglass said, "No such order could have emanated from President Lincoln." To end the confrontation, which was blocking the entrance, one officer escorted Douglass in and then tried quickly to escort him out the exit before he saw President Lincoln or President Lincoln saw him. However, Douglass asked a passing guest to tell Lincoln that he was being prevented from seeing him. The appeal reached the president, and, finally, Frederick Douglass was ushered into the crowded East Room where President Lincoln was greeting a long line of visitors.[28]

"Here comes my friend Douglass," Lincoln said, in such a loud voice "that all around could hear him."[29] Taking Douglass by the hand, Lincoln said, "I am glad to see you. I saw you in the crowd today listening to my inaugural address; how did you like it?" Douglass replied, "Mr. Lincoln, I must not detain you with my poor opinion, when there are thousands waiting to shake hands with you." "No, no," Lincoln said, "you must stop a little, Douglass; there is no man in the country whose opinion I value more than yours. I want to know what you think of it."

"Mr. Lincoln," Frederick Douglass replied, "that was a sacred effort."

The Lincoln Memorial and the Transformation of Memory

The decision to place Lincoln's words in the Lincoln Memorial predated architect Henry Bacon's involvement. The McMillan Commission of 1901, which revived Pierre-Charles L'Enfant's original imperial plan for the capital in the wake of the Spanish-American War, selected the choice site on which the Lincoln Memorial was built. They envisioned a neoclassical temple, similar to what was eventually built, but they recognized that the words inside were as important as the architecture. One of the commission's reports stated that the memorial "has for its chief function to support a panel bearing an inscription taken either from the Gettysburg speech or from some one of the immortal messages of the savior of the Union."[30] The commission's recognition that the memorial was meant primarily to "support" the text inside buttresses a reading of the memorial that emphasizes the importance of Lincoln's words for national identity and the nation's civil religion.[31]

However, the many interpretations offered of the Lincoln Memorial that do not focus on its words, particularly those by Sandage, Savage, and Thomas, are not only compelling but offer crucial insights into the meanings of the memorial over time. Christopher Thomas, especially, has offered comprehensive and perceptive coverage of the Lincoln Memorial that is unlikely to be surpassed.[32] For instance, Thomas powerfully conveys how the memorial was part of a surge of nationalism and even imperialism that swept through the country during and after the Spanish-American War of 1898.[33] As Thomas argues, the monument is as much about the era in which it was built as it is about Lincoln.[34]

New technologies of memory were leading to new ways of conceptualizing heroism and history as the Lincoln Memorial was being built. Even as the iconic presidential monument was reaching its culmination in the Lincoln Memorial the transformation of this kind of commemoration was imminent. New memory technologies were leading to new ways of conceptualizing heroism and history. An iconic monument in an age of cameras, motion pictures, voice recordings, and documentary evidence was no longer seen as a sufficient guarantor of truth—for memory itself, as Pierre Nora suggests, was no longer trusted to the same degree.[35] The preservation of presidential relics found at Mount Vernon was a precursor to the new mode of commemoration that was emerging.[36] Art critic Royal Cortissoz warned Bacon to "shrink from turning the thing [the Lincoln Memorial] into a miscellaneous, museumy place for the army to deposit 'relics' in."[37] Yet the process of creating an archival form of commemoration that displayed relics in museums was not to be repressed. National presidential commemoration embraced relics and validated itself through archives in the new commemorative form of the presidential library—the subject of much of the rest of this book.

1 A Shift in Commemoration
The Roosevelt Presidential Library

On 12 April 1937, Franklin D. Roosevelt made a sketch of the first federally administered presidential library, a new kind of institution that shifted presidential commemoration into the realms of the archive and museum. Roosevelt drew a two-story Dutch colonial–style building faced in stone, with a full-length porch, small windows, and a steeply pitched roof, like the houses he remembered from his childhood in New York state. He labeled the two views "Ground Plan" and "Front Elevation" and signed the drawing with a flourish, "FDR."[1] Roosevelt had collected many things since his childhood, from books to stuffed birds, from model ships to millions of government documents relating to his public service. As a student of history, he knew the danger of leaving the fate of these collections to chance. They needed an archive in order to remain intact after his death and thereby remain a testament to his life. To appeal to the public, FDR wanted a tourist-friendly history museum to be part of his library, and he hoped that it would draw "an appalling number of sightseers."[2]

On viewing Egypt's pyramids during World War II, Roosevelt commented that "man's desire to be remembered is colossal,"[3] and what he observed about the pharaohs was true of himself. Roosevelt so desired to be remembered, and to be remembered in a particular way, that he altered the essential terms of commemoration for the American presidency. No previous president had presumed to memorialize himself; self-aggrandizing monuments were thought to be for monarchs, not the elected leader of the United States. American leaders submitted their bid for immortality to posterity, and some were commemorated with statues, preserved homes, obelisks, and even temples, while others within a few generations were nearly obliterated from public memory. Never before had a president designed his own national memorial. Compared in size to the monuments with which previous leaders in world history have been commemorated, the Roosevelt Library is relatively modest. But it was audacious in its ambition to preserve not just the Roosevelt name, but also a narrative of the

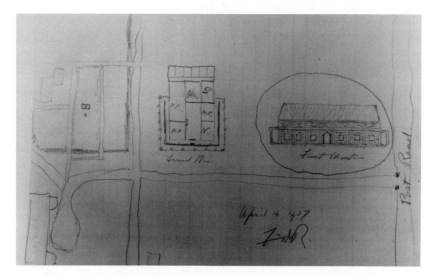

FDR's sketch from 1937 of his future presidential library in Hyde Park, New York.
Photo courtesy Franklin D. Roosevelt Library.

man's life and a vast variety of relics for as long as the United States remains
in existence.[4]

Roosevelt's library, the first federal presidential library, set a precedent.
Currently eleven presidential libraries run by the National Archives and
Records Administration draw thousands of scholars and over a million
tourists each year.[5] The national cultural impact of the presidential library
today directly flows from Roosevelt's plans for self-commemoration.

As an intervention in public memory, the presidential library functions
in several ways. For tourists, a presidential library presents an ideologically
charged narrative that valorizes a presidential life, helping to incorporate
it into the nation's civil religion. Informing and validating a presidential
library's museum are archives that preserve documents and other presidential possessions as national relics. Finally, presidential libraries through
their sites project an aura of the sacred by entwining an individual's life with
national history to create a narrative circuit that concludes with a presidential grave. Presidential libraries as institutions help create narratives about
national history not only through their sites and museums but through the
accessibility and use of their archives. This accessibility, as will be seen,
Roosevelt secretly hoped to prevent even as he publicly brought it about.

Sites of memory, like presidential libraries, have come under increasing
scrutiny by scholars who examine the landscape of public memory.[6] John

Franklin D. Roosevelt Library, designed in a Dutch colonial style. Photo courtesy Franklin D. Roosevelt Library.

Bodnar has written that "public memory is produced from a political discussion that involves . . . fundamental issues about the entire existence of a society: its organization, structure of power, and the very meaning of its past and present."[7] As sites of memory, presidential libraries have embedded within them an ideology that attempts to reify reverence for the presidency. This chapter explains why and how this new site of memory was created and examines its cultural effects.

Presidential Records and Relics

One of FDR's goals in creating a federally administered Roosevelt library was to escape a pattern of destruction and disbursement that had affected presidential records since George Washington's death. The private ownership of presidential papers was a peculiar national tradition established when Washington, at the end of his second term, shipped all of his documents to Mount Vernon.[8] During retirement, Washington wanted to erect a stone building at Mount Vernon "for the accommodation and security of my Military, Civil and private Papers which are voluminous and may be interesting."[9] Washington had in mind a precursor to the presidential library, but he was unable to carry out his plan, and on his death his papers went to his nephew, Bushrod Washington.[10] Bushrod lent large portions of the papers to the chief justice of the Supreme Court, John Marshall, who confessed that after many years they were "extensively mutilated by rats and otherwise injured by damp."[11] The remains of Washington's papers, like the remains of most presidential papers, were eventually purchased by the Library of Congress, but only after many were lost forever. Even some presidential papers that found their way to the Library of Congress had unusual restrictions placed on them. For instance, many of Abraham Lincoln's papers were sealed and unavailable to historians until 1947.[12]

Webb Hayes, the son of late-nineteenth-century president Rutherford B. Hayes, created an institution that provided a model for Roosevelt's library. In 1910, Hayes deeded his parents' twenty-five-acre estate, Spiegel Grove, to the state of Ohio under the condition that "a suitable fireproof building" be erected "for the purpose of preserving and forever keeping" the records and relics of his parents.[13] The Hayes family and the Ohio legislature provided the money for the neoclassical library, privately administered by the Ohio Historical Society and the Hayes Foundation. Until Franklin Roosevelt, however, no president seems to have looked to the Hayes Library as a model for preserving presidential papers and collections. President Roosevelt instructed the director of the National Archives, Robert Connor, to investigate the Hayes Library and learned that it was "a veritable gold mine for historical scholars."[14]

Even before Roosevelt investigated the Hayes model, however, I believe two other commemorative events helped shape his vision of presidential commemoration. The first was the founding of the National Gallery of Art by Andrew Mellon, which gave Roosevelt a lesson in how to build an institution from scratch and persuade the federal government to administer it in perpetuity. The second was the controversy surrounding the design and building of the neoclassical Jefferson Memorial, which may have led Roosevelt to create his library outside the capital, using a domestic architectural idiom.

Mellon's National Gallery and the Jefferson Memorial

Andrew Mellon, treasury secretary for three Republican presidents during the booming 1920s, epitomized the mysteries of public and private finance for that era.[15] At the 1926 Democratic National Convention, Franklin

Roosevelt said, "Calvin Coolidge would like to have God on his side, but he must have Mellon."[16] When the Great Depression hit, however, Mellon's reputation became as tarnished as it had been bright. His son, Paul Mellon, recalled reading a scrawled poem above a urinal in 1934 that illustrated how far his father's reputation had fallen:

Hoover blew the whistle
Mellon rang the bell
Wall Street gave the signal
And the country went to hell.[17]

After Roosevelt became president, his administration launched a highly publicized investigation into Mellon's taxes, charging that the former treasury secretary had violated the very laws he was pledged to uphold. Mellon had for years deducted from his income on his tax returns the purchase prices of many expensive works of art—including paintings by Raphael, Titian, Vermeer, and Rembrandt.[18] Mellon claimed that the prices of his masterpieces could be deducted because the art was officially owned by a nonprofit trust.

On 22 December 1936, during the Roosevelt administration's investigation against him, the eighty-one-year-old Mellon wrote Roosevelt a letter offering to donate his collection to the United States in order to found a "National Gallery of Art." Roosevelt was delighted with Mellon's proposal to give to the nation a priceless art collection and also pay for the construction of a massive museum in which it and future donations could be displayed. All Mellon wanted in return was for the National Gallery to be supported by annual appropriations from Congress and to be chartered by the Smithsonian Institution, assuring Mellon a form of immortality. Mellon was later asked why he would give his art collection to the very government that was attacking him. He replied, "Every man wants to connect his life with something he thinks eternal."[19]

In a letter marked "Personal and Confidential," Attorney General Homer Cummings told Roosevelt that, under the proposal, Mellon's trustees would outnumber government appointees and would appoint their successors. "The net result is that they will control the management of the Gallery, the site, and the contents thereof for all time . . . . The anomaly is therefore presented of government property being mnaged by a private group."[20] Roosevelt did not see this concern as serious. In fact, it appears that FDR tried to follow this precedent in creating his presidential library.[21] Cummings also objected that in the proposal "the faith of the United States is pledged" to support the National Gallery. "A question of taste and propriety is raised by this phraseology, but it was a form insisted upon by Mr. Mellon's attorney."[22] Roosevelt insisted on similar language when he deeded his presidential library to the United States.[23]

While the National Gallery provided Roosevelt with an institutional framework to follow in preserving his collections with assistance from the federal government, the relative failure of the Thomas Jefferson Memorial, the last great neoclassical presidential monument built in Washington, D.C., may have spurred Roosevelt's presidential library as well. The Jefferson Memorial was authorized by Congress at the height of the New Deal to give Democrats something approaching equal commemorative space with Republican Abraham Lincoln. Designed by John Russell Pope, also the architect of Mellon's National Gallery, the Jefferson Memorial was based on ancient Rome's Pantheon, a form particularly suited to the commemoration of the classically minded Jefferson, who had used the domed temple as his model for Monticello.[24]

But while the neoclassical design of the Lincoln Memorial was hailed by many two decades earlier, some advocates of modern design considered neoclassicism to be anachronistic in the late 1930s. The Magazine of Art criticized Pope's design with an open letter to President Roosevelt: "An enlightened government must realize that the stir which the announcement of the proposed Jefferson Memorial has occasioned, is not due solely to the Jefferson Memorial itself, but is due in large measure to the pent up feeling against a long series of dreary, costly, pretentious, inefficient, and dishonest buildings."[25] Moreover, several of Washington's famous cherry trees had to be destroyed during construction. As a supporter of the Jefferson Memorial and an avid reader of the New York Times, FDR was probably chagrined to read, on 8 April 1937, as the controversy moved to its height: "Plan for Jefferson Memorial Is under Attack; New Site and Design Urged upon Congress."[26] Angry women chained themselves to the cherry trees in an unsuccessful attempt to prevent their destruction. Some protesters even entered the White House to try to gain an audience with President Roosevelt. Although construction of the Jefferson Memorial continued, in spite of stiff opposition, Roosevelt was concerned with how he himself would be commemorated. Four days later, FDR was thinking about a different kind of presidential commemoration as he sketched his library.

FDR and the First Federal Presidential Library

Roosevelt's library was, like the National Gallery, to be privately constructed but operated by the federal government. In late 1937 Roosevelt
asked architect Henry J. Toombs, a personal friend with whom he had previously worked on small architectural projects, to draw up a design based
on his sketch for a new building next to his family home at Hyde Park, New
York.[27] Toombs soon sent the plans, remarking in the enclosed letter that
"I tried to arrange a plan as closely as possible to the plan you sketched for
me. . . . The stack area will take care of your files and while it has been very
difficult to arrive at the proper amount of exhibition space, I think what I
have is about right."[28] Roosevelt replied that Toombs had not taken into account the number of tourists that would visit the site. FDR thought that in
the summer there might be as many as 3,000 visitors a day:

> That is an appalling number of sightseers to handle, and these visitors
> would have to go in and pass through the rooms and exhibition halls
> and out again on regular tour. That makes me think that what we call a
> reading room would not be a reading room at all for students but rather a
> very carefully designed living room which would contain portraits, several
> of my favorite paintings and perhaps a thousand of my books . . . [with]
> visitors to pass in one door and out another through an isle formed by
> stanchions and ropes. This room, incidentally, I could use myself in the
> work of preparing the collections during hours when the public was not
> admitted.[29]

FDR's desire to convert the research room into a display room for paintings and books shows Roosevelt's understanding of the need to appeal to
tourists, even if it meant sacrificing facilities for researchers. Roosevelt
understood that most tourists would have little interest in using the archive, even if it was what validated the site and informed the displays. The
research room was instead to become a subsidiary presidential workspace,
a room where Roosevelt could lavish attention on the objects he proposed
to display in the museum and store in the archive. FDR's papers and collections were to be stored mostly out of sight, in a National Archives' reposi-
tory that was to be part of the building. In terms of display, and thus of the
relationship between most visitors and the archive, many of the traces of
presidential labor were to be hidden. And the building itself was even larg-

er than it appeared, for Roosevelt as designer had minimized the apparent size of the library by drawing upon domestic architectural metaphors. The Roosevelt Library's design included a full basement and a steeply pitched roof that made it a three-story building of approximately 40,000 square feet— twenty times the size of a comfortable middle-class home.[30] Although no one would easily connect the Roosevelt Library with the overtly magnificent Jefferson Memorial, it was actually larger in terms of floor space.

As important as the public display of his collections and memorabilia was to Roosevelt's plans, the museum alone was not enough to justify creating the first federal presidential library. FDR knew that every government activity required a coalition of groups who will benefit and will therefore lend political support. After deciding on Hyde Park as the site and himself as master designer, FDR wooed professional historians, perhaps the most important constituency for his plans. One of the first approached was Samuel Eliot Morison, professor of history at the president's alma mater, Harvard. Roosevelt told Morison that

> my own papers should, under the old method, be divided among the
> Navy Department, the Library of Congress, the New York State Historical
> Division in Albany, the New York City Historical Society, Harvard
> University, and various members of my family. . . . If anything is done in
> the way of assembling a fairly complete collection in one place, the effort
> should start now, but it should have the sanction of scholars.[31]

Morison replied that he liked the idea for what he called the "New Deal Archives" but still thought that Roosevelt's official state papers should be deposited with the National Archives in Washington, D.C.[32] Roosevelt was undeterred, however, and wrote to another professor that "the creation of a center devoted to the history of this period must have the support of the fraternity of historians."[33]

On 4 July 1938, Roosevelt met at the White House with National Archives director Robert Connor to enlist help in creating his new institution. Roosevelt told Connor that he had ruled out the Library of Congress and the National Archives for his papers. Moreover, he warned, concentration in Washington, D.C., could lead to a disaster for national records if war broke out and the capital were attacked. FDR described how the national archives of Spain had been severely damaged during the recent Spanish Civil War and related the anxiety French government officials had expressed to him about the concentration of France's national records in Paris with war looming in Europe.[34] Roosevelt proposed constructing a combined archive and museum in Hyde Park with private funds and then making the building a branch of the National Archives. But to start this process, FDR needed to begin a private fund-raising campaign to build the facility. Though well off, FDR did not have the personal wealth needed to build an impressive memorial. Eventually $400,000 came from 28,000 donors to build the Roosevelt Library.[35]

The loss of many presidential records, and the limited access granted to some of those that remained, gave Roosevelt a compelling rationale for creating his archive. Professional historians, Roosevelt judged, would come around to his plan if they could be made to see its advantages for their profession. On 1 November 1938, Roosevelt invited a select group of historians and archivists to lunch at the White House on 10 December: "I am asking a small group of people from different parts of the country to come together to discuss with me a matter which lies very close to my heart. . . . I am enclosing a short and very sketchy memorandum which I hope you will be thinking over."[36] The two-page single-spaced memorandum that FDR included was actually a detailed summary of the variety of papers and other collections that he had gathered over his life. Roosevelt stated that with the new facility his collections would remain "whole and intact in their original condition, available to scholars of the future."[37]

The historians discussed with Roosevelt his planned archive, and after lunch FDR called a press conference to announce his plans. Professor Morison, who had been won over, stood near him to show the historians' support. Professor Morison said to the press, "President Roosevelt has proposed, for the first time, to keep all of his files intact . . . under the administration of the National Archives so that . . . they will be under public control and will not be subject to dilapidation or destruction or anything else."[38] The president needed to create this impression to gain press support, which in turn would garner congressional support. On the following day, the New York Times headline announced: "Roosevelt Estate to House Archives, Go to Public Later," and beneath, "Historians Back Idea."[39]

Not all reaction was positive, however. The Chicago Tribune printed an editorial cartoon captioned, "He Did His Shopping Early," showing a rotund FDR dressed up as Santa Claus leaving a weighty present in a stocking. The stocking was marked, "Hyde Park Memorial to Franklin D. Roosevelt, to be enlarged by public subscription and forever maintained at government expense. To be grander than Mount Vernon or Monticello." At the far left of the cartoon FDR-as-Santa walks away and says, "Won't he be Surprised—Bless His Heart," as he looks back at his card, which is engraved, "To Pres. Roosevelt from F.D.R."[40]

Unmoved by the criticism, Roosevelt appointed a committee composed mainly of professors and archivists to make recommendations about the organization of the facility. On 17 December 1938, the committee decided to name the site the Franklin D. Roosevelt Library.[41] The term "library" was chosen over "archive" because it was thought that it would seem less alien to the public. The library was to include Roosevelt's extensive collection of books, but that was only a small portion of its proposed contents. The name was also chosen because of the precedent established by the Rutherford B. Hayes Library. After the morning session, the committee reconvened at the White House for lunch with President Roosevelt. FDR, almost certainly with Andrew Mellon's National Gallery in mind, wondered if some designation could be found that did not use the Roosevelt name. "What about the Hyde Park Library?" Roosevelt asked, at which some committee members scoffed.[42] FDR eventually agreed to the name "Roosevelt Library" because, as the committee stated, "the President's personal and official papers . . . constitute the principal reason for establishing the Library."[43]

A draft of the legislation by the Justice Department establishing the Roosevelt Library as part of the National Archives was submitted to Congress four days after the library committee's first meeting.[44] The legislation languished in Congress for some months, however, and one Republican congressman complained that "only an egocentric maniac would have the nerve to ask for such a measure."[45] Columnist John T. Flynn compared Roosevelt to a glory-mad Egyptian pharaoh and said FDR wanted a "Yankee Pyramid."[46] Nevertheless, the legislation finally passed Congress in July 1939, which at that time had a substantial majority of Democrats in both houses. Roosevelt, following Andrew Mellon's example, was able to insert language into the bill promising that the federal government would "provide such funds as may be necessary . . . so that the said Library shall be at all times properly maintained."[47]

At the cornerstone-laying ceremony on 19 November 1939, FDR said: "Of the papers which will come to rest here, I personally attach less importance to the documents of those who have occupied high public or private office than I do the spontaneous letters which have come to me . . . from men, from women, and from children in every part of the United States, telling me of their conditions and problems and giving me their own opinions."[48] Roosevelt did value expressions of popular opinion, but his statement screened his desire to prevent access to many of his own sensitive papers.

We can discern this in FDR's desire to select his close advisor Harry Hopkins as the library's first director, which would have given Roosevelt indirect control of his sensitive archival materials. National archivist Robert Connor wrote in his diary, "Wow! Was that a blow!"[49] Connor convinced the president that an archivist would be better for the position, but only after Supreme Court Justice Felix Frankfurter, one of FDR's appointees, warned Roosevelt against choosing a "court historian." Connor instead recommended professional archivist Fred Shipman, and Roosevelt acquiesced. By 1941, when the museum portion of the Roosevelt Library opened to the public, Connor confided in his diary, "The President still thinks of the library as his personal property."[50]

Indeed Roosevelt did. In 1943, he wrote a memo to director Shipman that revealed his intentions. Roosevelt, like Andrew Mellon with the National Gallery, wanted to exercise some control over his institution even after his death, through people of his own choosing:

> Before any of my personal or confidential files are transferred to the
> Library at Hyde Park, I wish to go through them and select those which
> are never to be made public. . . . If by reason of death or incapacity I am
> unable to do this, I wish that function to be performed by a Committee of
> three, namely, Samuel I. Rosenman, Harry L. Hopkins and Grace Tully, or
> the survivors thereof.
>
> With respect to the file known as "Famous People File," the same
> procedure should be followed. Those which are official letters may be
> turned over to the Library, but those which are in effect personal such
> as, for example, the longhand letters between the King of England and
> myself, are to be retained by me or my Estate and should never be made
> public.[51]

Roosevelt, five years after he began selling his new institution as an accessible archive, here privately revealed that access to sensitive materials was to be almost the opposite of his public statements. In 1947, however, after Roosevelt's death, New York Judge Frederick S. Quintero ruled that Roosevelt's public utterances were a "valid and effective gift of all of his papers . . . to be placed, maintained, and preserved in the Franklin D. Roosevelt Library."[52]

The ruling eventually gave the public access to all of the materials in the Roosevelt Library's archives consistent with respect for the feelings of living persons and the requirements of national security. Roosevelt ended up creating, in spite of his contrary private desires, an institution that fulfilled the roles that he publicly advertised for it, providing unprecedented public access to sensitive government materials decades sooner than they otherwise would have been available. In no other major nation can citizens so easily obtain access to previously secret, sensitive, personal, as well as banal, documents and collections as one can in a presidential library.[53] British citizens wishing to see the handwritten correspondence between King George VI and President Roosevelt, for instance, would probably find this difficult in England. But at the Roosevelt Library, within half an hour of entering the library's archive, a researcher assisted by professional archivists would be able to see copies of documents that Roosevelt thought should be sealed forever.

A Commemorative Shift

On 12 April 1945, as World War II was drawing to a close, President Roosevelt died of a cerebral hemorrhage in Warm Springs, Georgia. The president's body was taken by train to Washington, D.C., and then on to Hyde Park, and during the journey thousands of people lined the tracks to pay their last respects to the president. Roosevelt was laid to rest near the Roosevelt Library, where his grave completed the monument that he had created for himself. The library helped to ensure the continuance of Roosevelt's memory after his death through his museum and archive, which would help to project his life and image into the future. At the Roosevelt Library, FDR thought of himself as a tourist object and placed himself within a narrative circuit of the settings and objects that framed his life, from the Roosevelt family mansion in which he grew up, to his personal collections, to his presidential work, and, finally, to the large stone that he designed for his grave. The narrative generated confers authenticity on the complex through the telling of a cyclical story reinforced by relics, which concludes by returning Roosevelt to sacred American soil.

The narrative circuit that Roosevelt designed for himself is structured around the idea of mystified presidential labor. As Dean MacCannell has written, many tourist sites, such as the pyramids of Egypt or Saint Peter's

FDR's family mansion, Hyde Park, New York. Photo courtesy Bess Reed.

in Rome, are opulent displays of stored labor power that present the production and storage of work as a form of collectible authenticity.[54] The Roosevelt Library is meant to store and display every preservable trace of Roosevelt's life and labor for as long as possible. The archived traces of Roosevelt's labor become the sacra of the presidency at the site. Archived traces become sacred presidential remains. The mystified quality of this labor is emphasized by Roosevelt's plan to restrict access to the archive, which was to be seen even more than it was to be used.

The commemorative transition that the presidential library represents may be described in part as a shift from a Classical to a Catholic mode of commemoration.[55] In Classical commemoration, an abstract or representational monument, such as the Washington Monument or the Lincoln Memorial, visually attests to the heroism of a president. In presidential libraries, a comparatively Christian mode of commemoration, objects used by a president become relics and are stored and displayed in a federal facility that affirms a heroism that is supposedly already accepted. In other words, the touch of a president potentially transforms any object into a relic to be kept by a presidential library. As stated in the previous chapter, Royal Cortissoz, author of the inscription inside the Lincoln Memorial, foresaw this

The rose garden grave of Franklin and Eleanor Roosevelt, Hyde Park, New York. Photo courtesy Bess Reed.

transformation of presidential commemoration into a "museumy" collection of relics and feared it.

Roosevelt was able to conceive of an archival memorial in part because of shifts in media technology and culture that occurred before and during the twentieth century.[56] These shifts increased the importance of archives for preserving new forms of memory, making it possible for Roosevelt to think of an archival commemoration. Donald M. Lowe and others have analyzed how shifts in media technology layer different modes of perception: "Culture can be conceived of as oral, chirographic [handwritten], typographic, or electronic, in accordance with the communications media which sustain it. Each of these four types of culture organizes and frames knowledge qualitatively in an entirely different manner than the other three. And . . . each subsequent type is superimposed on the previous one."[57] Roosevelt's political career stretched from a typographic culture characterized by print media to the beginnings of a culture that relied more on such media as "telegraph, telephone, phonograph, radio, film, television, audio-video tape and disc, computer, plus others yet to come."[58]

The presidential library that Roosevelt designed was capable of storing and displaying both old and new forms of memory. In addition to its millions of government documents, it also preserves thousands of photographs, miles of film and audiotape, and every relic of Roosevelt's experience that he thought significant, down to a horseshoe that he found in the Sahara during World War II.[59] Collections can be a way to project an ego ideal—for instance, a collection of paintings, such as Andrew Mellon's, can represent a collector's aesthetic sensibility, intelligence, and wealth.[60] The Roosevelt Library took this process one step further by combining a museum with a personal and national archive. Through the organization of his presidential library into a tourist site and museum, Roosevelt was able to elevate the idiosyncrasy of his collections to the level of national relics.[61]

The Roosevelt Library's Life Cycle

Changes in cultural technology made possible—and have continued to affect—the presidential library as an institution. Through FDR's live radio Fireside Chats, to his nearly weekly appearances in filmed newsreels, to the previously unprecedented reproduction of his images throughout American culture, Roosevelt was able to become an effective shaper of his image in the mass media.[62] Herbert Hoover, while he was president, received, at most, 600 letters a day, while FDR sometimes received as many as 6,000.[63] This proliferation of letters, many of which are stored at the Roosevelt Library, is evidence that FDR forged a more powerful connection with the public through the mass media than did most of his predecessors. Some Americans, inspired by Roosevelt's image, even created folk-art representations of the president that are stored at the library. One, a sphinx with Roosevelt's face and characteristic cigarette holder that was part of the Roosevelt Library's early displays, manifests a popular appreciation for the mystery of FDR's political success, a mystery connected to Roosevelt's mastery of new media technologies.

The Roosevelt Library was first opened to the public in 1941, but wartime restrictions on travel held down admissions until the second half of the 1940s. From 1947 to 1986, however, admissions averaged nearly 200,000 annually, an impressive figure for an institution that is a substantial drive from any large city. By the late 1980s, a slow and steady decline had set in, and by 1994 admissions had dropped to 136,000.[64] The displays of Roosevelt's relics, from his christening gown to his extensive political memorabilia, began to lose some of their appeal as living memory of Franklin Roosevelt

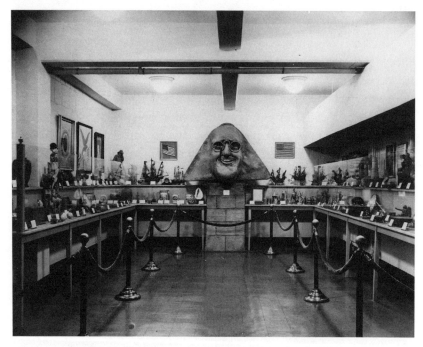

A large papier-mâché sphinx in an early exhibit from the 1940s at the Franklin D. Roosevelt Library in Hyde Park, New York. Photo courtesy Franklin D. Roosevelt Library.

passed away. As Pierre Nora has written, sites of memory can become "like shells left on the shore when the sea of living memory has receded."[65] As the tide of living memory that Nora refers to withdrew, the Roosevelt Library faced what its director at the time, Verne Newton, called "a demographic crisis."[66] To reach a new generation of patrons who "processed information in a fundamentally different way," Newton believed that "the Roosevelt Library would have to reinvent itself or eventually die."

When Newton became director, in the early 1990s, the exhibits had only been revised twice since the library opened and were largely static displays of relics in glass cases accompanied by extensive wall text. Newton spent time observing visitors in the Roosevelt Library's museum and found that although the declining numbers of older tourists were engaged, younger visitors were restless and bored. He stated that "the way this new generation receives its information is through interactive video and audio displays, and this was our guiding philosophy as we redesigned the museum." Newton had the library create its own video game that confronts visitors with the same information FDR had as president, for instance about whether to send destroyers to Britain during the early days of World War II. The visitor must then choose among various options. The thinking was that younger audiences would be more interested in this game than in Roosevelt's relics, and the library even contemplated expanding the computer game so that it could be marketed nationwide. Another new display re-creates the White House's wartime map room and uses a visitor-activated recording of a voice actor to create an imagined fragment of one of Roosevelt's workdays during the war. The game and re-creation were meant to make a president who seems almost as distant for some younger visitors as the Founding Fathers seem more relevant. Newton stated that the Roosevelt Library, in order to survive, "must become a mini-Disneyland. It needs to entertain, educate, and even create a marketable product."

The Roosevelt Library, like succeeding presidential libraries, has gone through a life cycle in its displays and also in the way its archive is used. A presidential library is created through a fund-raising campaign, its museum is opened to tourists, and then its archive is opened to scholars.[67] In a presidential library's first decades, archivists catalog and organize presidential materials, which are slowly declassified and released for use by scholars, who then write histories and biographies. These books often revive interest in a presidential library's subject, even if they sometimes create unflattering portraits of presidential lives.[68] Since 1950, hundreds of books on Roosevelt, the Great Depression, and World War II have been written by making use of the Roosevelt Library's archive. When eventually the interest of scholars, as with tourists, subsides, it becomes a continuing challenge for presidential libraries to justify their existence. The Roosevelt Library, like many presidential libraries, currently has a successful program to encourage the use of its archive by high school and grade school students.[69] President Roosevelt, who originally wanted to eliminate the room at the library for researchers and thought many papers should be preserved but sealed forever, might be disquieted by the sight of students working with the raw materials of his history at the Roosevelt Library.

The Presidential Library

The unusual hybrid commemorative institution that Franklin Roosevelt invented came to seem natural and necessary to his successors, and every president since has had a hand in the creation of his own presidential library. Presidential libraries have increased dramatically in size and cost but have not changed essentially from the model laid out by FDR. The presidential library as an institution is one reflection of what Arthur Schlesinger called the "imperial presidency." Schlesinger identified Roosevelt as the first in a long line of presidents who took on, and sometimes abused, increased powers that resulted from World War II, the Korean and Vietnam wars, and the Cold War. Not only did those who occupied the presidency since the 1930s have greater power than nearly all of their predecessors, but their postpresidential roles were also dramatically enhanced. The presidential library has come to function as the base for what Senator William Roth once called "the imperial ex-presidency."[70] The presidential library functions as the most important institution for the expansion of the civil religion of the American presidency, continuing in a new form the structure of reverence initiated by the creation and use of such memorials as the Washington Monument and the Lincoln Memorial. With the presidential library, however, every president—not merely the exceptional—has a national monument. Presidential libraries reify an ideology that claims all presidents as exceptional human beings and leaders worthy of reverential commemoration.

The presidential library is based upon the idea of the archive as the effective storage system for contemporary memory. As Pierre Nora has written, "Modern memory is first of all archival. It relies entirely on the specificity of the trace, the materiality of the vestige, the concreteness of the recording, the visibility of the image . . . [for] society as a whole has acquired the religion of preservation and archivalization."[71] Yet, while presidential libraries are part of a societal urge for archives that has been called archive "fever" or "sickness,"[72] the displays in presidential libraries, while continuing to construct a veneration for presidential relics, increasingly revolve around re-creations and simulations. Relics provide the authenticating foundation on which replicas and re-creations have been built in the commemorative space of presidential libraries. Although the Roosevelt Library did not originally have any replicated presidential spaces, its recent remodeling has given it three: its World War II map room, a re-creation of part of Roosevelt's Oval Office, and a re-creation of part of Eleanor Roosevelt's post–White House office.[73] Some presidential libraries, such as Ronald Reagan's in Simi Valley, California, have created a simulated "meet the President" display, using interactive CD-ROM technology.

Presidential libraries, with their museum collections, archival holdings, houses (usually administered by the National Park Service), and graves, mark a shift in commemoration reflective of changing technologies of memory. They are constructed to high standards and are designed to last for hundreds of years. Inside, rather than unchanging permanence, however, are museum displays of presidential stories and American history that change over time. Each generation of presidential library directors, curators, and archivists—who might be thought of as priests and priestesses within contemporary archival temples—reconstructs the story of their president for every new generation of visitor. The technology of display changes as well, from glass cases filled with relics, to computer-controlled exhibits that simulate a visitor's meeting with a president.

2 The Rhetoric of the Replica
The Truman Library's Oval Office and Benton Mural

As tourists enter the Harry S. Truman Presidential Museum and Library in Independence, Missouri, they face Thomas Hart Benton's mural *Independence and the Opening of the West*, which frames the entry to one of the library's chief attractions, a 94-percent-scale replica of the Oval Office. The mural and Oval Office replica at the Truman Library form a rhetorical pair, one that gains resonance because it exists within a national memorial—part of the landscape of public memory and national identity formation in the United States.[1] Although carefully coded to appear objective, these memory sites often carry a heavy ideological charge. Such is the case with the pairing of the Truman Library's Oval Office replica and Benton's mural, which were both created in the late 1950s.[2] The mural and replica take visitors on a chronological and geographical journey from a stereotypical depiction of the nineteenth-century American frontier into a re-creation of probably the most mythologized room of the twentieth century, the Oval Office. In the process, tourists become part of an allegory of white American victory on the western frontier and in the Cold War.

As visitors walk toward the Oval Office replica, they view Benton's huge mural crowded with Native Americans, white settlers, black workers, and covered wagons. The mural is a projection of the ideology of Manifest Destiny, with nonwhite ethnic groups, however ethnologically accurate their portrayal, depicted as subordinate to white Americans. As viewers pass through a doorway in the center of Benton's painting they face a glass display case with Truman's famous sign, "The Buck Stops Here!" which highlights Truman's refusal to duck his presidential responsibilities, especially in the conduct of U.S. foreign policy at the beginning of the Cold War.[3] Moving beyond this sign, tourists walk into a precisely rendered replica of the Oval Office. As visitors view the room, its function and contents are carefully described by President Truman himself, in a recording made for the library in 1964.[4] The replica comes synecdochically to represent the U.S.

Independence and the Opening of the West, Thomas Hart Benton, 1958–1961. Harry S. Truman Library, Independence, Missouri. Photo, E. G. Schempf.

government, for it re-creates the most important nerve center of Cold War America. Just as Benton's mural portrays the victory of white settlers over Native Americans, the Oval Office replica projects American steadfastness in the face of a global threat.

The memorial works by creating a passage through fictive time and real space, dramatizing the larger historical processes through which Truman became president and visualizing the world in which white Americans rose to global power. In so doing, the replica creates a sense of the uncanny through the appearance in Missouri of an empty double of the Oval Office narrated by Truman's disembodied voice. Like the replica, the Native Americans in Benton's mural may also be described as uncanny.[5] As Renée Bergland writes, "By discursively emptying physical territory of Indians and by removing those Indians into white imaginative spaces"—as happens in Benton's mural—"spectralization claims the physical landscape as American territory . . . [but] the Indians who are transformed into ghosts cannot be buried or evaded, and the specter of their forced disappearance haunts the American nation and the American imagination."[6] Viewed in this context, the rhetorical pairing of Benton's mural and the Oval Office replica constructs an American history and an idealized American subject haunted by specters of death—on the western frontier and in the Cold War.

The original Oval Office replica, Harry S. Truman Library, Independence, Missouri, 1952–1957. Photo courtesy Harry S. Truman Library.

Benton's *Independence and the Opening of the West*

When Benton was commissioned to paint the Truman Library's mural in 1958, the fame of such abstract painters as Jackson Pollock, Willem de Kooning, Helen Frankenthaler, and Mark Rothko was at its height. Benton's Regionalist style by that time was considered not merely anachronistic but reactionary.[7] However, the library sought a narrative painting that tourists could understand, and Benton was a famous Missouri artist who could create a product to fill this need. Early in his career, in the 1910s and 1920s, Benton chose his artistic precursors as much from Old Masters such as Michelangelo and Rembrandt as from the modernists.[8] In appropriating Mannerism and the Baroque and fusing it with a democratic view of American history—as well as with some of the techniques of modern art—Benton sought to create an art that would be expressive of modern times while at the same time appealing to a popular audience.[9] Few twentieth-century artists have attempted a combination as ambitious and at the same time as potentially absurd as Benton's. Through his paradoxically progressive and conservative art, however, Benton was capable of addressing serious social issues. For instance, in the mural A Social History of Missouri, painted for the Missouri Capitol in 1936, Benton depicts the grisly lynching of a black man against a fiery background, implicitly criticizing the all-white crowd in the foreground that listens to a political speech while ignoring the crime.

Although Benton's work has received significant academic attention, especially since the 1970s, the Truman Library's Independence and the Opening of the West has not been extensively analyzed and has never been examined in relation to the Oval Office replica that it frames. The most detailed discussion of the painting is found in Benton's own writings, which tell how the Truman Library's first director, David Lloyd, an admirer of Benton's work, brought Truman and Benton together. Benton described how "the aura of the Presidency" still clung to Truman as the former president worked in retirement at his new library and noted that "people who had known Harry Truman all their lives called him Mr. President."[10] The library the ex-president worked in was an impressive modernist building of white limestone designed by the Missouri firm of Gentry and Voskamp, which simultaneously evoked twentieth-century American government and Queen Hatshepsut's temples in ancient Egypt. Benton went on to describe the meeting between himself and Truman: "The President [was] apparently impressed by the array of historical facts I could assemble. . . . He told me he had not known that artists could entertain such interests. With his Library mural in mind I said, 'Mr. President, when I am commissioned to paint a piece of history, I take the trouble to know it.'"[11]

The painting visually expresses the ideology of Manifest Destiny in which both Truman and Benton were steeped. The mural has the effect of surrounding the Oval Office with inevitability, by paralleling the success of earlier generations of white Americans on the western frontier with the success of twentieth-century Americans on a global stage.

Truman insisted that no portrait of himself be included in the mural, to Benton's great relief, but initially they could not agree on a precise subject for the painting. Truman at first thought Benton should paint a historical panorama filled with characters and events from Thomas Jefferson's Louisiana Purchase through the early years of Independence, Missouri. When Benton told him he could not paint in detail more than fifty years of history, Truman replied, "Well, what the hell is it you can paint?" Benton proposed

The Harry S. Truman Library, designed by Gentry and Voskamp, 1952–1957. Photo courtesy Bess Reed.

that the mural depict the bustling life of Independence during the settling of the West in the mid-nineteenth century, with the figures being not historic but "symbolic."[12] Truman agreed, and under the ex-president's eye Benton worked on the $60,000 mural for most of the next three years.[13] As was his usual practice, Benton proceeded slowly and carefully, making numerous preliminary drawings, constructing a plastilene model of the composition, and conducting extensive research—including travel and sketching among the Cheyenne and Pawnee peoples of Nebraska and Oklahoma. As the work progressed, Benton even invited President Truman to climb his ladder and paint a small piece of the mural's sky, giving the painting an added touch of presidential authenticity.

The Opening of the West

Benton's mural represents the struggles—physical, cultural, and historical—surrounding the success of white Americans in North America. The painting is structured around a conflict between white settlers and Native Americans that is about to break out in the mural's center. Roads, hills, and clouds swirl across the landscape, seeming to push the figures toward

President Harry S. Truman (right) with Thomas Hart Benton (left), about 1959. Photo courtesy Harry S. Truman Library.

a bloody battle. Benton's colors are bright and rich: intense copper-green foliage, azure skies, lavender-tinged clouds, warm sienna fabrics, indigo jeans, and skin tones of cinnamon, tan, chalk, and dark brown. The intensity of Benton's palette helps to heighten the mural's tension.

In the period portrayed in the mural—between the 1830s and the 1860s—Independence was a jumping-off point for American settlers heading west to Oregon and California and a supply station for traders traveling back and forth along the Santa Fe Trail. From before the Mexican-American War until Reconstruction—when Independence was eclipsed by nearby Kansas City economically and politically—the future birthplace of Harry S. Truman helped white Americans achieve western settlement. In an essay about the mural Benton wrote for the Truman Library, he described Independence during this period:

> Milling in the new town's streets were hunters, fur trappers of the high Rockies . . . Indians of adjacent areas . . . soldiers, literary celebrities . . . profit seekers of every shade and degree of honesty looking to the Indian

Detail, center, *Independence and the Opening of the West*, Thomas Hart Benton, Harry S. Truman Library, Independence, Missouri. Photo, E. G. Schempf.

trade or further to the Spanish trade of Santa Fe. . . . Set up at a strategic conjunction of river and trail and at a time when American urges westward were reaching to climactic proportions, it was given to Independence to play a first and major part in the continental destiny of the United States.[14]

For Benton, and for Truman, the mural was not simply a portrayal of one town's history, but a grand history painting of "American urges westward" that rationalized the dispossession of Native Americans. These urges seemed to be described by Benton as an almost physical need of white

Americans to possess and domesticate the body of wild America. The needs and desires of Native Americans within this matrix of Manifest Destiny were largely reduced to stereotyped expressions of aggression, alterity, and loss.

Benton's mural was a late contribution to the depiction of Manifest Destiny that drew upon the visual tropes of earlier paintings of this theme, such as Emanuel Leutze's 1861 painting *Westward the Course of Empire Takes Its Way*. Benton's mural, like images of the century before, drew upon the same pool of rhetorical resources for imagining these migrations—the compulsion of whites to spread across the continent, the glorification of their hard work, and the perils of dealing with the Indians who are forced to make way for settlement.[15] Robert N. Bellah states that "civil religion . . . can be overtly or implicitly linked to the idea of manifest destiny."[16] It is not surprising that Benton's imagining of Manifest Destiny and Indian conduct were founded on old and resonant expressions of white American power. In his mural, Benton drew on the dichotomy between "good" and "bad" Indians that had been developed over the course of European settlement.[17] "Good" Indians engaged in peaceful trade and scouting and helped negotiate between white Americans and hostile Indian groups, while "bad" Indians violently resisted territorial encroachment. The left half of the mural represents this contrast: "good" Indians are shown busily at work in the fur trade, while "bad" Indians threaten settlers and get drunk.

However, Benton's mural also reflected changing ideas about Native peoples in mid-twentieth-century white America, when the cultural stereotype of the noble but doomed Indian reached equality with and then surpassed that of the bloodthirsty savage in need of eradication.[18] By the mid-twentieth century, the literary and artistic tropes asserting an uncanny or ghostly presence of Indians in America were mirrored by the long-term isolation of many Native Americans on reservations. It remained the work of art, literature, and film to rationalize the marginalized existence of Indians in the American experience and to explain it in ways that supported past narratives of white power. Although Benton follows in this tradition, he was careful to create an ethnologically accurate portrayal of the Cheyenne and Pawnee people in the mural based on firsthand observations.[19] The Indians Benton painted are busily engaged in labor and trade and depicted physiognomically and materially as representations of particular ethnicities engaged in specific historical practices, which were the result of Benton's sketching trips to the Cheyenne and Pawnee reservations. Benton described how he drew "bucks" and "squaws" on his sketching trips—seemingly unaware of how loaded these racist terms were, for at the same time he critiqued the cruel racism expressed by the local whites toward Native Americans.[20]

In the mural's center, four armed white men on the Oregon Trail (spread out along the top and right side of the doorway) prepare to defend the women and children at their camp from two approaching Pawnee men. The two white men on either side of the mother and children, directly over the doorway, stand with their rifle muzzles pointing into the golden air. Their expressions, verging on hostility, are echoed by their snarling dog that crouches ready to attack. In spite of this reception, the first Indian approaches the settlers offering a "peace pipe,"[21] an image recognizable to viewers of Hollywood Westerns. The approaching Pawnee man also wears a red trade blanket over his body—a sign of previous contact with whites that, with the peace pipe, serves to identify him as a good Indian. Two eagle feathers, one above and one below, pierce his hat. These feathers symbolize Tirawa, the all-knowing sky spirit who stands above the clouds, and indicate Benton's understanding of the signs used by the Pawnee to indicate chiefly status.[22] Although this Pawnee man's face is unreadable because it is turned away from the viewer, he is clearly marked as representing the possibility of peaceful accommodation between whites and Native Americans.

This possibility is undermined by the image of a Pawnee warrior who crouches behind the chief wearing beaded leggings, with a painted breechcloth and carrying a shield. He menaces the family as he climbs up the slope, preparing to launch an arrow against them. Benton uses the friendly chief and the stalking warrior to heighten the danger in the scene. Benton wrote in his description of the painting that "the whites are suspicious, as they usually were with Indians whose unpredictable behaviours, volatile temperaments, and ways of thinking they did not understand. Some justification of that suspicion is indicated by the Pawnee warrior . . . who though probably aware of the peaceful pipe offering has ideas of his own."[23] To develop his narrative formula, Benton portrays the Pawnee warrior using the peace pipe as a ruse for an attack. But for the Pawnee, ceremonial pipes were sacred gifts of the sky gods and were smoked as sacrifices to them during ceremonials that consecrated crops, war, and hunting.[24] These spirits' wrath over a warrior's failure to respect the pipe would have been devastating, making Benton's portrayal of this Pawnee warrior's plans for surreptitious attack implausible.

Even though it is white men who wield the deadliest weapons in Benton's painting, the white women and children also have important symbolic roles. A woman looks out from inside a wagon at the rear of the camp, sur-rounded by a halolike glow of late afternoon sunlight that suggests divine sanction for her family's settlement. In the near-ground, a pioneer mother cradles her young son, who turns away from the Indians in fear and nestles into her chest. The woman bends her body, exhausted from the journey, as she holds a spoon ready to stir a cooking pot on the settlers' fire. Here Benton portrays the difficulties faced by pioneer women. But like the men, this woman expresses not fear but weary determination.[25] Moreover, Ben-ton suggests that the children she rears will also be up to the task, for her older son beside her clutches a stick that parallels the rifle above him. This parallel is more than a formal device; it presages the boy's future ability to handle deadly weapons and the readiness of the pioneers' descendants to defend white America's future interests.

A viewer studying this painting can predict the resolution of Benton's fictional meeting. If, as seems certain, the Pawnee warrior shoots an arrow at one of the whites, the settlers will use their shotguns to shoot him dead. This will lead to an escalation of violence with one outcome: the eventual victory of whites and the displacement of Native Americans to reservations. The cycle begins with Benton's "unpredictable" Pawnee warrior, who in fact is as predictable as the working of a gear in the ideological clock of Mani-fest Destiny. The image of the threatening Indian was, from the seventeenth through the twentieth centuries, a well-worn trope that acknowledged the violence and anxiety caused by settlement and then used this violence to help justify white colonization of the West.[26]

In the twentieth century, this trope was most powerfully and pervasively deployed by Hollywood from the 1940s to the 1960s, a peak era of the West-ern in film and television.[27] As Edward Buscombe puts it, "The Western had always offered violence as the solution to the threat of lawlessness, but in a ritualized form, removed from everyday reality by the distance of time and place."[28] One of the cultural effects of the Western, especially during the first two decades of the Cold War (1946–1966), was to recast the era's in-ternational tensions into a nostalgic and heroic past, to provide Americans with a sense of moral certainty in the face of life and death conflict. As Stan-ley Corkin has written, "The western was well suited to convey important ideological rationales for postwar U.S. foreign policy, including the inevi-tability of American expansion and the strategies of hegemony that guided the Truman administration's foreign policy."[29] Filmed Westerns were in-fused by imagery from the rich tradition of American landscape painting in the nineteenth century.[30] Benton's painting was borrowing some of this imagery back from Hollywood and using it as an effective framing device for one of the most potent symbols of the Cold War, the Oval Office. This transformed one of the subtexts of the Western—its recasting of the Cold War—into a lived museum experience at the Truman Library. White women and children were made safe by their men in Benton's painting, just as the world was being protected by the United States from the Soviet Union and Communism during the Cold War.

Native Americans

Although Benton's mural appears as a unified, if imaginary, landscape, it can also be read as a continuous narrative—reflecting the Native American past on the left, the conflict surrounding Manifest Destiny in the painting's "present" in the center, and the future of the United States as foreshadowed by the town of Independence on the right. The reservation era, from 1860 to 1934, firmly fixed the Indians in the left of the mural as part of America's colorful heritage and helped to make them seem to disappear into ghosts of the past that haunt the United States and yet cannot significantly change the shape of its future.[31] The language that Benton used to describe the scene is further informed by larger racial stereotypes of Indians and whites. In his essay describing the mural Benton wrote: "The Indians were individualistic and acted more frequently on purely personal initiative than the whites who traversed the prairies. The whites knew the value of disciplined cooperative action. That is one reason why they dispossessed the Indians even though obstreperous whites frequently enough forgot their group responsibilities."[32] Benton's claim that whites triumphed over the Indians because of their "disciplined cooperative action" ignores the historical reasons for the dispossession of Native Americans in order to generate a representation of white cultural and ethnic superiority.[33] The spread of deadly European diseases, combined with the weapons made available to whites by industrialization, devastated Native American populations and were the real reasons for Native American dispossession, rather than Benton's false contrast of cooperative whites and individualistic Indians.

In spite of Benton's racist comparison between whites and Indians, in his mural a majority of the Native Americans are "good" Indians who work hard, have sophisticated cultures, and develop economic relation-

Detail, left, *Independence and the Opening of the West*, Thomas Hart
Benton, Harry S. Truman Library, Independence, Missouri. Photo,
E. G. Schempf.

ships with European Americans. Benton's "good" Indians represent one
reason that Native Americans as cultural figures can become uncanny specters—because they were noble people who did not deserve to be dispossessed but nevertheless were forced to make way for the expansion of the
United States. Benton gives examples of five "good" Indians, in addition to
the chief who offers his peace pipe in the central scene, most of whom are
productively involved in trade.[34] At the same time, a second dichotomy of
women and elders as "good" Indians and youthful warriors as "bad" ones

is also depicted. In the background, two Indian women tan a hide, a Cheyenne woman carries a load of pelts toward a trading site, and finally, in the foreground, an older Cheyenne man negotiates with a white trader over red fox furs. The Cheyenne man's younger companion stands behind him leaning on a rifle—the only young Native American man shown demonstrating nonviolent behavior. These two Cheyenne men, illustrating the virtuous rewards of trade, bargain over pieces of cloth, beads, and iron tools. But a barrel of whisky behind the frontiersman signals the negative side of the Indian trade and the corrupting effects of alcohol. Benton's "bad" Indians are either drunken, aggressive, or both. The most threatening figure is the central Pawnee warrior who stalks the settlers over the door, but in the background three warriors with feather headdresses and long, sharp lances prepare to ride out of a tipi encampment, perhaps to stage a raid. Their exuberant departure is marked by a fourth warrior who fires his rifle randomly into the air, startling the horses—all of them "no doubt stimulated," Benton wrote, "by trader's beverages."[35]

Independence, Missouri

While the Native Americans on the left are part of this noble, savage, and lost past, Benton portrays the early period of Independence depicted on the mural's right as a prelude to America's prosperous future. The image of Independence represents a way of life that is just beginning—one that presages modern commerce and industrialization. In fact, Benton's depiction of Independence is a blueprint for the economic and political structures that would supplant most native ways of life: it features commerce bolstered by trade routes on rivers and land, farming, fenced boundaries, and the beginnings of manufacturing. A two-story clapboard store, with living quarters above, stands beside a road filled with a line of covered wagons moving west to fulfill the nation's Manifest Destiny. The last wagon is being filled with barrels of food, furniture, and a plow, and as a man waves his hat at the immigrants, a young girl pauses in her work to watch the wagons leave. On the near side of the triangular scene, men walk into town with the cattle that will pull the next group of settlers west. A line of rail fencing disappears into the distance, testifying to the presence of land ownership and the settled life of white farmers that has replaced the Native Americans' fur-trading economy.

Detail, right, Independence and the Opening of the West, Thomas
Hart Benton, Harry S. Truman Library, Independence, Missouri.
Photo, E. G. Schempf.

Two African American blacksmiths in the middle ground to the right of
the door occupy the most prominent position in Benton's Independence
and represent the circumscribed role of ethnic diversity in the mural. In
contrast to the sometimes treacherous behavior of the painting's Indians,
these two men, like others on this side of the painting, contribute vigor-
ously to the new American social order. The blacksmiths' skilled labor is
emphatically detailed: the nearer smith heats iron over glowing coals and
furrows his brow as he concentrates on carefully bending hot iron, while

the second forges a horseshoe. Behind them, a white man brings a wheel to the shop for repair. Given the era Benton depicted and the fact that the scene takes place in Missouri, a slave state, it is impossible for the viewer to know with certainty whether these are slaves or free men. However, their strong and heroic visual impact implies that they are free, and it seems likely that Benton's depiction of the blacksmiths refers to a free black man named Hiram Young, who was the most sought-after wagon maker in antebellum Independence.[36] Next to the blacksmiths, a vaquero recently arrived from his journey along the Santa Fe Trail struggles to hold a mule that shies away from the forge. The provisioning period of Independence during the settling of the West foretells a future in which Mexican Americans and African Americans are part of society, but Native Americans are not.

Benton matured as an artist and Truman as a politician during a period of increasing awareness among some whites of the intolerable situation of black Americans. Although Franklin Roosevelt as president acknowledged the plight of African Americans, President Truman made more significant progress through such actions as his Executive Orders to desegregate the armed forces and to guarantee fair civil-service employment.[37] The diversity of Benton's mural may attest to Truman's strong civil rights record, at that time better than any other president's since Lincoln's.[38] Images of the final plastilene model of the mural that Benton showed to Truman prominently portray the African American smiths in the near-ground, which suggests that Truman supported their inclusion.[39] But although two black men were included, the role of African Americans was at the same time limited.[40] In *Independence and the Opening of the West*, there are no black, Native American, or Hispanic children, although there are four white children.[41] This sends a powerful message: the future of the country lies with white Americans.

Benton is careful, however, not to idealize the white settlers completely. Although they hold the technological, numerical, and physical high ground in the center of the painting, they are not entirely admirable. They are the ones who are dispossessing the Native Americans and who, in response to the peace pipe, threaten the Pawnee with three rifles and an axe to one bow and arrow. Although Benton does not make the settlers saints, he admires their grit and hard work. The mural portrays a nation of different cultures and ethnicities, but with one dominating. The display of racial diversity constructs a world in which the white settlers are literally and figuratively on top. The other races are laborers or nonwhites that help to locate the white center, showing how it accommodates and yet controls these minorities.

Below the main mural is a predella, rendered in smaller scale, which continues Benton's theme of Manifest Destiny by depicting the superiority of the economy of the United States. On the left, the *Saint Louis* is being unloaded on a Missouri River landing, an example of the type of paddle wheel steamer that was vital to domestic trade in the nineteenth century. The goods are being transferred onto a freight wagon, one in a line of wagons heading into town. A long warehouse, interrupted by the doorway, connects the landing with Independence on the right. At the warehouse, an unhitched team of oxen waits beside a wagon for the settlers to buy provisions. Benton portrays Independence as an orderly economic center with greater permanence and prosperity than the nomadic Native American village above. The Indians are nowhere to be seen in the predella, for they have been erased from civilization by the men and women who work in Independence. As Benton wrote, work and commerce transformed Independence "from a quiet backwoods settlement" into "a gateway of destiny" for the United States.[42]

In an interview for the Truman Library, Benton was asked if he had a message that he wanted viewers of the painting to receive. He said,

> I did want them to get the sense that America was made, built up into the powerful country it has become, very largely by the actions of the common people spreading out over the frontier. . . . The mural was conceived as a folk story and if it has a deliverable message, that would be about the preeminence of the folk in the development of our country.[43]

It was the folk, the common people, who, in Benton's view, transformed the United States from a relatively small and insignificant country into the economic, political, and military superpower it became in the twentieth century. The painting heralds Independence as a microcosm of American society, one that helps explain how Manifest Destiny formed an integral part of the foundation of twentieth-century America and the twentieth-century American presidency. And the mural prepares viewers for the culmination of American power symbolized by the Oval Office replica.

The Truman Library's Oval Office

Visitors move through a doorway in Benton's fictive historicizing image, pass through an interpretive gallery with the original "The Buck Stops

President Harry S. Truman seated at the desk in the Oval Office replica in the
Harry S. Truman Library, Independence, Missouri, c. 1960. Photo courtesy Harry S.
Truman Library.

Here!" sign, and then enter the replica and become part of the Truman Library's American story. The Oval Office replica shares with Benton's mural
a cinematic quality, but with a difference: where Benton's mural reminds
viewers of classic Westerns, the Oval Office recalls films about Cold War
anxiety, doubly enveloping viewers in these imaginings of American power.
Visitors stand inside the curved walls of the room in a space marked off by
a white railing, from which they can see Truman's desk, filled with pens,
clocks, photographs, and an old-fashioned black telephone. The American flag and the president's flag stand behind the desk before three large
windows. Prominently displayed across the room is the globe that General
Dwight D. Eisenhower presented to President Truman at the end of World
War II, which signals the importance of the global role of the United States.
The replicated Oval Office seems to be presented to the viewer at a moment
of ease, when the office is uninhabited and no crisis looms.

In walking from the painting into the replica, tourists reenact Truman's
journey from his common pioneer roots of Independence, past the Indians,

Oval Office replica. Harry S. Truman Library, Independence, Missouri. Photo, Abbie Rowe, courtesy Harry S. Truman Library.

the black men working the forge, and the settlers, into the twentieth century of the Oval Office—the American high ground of the Cold War. The tourist is the animate figure here, possibly a successor to the pioneers and traders in Benton's mural, living for a moment in an eerily empty Oval Office. Tourists re-create that journey and are faced with this room where a common man, supported by the grit of his ancestors, stood ready to wield and accept his unprecedented powers and responsibilities. The narrative of American success found in Benton's mural has been expanded to cover a world stage where the United States is struggling with the Soviet Union. Nuclear weapons were a key part of this struggle, and their existence provides a subtext that haunts the Oval Office replica.

This replicated room comes to life as Truman's recorded voice comes over hidden loudspeakers, activated by motion sensors:

I am glad you have come to this historical institution. You are very welcome. This is Harry S. Truman speaking. This room is an exact reproduction of the Presidential Office in the West Wing of the White House, as it was in the early 1950s. The furniture, the rug, and the drapes are duplicates of those in use at the White House when I was President of the United States.[44]

One afternoon, as I stood behind the railing that keeps visitors from moving beyond the edge of the replica, a United States Marine and his family came in behind me. As Truman's voice described the reproduction of his Oval Office, a boy of about seven or eight years told his father, in a tone of pleasurable deduction, "That's Harry Truman!" His father said, "That's not the President, son. That's an actor." In the midst of the largest collection of Truman materials and displays in the world, the sense that Truman's recorded voice would be an actor's impersonation offered an insight into the uncanny nature of the replica. In the Truman Library, where simulation and authenticity are closely paired, the truth of history is disrupted as much as reinforced by displays that seek to verify historical reality through simulations.

The Oval Office replica seems to be the most popular display at the Truman Library.[45] Most visitors, on entering the library, observe Benton's large mural only for a minute or so (although even in that length of time I believe a majority absorb its message about Manifest Destiny, because it is so obvious) and then head directly into the Oval Office. As Truman Library archivist Raymond Geselbracht noted, "The Oval Office is the main symbol of presidential power for Americans."[46] And since the real Oval Office is almost never open to tourists, the replica's mystique is enhanced.

But the Oval Office's ascension to the status of premiere presidential symbol only predated Truman's presidency by a few decades. It was first constructed in 1909 in the West Wing next to the White House, based on President William Howard Taft's sketches, which were inspired by the oval Blue Room in the White House.[47] Architect Nathan Wyeth used Taft's sketches to create "a dignified treatment" for the Oval Office "in keeping with the high purpose it is to serve"—as the presidential workspace for the twentieth century and beyond.[48] Taft continued to hold public ceremonial occasions in the White House, however, worrying that it might weaken his authority to appear before the public in the new office, which lacked the White House's history.[49] But in 1915, with the press in attendance, President Woodrow Wilson placed the first transcontinental telephone call from the Oval Office to San Francisco, helping make the room into a space that symbolized presidential power.[50] In 1934, Franklin Roosevelt had the Oval Office redesigned and rebuilt by architect Eric Gugler and had the room moved to where it stands today, in the southeast corner of the West Wing.[51]

Over the main doors of Gugler's Oval Office heavy cornices rest on bundled fascia, while minor doors and bookcases are crowned by shell-shaped niches, creating a rhythmic march of neoclassical architectural motifs around the room. It is this second Oval Office, the one Truman used as president, which is replicated at the Truman Library.

The idea for creating a replica of this office dates from Truman's second term (1949–1953), when the White House itself was completely rebuilt. By the time Truman became president in 1945, the White House was near structural collapse, and pictures from the three-year reconstruction completed under Truman's direction show that little remained of the original building. White House historian William Seale writes that the new structure's "reinforced concrete poured on a steel bedding" made "each room in a sense a cage of steel." The White House essentially became a replica of itself during Truman's term (with the addition of a nuclear bomb shelter buried deep under its foundation), possibly providing inspiration for Truman's Oval Office replica.[52] In any case, the reconstruction of the White House and the idea for the replica occurred at roughly the same time. The rebuilt White House was completed in 1952, the same year that the architectural firm of Gentry and Voskamp presented a preliminary presidential library plan to Truman that featured an Oval Office replica.[53] A search through archival materials in the Truman Library did not reveal the identity of the replica's originator, and no one at the library today seems certain of who first thought of it—Truman, one of his advisors, or one of the library's architects. In a sense, it does not matter; by 1952, the Oval Office was seen as the room that most symbolized the presidency.

The Truman Library's reproduction was originally meant to be full-scale, not the 94-percent-scale replica that now exists. But the library's architects based their design on incorrect measurements of the Oval Office provided by the General Services Administration, using only slightly larger dimensions to construct the exterior walls in which the replica was to be built. The architects and staff of the Truman Library were distressed when this mistake was discovered before the library opened, but it was too late and too costly at that point to rebuild the exterior walls.[54] As a result, the replica was scaled down from the Oval Office's true dimensions of 35 feet 10 inches by 29 feet, to 32 feet 9 inches by 27 feet 3 inches. But the average tourist is unlikely to notice the replica's reduced size, because it looks just like the Oval Offices seen in Hollywood films and television programs—which are, of course, also replicas.

Interior of the White House during its reconstruction, c. 1950.
Photo, Abbie Rowe, courtesy Harry S. Truman Library.

Oval Office sets had already been built by the film industry by the time the replica was built for the Truman Library. One of Hollywood's first Oval Office sets was featured in the 1944 film *Wilson*. In that movie, President Woodrow Wilson learns while in the Oval Office that he has failed to get the League of Nations treaty through the Senate, making a second world war likely. He decides in the Oval Office to launch his doomed national tour in favor of the League, which will end in his paralyzing stroke. The office is the scene of Wilson's greatest tragedy, as well as his greatest moral authority. Many films and television programs produced after World War II

THE RHETORIC OF THE REPLICA   63

Aerial view of the Harry S. Truman Library showing the oval form of the replica of the Oval Office, 1957. Photo courtesy Harry S. Truman Library.

that feature an American president also feature an Oval Office replica, reinforcing it as a symbol in popular culture. A few examples of the dozens of films with Oval Office replicas include *Fail Safe* (1964), *Superman II* (1981), *Nixon* (1995), *The American President* (1996), *Independence Day* (1996), *Thirteen Days* (2001), and the recent television series *The West Wing*. Truman archivist Raymond Geselbracht observed, "When you look at these things from the museum's perspective, you find that there are actually very few symbols of the presidency that have real resonance with the American people, and the Oval Office is one of them."[55] The replica's effectiveness is enhanced because, like Benton's mural, it immerses the viewer in the world of Hollywood archetypes.

Replicas and dioramas were important in museum displays, however, long before the film industry's Oval Office replicas were built. Replicas of architecture, with indigenous people working at imagined daily activities, were introduced at the 1889 Paris Exposition.[56] By the early twentieth century, anthropologist Franz Boas was creating dioramas of Native American cultures for Harvard's Peabody Museum.[57] In the 1920s, the Metropolitan Museum reconstructed a bedroom from ancient Pompeii,[58] and by the 1950s, Walt Disney was miniaturizing his vision of an early-twentieth-century American Main Street. This multiplication of replicated and reconstructed spaces in museums and tourist sites set the stage for the Truman Library's Oval Office re-creation as a museum display. The simulacrum of American culture expressed by the replicated Oval Office parallels the re-created worlds of Disneyland, which opened in Anaheim, California, in 1955, two years before the Truman Library. Both Disneyland's Main Street and the Oval Office replica present the architecture for imagined stories of an ideal America. As my late mentor Reyner Banham once wrote, "Disneyland was a set for a film that was never going to be made, except in the mind of the visitor."[59] This is essentially the process at the Oval Office replica—it is an empty set, a space for visualizing allegories of American power.

The replica is not only a symbol and sign of the American presidency and of American power, but also functions as an architectural container for additional symbols, such as flags, pictures of American leaders, the globe, and the Presidential Seal. In 1946, President Truman himself approved a redesign of the Presidential Seal—found on his rug in the Oval Office, on the Presidential Flag, and now everywhere the Presidential Seal is used. The Presidential Seal had long portrayed an American eagle facing the arrows of war, but at the dawn of the Cold War Truman ordered that the eagle be reversed to face the laurel leaves of peace.[60] Truman also, however, suggested that lighting emanate from the arrowheads in the left claw of the eagle as a "symbolic reference to the tremendous importance of the atomic bomb" but was dissuaded by his advisor, Clark Clifford.[61] The earlier Presidential Seal is carefully embossed on the ceiling of the Truman Library's replica, just as it is in the real Oval Office. Looking from rug to ceiling, one can compare the earlier and later versions. With the first use of nuclear weapons in 1945 and the advent of the Cold War, a new and disturbing power was located in the Oval Office and centralized in the president. It is not surprising that Truman sought with the new Presidential Seal to reassure Americans and the world that this power would be used responsibly.

Truman is the only president ever to use atomic weapons in war, and this is the action for which he is most remembered. On 14 August 1945, from the Oval Office, Truman announced Japan's surrender. In Truman's Oval Office the further development and possible use of nuclear weapons was discussed during his presidency, including his rejection of General Doug-

President Truman announcing Japan's surrender from the Oval Office, August 1945.
Photo, Abbie Rowe, courtesy Harry S. Truman Library.

las MacArthur's plan to drop fifty atomic bombs on China in an attempt to
win the Korean War.[62] The knowledge that a full-scale nuclear war would
obliterate not only the White House and the Oval Office but also other major
cities in the United States—as seen in a 19 November 1945 *Life* magazine illustration of an imagined atomic attack on New York City—is an unwritten
theme that hangs over the replica. The replica gives tourists a stabilizing,
symbol-laden environment in which to feel this anxiety and visualize this
authority.

The Rhetoric of the Replica

The Oval Office replica in the Truman Library is the culmination of the
narratives constructed by the museum's exhibits. In contrast to the replica
and the mural, which are more permanent, the remaining exhibits have been
redesigned a few times since the library opened nearly fifty years ago. The current exhibits, completed in 2000–2001, contextualize the narratives found in

Truman's presidency "for new generations of visitors for whom Harry Truman seems almost as distant as George Washington."[63] The interactive exhibits include stories and displays about the decision to drop nuclear weapons on Japan, the implementation of the Marshall Plan, the formation of NATO, the Korean War, and progress on civil rights (see chapter five). The mural and the replica anchor the stories that simultaneously identify the president as a common man—the grandson of Benton's folk, as it were—and exemplary leader during a period of almost continual crises. The replica is the museum's emotional core, but it also heightens the contradictions within the museum's narratives. The tension between the president as average American (representing the republican ideal that anyone can become president) and the president as an extraordinary leader (and white and male) is displayed in the museum exhibits and in the presidential desk surrounded by symbols of state power.[64]

As was mentioned in the last chapter, Dean MacCannell has argued that many tourist sites—from the pyramids of Egypt to Saint Peter's Cathedral—are opulent displays of stored labor power that represent a form of collectible authenticity.[65] Labor at the Truman Library is displayed and stored in several ways in order to valorize presidential work. For instance, the Oval Office itself is a set piece of pristine stillness that displays an absent presidential labor—the products of which are displayed in the museum's many exhibits and preserved in the library's vast archive of Truman-related documents, films, photographs, and audio records. These archives are meant to keep every preservable trace of Truman's presidency for as long as the United States remains in existence. The rhetoric of the replica sacralizes this preserved labor and makes the replica a metaphor for a system of government that is quite literally represented by an office.

The Truman Library's pairing of Benton's Independence and its Oval Office replica creates a combined meaning about American history and identity. Benton's mural creates a narrative that legitimates the governance of white Americans from the Oval Office by making the settling of the West analogous to the preservation of the American way of life during the Cold War. The paralleled narratives, however, are haunted by the deaths that sustain them—from the dispossession and spectralization of Native Americans on the frontier, to the repressed possibility of nuclear war that haunts the Oval Office. The ideal white American subject that is generated is steadfast in the face of these deaths, actual and potential. Independence and the Opening of the West presents an origin myth—a sacred vision—of American history that informs the Oval Office, while at the same time the rhetoric of the replica informs the viewing of Benton's Independence. Benton said of his painting, "In the mural you see the old town of *Independence*, the Rocky Mountains, the Great Plains, Chimney Rock of western Nebraska—all in one scene. That's impossible except in your imagination."[66] Likewise, the landscape of memory at the Truman Library simultaneously acknowledges and represses the death that drives its narratives, because the human costs that enable these narratives can only be comprehended—and even then, with difficulty—through the imagination.

The replica at the Truman Library has been so effective at evocatively commemorating Truman's presidency that Oval Office replicas have subsequently been built at the Kennedy, Johnson, Ford, Carter, Reagan, and Clinton libraries. These presidential dioramas, in their different ways with their different stories, continue the project of using the landscape of public memory to naturalize narratives of white supremacy and presidential power in order to make them appear as objective history rather than constructed myth.

3 Symbolic Power, Democratic Access, and the Imperial Presidency
The Johnson Library

The Lyndon Baines Johnson Library in Austin, Texas, designed by architect Gordon Bunshaft (1909–1990) of the famed Skidmore, Owings, and Merrill firm, was a turning point for the institution of the presidential library. It was the first to be affiliated with an academic institution, the University of Texas, the first to have the benefits as well as the problems associated with high-profile architecture, and the first to feature extensive use of film and video in its museum displays. The Johnson Library was the culmination of the presidential library's memorialization of the imperial presidency up to that time.

One of the themes of this book is that the presidential library not only symbolizes the imperial presidency but also symbolizes presidential personalities. The authority of the imperial presidency exceeds a strict reading of the U.S. Constitution, and this power can sometimes foster presidential egos.[1] The Johnson Library is a potent expression of the imperial presidency and presidential narcissism, but it is by no means the only example.

Johnson said his ambition was "to have the best Presidential Library in the world,"[2] which meant having a bigger and better building than his predecessors. Roosevelt himself had largely designed the Roosevelt Library in a Dutch colonial style, while the next two presidential libraries, for Truman and Eisenhower, were bland modernist buildings designed by little-known architects. In contrast, the Johnson Library's 85-foot-high travertine-clad form set a new architectural standard for presidential libraries while also symbolizing the personality of the thirty-sixth president. The building symbolizes that Johnson was, in Bunshaft's words, "an aggressive . . . big man,"[3] who forcefully used the federal government to prosecute the Vietnam War as well as to broaden civil rights and promote social programs. Johnson's belief in raw power, personal and governmental, is built into this stark and yet refined building that has been visited on average by more than

The Lyndon Baines Johnson Library in Austin, Texas, designed by
Gordon Bunshaft of Skidmore, Owings, and Merrill, 1965–1971.
Photo, Frank Wolfe, courtesy Lyndon Baines Johnson Library.

250,000 tourists and scholars a year since it opened, the highest annual
attendance of any presidential library, which no doubt would have pleased
Johnson, who insisted that no admission could be charged at his presidential library.[4]

On the outside, Bunshaft's design is austere and, for much of its surface,
windowless, but inside thousands of red archival boxes stamped with gold
presidential seals are spectacularly revealed through a glass-walled atrium

The Great Hall of Achievement, Lyndon Baines Johnson Library, showing the ceremonial staircase and the archival stacks behind glass. Photo, Frank Wolfe, courtesy Lyndon Baines Johnson Library.

four stories high. Robert A. Caro, one of Johnson's biographers, found "the Library's collection of 34,000,000 documents . . . loom[s] somewhat dauntingly over the researcher as he enters the building,"[5] but Caro has been allowed to read almost every document of the millions he has requested. He has constructed from these materials a compelling and disturbing narrative of Johnson's use and abuse of power.[6] The transparency of Bunshaft's design, in other words, is a metaphor for an access that is real. Arguably, a greater quantity of material is available to researchers on most modern presidents, because of presidential libraries, than for any other figures in history. The presidential library—especially Johnson's Library—manifests the dramatic increase in presidential power since the 1930s, but democratic access to most of their holdings has yielded publications, which, like Caro's, illuminate the sordid as well as positive aspects of presidential power and counteract the uncritical heroizing of presidents often found in the libraries' museum exhibits.

The story of the design and building of the Johnson Library, as well as the initial planning for its exhibits, reveals the process of a modern president's memorial representation. As with other presidential libraries, a large cast of characters was involved, including architects, exhibit designers, aides, supporters, and, most importantly, the president and first lady. They dealt with the memorial struggles of the moment, but they were creating a commemoration of the imperial presidency and Johnson's personality that would endure.

The Competition with the Kennedy Library

Lyndon B. Johnson was shadowed by comparisons with John F. Kennedy. As Johnson himself once said, Kennedy "was a great public hero, and anything I did that someone didn't approve of, they would always feel that President Kennedy wouldn't have done that . . . that he wouldn't have made that mistake."[7] The Johnson Library, from the beginning, competed—successfully, in most respects—with the John F. Kennedy Library in Boston for its architectural distinction, attendance, academic affiliation, and completion date. The person most responsible for its success, after Johnson himself, was his wife, Claudia, known as Lady Bird. In order to create a library that was both a paean to the Great Society that Johnson championed as well as to her husband's ego, Mrs. Johnson's taste and tact were called into action, signaling the ongoing transformation of the role of the first lady from a domestic helpmate into active partner.[8] The library also gave her an opportunity to present her own memory to the public. Kennedy had more style and glamour than probably any other president in American history, but in terms of concrete and marble reality, the Johnson Library was completed eight years before the Kennedy Library and has attracted more tourists and scholars, and some even prefer its architecture.[9]

President Kennedy began planning his presidential library during the first year of his presidency. A month before his assassination in November 1963 Kennedy had already selected a small site for it on the campus of his alma mater, Harvard University. To Kennedy must go the credit for the idea of associating a presidential library with a university and for connecting a presidential memorial and archive with future political leaders of American society. After Kennedy's death, the project advanced so rapidly that its completion was expected by the end of the 1960s.

President Johnson must have been aware of the extensive press coverage of the ambitious plans for the Kennedy Library. In December 1964, Jacqueline Kennedy's selection of its architect, I. M. Pei, was featured on the front page of the *New York Times*.[10] Jackie Kennedy was known for her exquisite taste,

The John F. Kennedy Library, Boston, Massachusetts, designed by I. M. Pei, 1964–1979. Photo, Benjamin Hufbauer.

and her selection of Pei launched him into the stratosphere of his profession. As Pei later recalled, his selection "opened the future" for him professionally, leading indirectly to his commissions for the National Gallery's East Wing in Washington, D.C., as well as for the Louvre's expansion.[11]

The Kennedy Library, however, had the longest gestation of any presidential library. Pei thought that the two-and-a-half-acre site that Kennedy had selected was too small and arranged instead for a twelve-acre site adjacent to Harvard that the president had also considered.[12] Pei's initial design for the larger site, a striking glass pyramid flattened at the top, was controversial. Critic Wolf Von Eckardt complained of the "banal symbolism of the pyramidal power of John Kennedy's achievement tragically truncated by fate."[13] More important, increasing numbers at Harvard feared that they would be overrun by a "gum-chewing, paper-throwing, sneaker-wearing crowd" of tourists that would descend on the Kennedy Library and pollute their campus, "like Goths overwhelming the intelligentsia."[14] After a decade of controversy and protests, the Harvard site was finally abandoned, and a redesigned Kennedy Library finally opened on the campus of the University of Massachusetts in 1979. In spite of a spectacular site overlooking Boston Harbor, the final design received a mixed critical response. As a review in *Progressive Architecture* put it, "The building's forms lack the underlying formal order one expects of a Pei work; and the blank surfaces fail, at close range, to exhibit the refined, eternal-looking qualities for which the firm is noted."[15] The only part of the original project that remained at Harvard was the Kennedy School of Government.

The Beginning of the Johnson Library

In spring 1965, however, there was every indication that the Kennedy Library would be a stunning success, and one that involved an institution—Harvard—that Lyndon Johnson, who graduated from Southwest Texas State Teachers College at San Marcos, both admired and resented. On 7 April 1965, when LBJ's attorney general, Nicholas Katzenbach, recommended yet another graduate of Harvard for a position in the federal government, Johnson could barely contain his annoyance. He said in a recorded conversation, "Can't you get me somebody in the Midwest or South or West? Do you know honestly that nine out of ten that I name are Harvard men?" Katzenbach, a graduate of Princeton and Yale, replied, "No, I didn't know that," and then heard Johnson's lecture about how he was going to try to break "this goddamned Harvard" hold on government positions through his new library:

> Now, I know it's a hell of a good school, and I'm for it and I don't mind them having thirty percent. . . . I'm going to start my Library, and I'm going to take a hundred people . . . and turn them out of Texas every year. That's what I'm going to do when I get out of here. Just go back there and teach, and make the University of Texas finance it. They've already agreed to put in $18, $20 million.[16]

Although Johnson exaggerated Harvard's hold on top federal positions, a large majority of them were indeed occupied by Ivy League graduates.

By the time Johnson had this conversation with his attorney general, he had been thinking about a memorial library for years. The idea apparently came to him by 1958, when he was majority leader of the Senate.[17] By that time, his good friend and Speaker of the House of Representatives, Sam Rayburn, had established a museum and library for the Rayburn papers in Bonham, Texas.[18] The Rayburn museum included a replica of the Speaker's office, where Mr. Sam, as his friends called him, sometimes worked. In November 1960, just after Johnson was elected vice president, the archivist of the University of Texas asked about acquiring Johnson's papers. Johnson's administrative assistant replied that Johnson "hopes to build or establish [a library] in his home community as did President Roosevelt and Speaker Rayburn."[19]

In January 1965, just after Johnson's landslide election to the presidency, Lady Bird took on three tasks: to contribute to the War on Poverty, to work for the beautification of America's cities and countryside, and to work on Johnson's presidential library.[20] She pulled off a coup for the library within weeks. She told William W. Heath, chair of the Board of Regents at her alma mater, the University of Texas at Austin, that she was considering locations for the library. Heath, who had a distant family connection to the president, won the approval of the Board of Regents for an unprecedented offer.[21] On 12 February 1965, he presented a proposal to Lady Bird and presidential advisors Clark Clifford and Horace Busby at the White House. All other presidential libraries before and since have been the products of extensive fund-raising campaigns. Heath instead proposed to have the University of Texas donate the land and provide the money to build the largest presidential library ever, as well as to create a new Johnson School of Public Affairs.

This proposal thrilled Lady Bird because she had always loved Austin and was not in favor of Johnson City, a small town, for the library.[22] When Johnson came home for dinner at 9 P.M., Lady Bird told him of the potential deal. Heath remembered that Lady Bird was crucial to the success of his offer: "Mrs. Johnson was a very strong ally. . . . [I]n fact we felt like she could sell him on whatever joint idea she and the rest of us came up with."[23] Johnson, clearly pleased, invited Heath for dinner and had what Lady Bird described as "a glowing, wonderful evening" in the White House discussing plans for the library and the School of Public Affairs, with the president waxing eloquent about how breaking the East Coast monopoly on political leadership could bring economic benefits to Texas.[24]

The president's longtime aide, Horace Busby, wrote a memo to Lady Bird emphasizing how the deal might even allow the Johnson Library to exceed Kennedy's:

> The exceptional factor of the University of Texas's offer is the University's willingness to provide grounds and buildings. Virtually all the energy expended on other Presidential Libraries has gone to the acquisition of these elements. But, the proposed "Johnson Library" would begin where

the Truman, Eisenhower and even Kennedy Libraries have, in effect, ended. This is the first occasion when the energies and efforts of friends and contemporaries could be directed beyond acquiring the physical mortar-and-stone facilities.[25]

Before the official exchange of letters in early August between Heath and President Johnson, the deal had already been sealed.[26] At the press conference announcing plans for the new library a reporter asked, "Have you designated members of your family to work on this?" The president replied, "I did not have to designate anybody. Mrs. Johnson appointed herself."[27]

Mrs. Johnson's Architectural Tours

And yet the mortar-and-stone facility was still crucially important. Here, too, the first lady played the leading role. Mrs. Johnson was a perceptive observer of both art and architecture, and LBJ relied on her taste. Her task was to make a presidential library work both in terms of its architecture and its displays.

In order to learn how presidential libraries functioned, she visited the Roosevelt, Truman, and Eisenhower libraries. She seems to have been most impressed by the Truman, which she first visited after Harry Truman said, "Come some time and I'll give you the five dollar tour myself."[28] She enjoyed the cartoons and the signed documents by presidents Jefferson, Jackson, and Roosevelt but was especially struck by two features: "There was a great mural in the Library by Thomas Hart Benton, called 'Independence and the Opening of the West,' which I liked very much. . . . There is also an exact replica of the Office of the President during Truman's term. How many succeeding Presidents may copy this idea?"[29] But she was troubled that Truman's documents in the archive were little seen or used. She wondered if "some more dramatic use" of the papers could be made. For instance, "they could be secure behind glass but some use could be made of color."[30]

Although she sought ideas at the presidential libraries, she was not impressed with their architecture. Like Jacqueline Kennedy, she wanted an architect whose name had cachet. In the receiving line at a White House event, President Johnson asked for the names of the best architects in the United States and received recommendations for such people as Philip

Johnson and I. M. Pei.[31] Pei, who was probably already seen as a Kennedy man, seems not to have been seriously considered. Lady Bird Johnson then examined the work of Philip Johnson and others, traveling to many locations, including Yale University, a microcosm of contemporary American architecture.

On 20 October 1965, she arrived at Yale, where her "eyes were out on stems."[32] Although she omitted this trip from her published diary, her secretary typed up her tape-recorded impressions:

> The President of Yale himself, Dr. Kingman Brewster—young, to me, handsome and very charming—met me at the airport . . . and then we set out on a walking tour of the Yale campus going by the IBM Building, designed by Bunshaft of Skidmore, Owings, and Merrill—a small jewel of glass and steel. And then on up to a half completed building by Philip Johnson—an enormous high-rise structure . . . of round pillars reaching to the sky. . . . And next to the Beinecke Rare Book Library by Bunshaft . . . I thought it looked cold, austere, severe on the outside. From the inside there was a magnificent way to display millions of dollars worth of rare books behind glass. . . . The outside shell of the building itself is composed of translucent marble some six or eight inches thick, which permits the light to filter through with great magnificence. No tomb of a pharaoh was ever designed with less thought of expense.[33]

Here, Lady Bird Johnson saw a realization of an architectural idea that she herself had thought of independently when touring presidential libraries—the display of stacks through glass. Although she considered some modernism "austere," she appreciated how Bunshaft was able to use the thinly cut and beautifully colored Vermont marble to spectacular effect. Mrs. Johnson, famous for her efforts at beautification in the United States,[34] recognized the beauty and appreciation for natural materials found in Bunshaft's design.[35]

She also critiqued other buildings that she saw, particularly the Art and Architecture Building designed by Paul Rudolph and the addition to the Yale Art Gallery by Louis Kahn. She commented:

> Neither appealed to me. I understood the phrase "brutalism" in architecture, which I had heard—the exposed concrete—the raw structural frame—the crude unfinished look—the deliberate defiance

of any need to be elegant or beautiful. And yet they are the great names in their profession. Somehow it reminded me of the Hans Christian Andersen story about the Emperor's new clothes.[36]

Brutalism in architecture was first analyzed extensively by British architectural critic Reyner Banham in 1955.[37] The movement took to extremes tendencies in modern architecture, such as exposing structural materials like steel and concrete rather than hiding them behind other materials, such as brick or marble. Even though she disapproved, Lady Bird understood this movement well.

Mrs. Johnson's favorite building that day was a dormitory by Eero Saarinen, famous for the TWA terminal at Kennedy Airport in New York, as well as the design of the Saint Louis Arch then under construction. She felt Saarinen had effectively blended his modernist residential colleges in with the older ivy-covered neomedieval buildings. Stiles and Morse Colleges were geometric in design, inspired by medieval Italian towers and townscapes. Nevertheless, she said, "that does us no good because Saarinen is dead, and what we are in search of is a living, malleable architect."[38]

She then took an architectural tour of New York, where she saw the New York State Theater at Lincoln Center, also by Philip Johnson, as well as other buildings. She later saw and admired Johnson's Amon Carter Museum in Fort Worth and his Dumbarton Oaks museum pavilion in the capital, both revealing a sense of order and delicacy combined with fine materials.[39]

She found similar qualities in Minoru Yamasaki's Woodrow Wilson School of Public and International Affairs then being completed on the campus of Princeton University, which she also visited.[40] Yamasaki had by that time been commissioned to design the Twin Towers of the World Trade Center in New York and had already designed the Science Pavilion for the Seattle World's Fair of 1962. The Woodrow Wilson School, surrounded by a portico, features 60 slender 28-foot columns, surfaced in white quartz, which visually support an upper story of offices around the perimeter of the building.[41] The wall surfaces behind the columns are of travertine, as are the floors inside. The graceful colonnade in Yamasaki's building, akin to some of those found in Philip Johnson's, was probably one of the features that attracted her. While narrowing her list, she said in her tape-recorded diary, "On my part there is no clear-cut choice. . . . But yet I want to attach some great and lustrous name to the Library so it will 'sell for what it's worth' in the eyes of the world."[42]

The Choice

By the end of 1965, there were three finalists for the Johnson Library: Minoru Yamasaki, Philip Johnson, and Gordon Bunshaft. Two architects with whom the Johnsons had already worked, Max Brooks and Roy White, accompanied Lady Bird on many of the architectural tours.[43] They and Heath, the chair of the Board of Regents, had their own ideas about the choice.

To help President Johnson make his decision, aides prepared a flip-book with a photo of each architect and some representative buildings. Heath noticed that LBJ seemed enthusiastic about Minoru Yamasaki, sharing an interest expressed to him by Lady Bird. But Heath, mistaking Yamasaki for an immigrant, felt that the library "ought to be designed by an American architect."[44] Actually, Yamasaki had been born in Seattle,[45] but Heath used another argument in his conversation with LBJ:

> This Japanese architect—one building that he did that we looked at was the Woodrow Wilson School. . . . It was sort of effeminate, so to speak. It's very graceful. And I know I remarked to President Johnson once when he was saying something about the Japanese architect, . . . "Mr. President, if this library was to have this big building to house the papers of some famous Queen—a woman—I would expect that it would be a beautiful and a dainty style of architecture [but] I can't see you in it as you have always been known as a man forceful, strong, who came from the harshest hills out here." . . . That was the last time he ever mentioned this Japanese architect. So it really was sort of a process of elimination.[46]

Roy White described what happened next:

> I've forgotten who found the picture, but there was a picture of Philip Johnson sitting cross-legged on the floor in his silken pajamas and the recipe for something made out of pansies that you eat. He was in this Chinese atmosphere or something or other and barefooted. Bill Heath said, "Well, Max, we ought to show this to Lyndon. That ought to cinch one thing." . . . They were just laughing about appearances. They all admitted that Philip Johnson was a great architect. . . . At any rate, the picture was shown to Lyndon. . . . That was the day it was narrowed down . . . that was the day they finally made a decision.[47]

Heath expressed the worst impulses of racism, sexism, and homophobia that existed in all of them. In particular, Heath appealed to Johnson's manliness in the selection of the architect, which would also be expressed in the building's final design.

Another reason for the selection of Gordon Bunshaft was that Max Brooks already knew him from MIT, where they had both earned their master's degrees in the mid-1930s.[48] It was already decided that the high-profile architect that was selected would work with Brooks's Texas firm of Brooks, Barr, Graeber, and White on the building. Moreover, they knew that Bunshaft was acceptable to Lady Bird.[49] As White said, they knew that in Bunshaft's buildings "she was struck by the . . . design and straightforwardness, beauty of material and so on, and the landscaping, everything."[50]

Before Bunshaft could get the job, he had to meet with President Johnson man-to-man. On 27 November 1965, Bill Heath sent a telegram to Bunshaft at his office at Skidmore, Owings, and Merrill (SOM) in New York City.[51] During this period, as Carol Krinsky writes in her definitive book on Bunshaft, "SOM set the standard for postwar office building in the United States, which in effect meant the world."[52] Bunshaft had been with the firm since 1937, two years after it had been founded, and was made a full partner in 1949.[53] In 1952, Bunshaft's Lever House in New York City, a twenty-four-story skyscraper with curtain walls of green glass, was completed. This design was one of the most influential in twentieth-century architecture, leading to hundreds of similar skyscrapers—some designed by Bunshaft himself—in cities throughout the world. As Reyner Banham wrote, "Its smoothly elegant solution . . . gave architectural expression to an age just as the age was being born, and while the age lasted, or its standards persisted, Lever House was an uncontrollable success."[54]

The building was so successful that it led to a deluge of commissions for SOM, which soon opened branch offices in other large cities, such as San Francisco, and its staff expanded to more than a thousand, unprecedented at the time.[55] In the 1950s and early 1960s, Bunshaft designed notable buildings for Pepsi-Cola, Heinz, Union Carbide, Manufacturers' Trust, Chase Manhattan, and others—a Who's Who of corporate America. He was known for his bold designs, fine materials, and innovative use of technology that, in his own words, "made companies and their officers look progressive."[56] As expensive as his buildings were, they proved their worth to the corporate bottom line. His Manufacturers' Trust bank building garnered so much attention after it was completed that the rate of new accounts tripled.[57] Bunshaft's design motifs changed over time, but one thing was constant: they conveyed monetary success. Frank Lloyd Wright, certainly thinking of some of Bunshaft's buildings, since he was the firm's most famous designer, sarcastically called the company "Skiddings, Own-more, and Sterile."[58]

Bunshaft's Trip to the Johnson Ranch

When Bunshaft arrived in Austin on 1 December 1965, he met Bill Heath, whom he described as "a real Texas old fellow."[59] Heath told him they were heading out to the Johnson Ranch for lunch and then would return to Austin, but they remained at the ranch from 12:30 until 10:00 that night. Bunshaft later described the visit:

> Johnson ate at one end and I was next to Mrs. Johnson . . . [who was] very cordial. After lunch, we got into this Lincoln Continental with the President driving, Mrs. Johnson in the middle, and me in front, the three of us, and Heath and Brooks in the back. And we started riding around the Ranch and looking at steers and what not with a Secret Service car in the back. We stopped at some prefab he was building there and there was some debate about putting a window in some wall. I told them it was a mistake . . . and he said "Naw," he was going to do it. . . . I have a feeling he was trying to figure out if I was some goddamned decorator or a man.[60]

In recalling that day, Bunshaft laughed, but his perception was quite accurate: his manliness was being measured. Bunshaft stood about 5 feet 11 inches, compared with Johnson's 6 feet 4 inches, but Bunshaft was sturdily built, had a gravelly voice, and was stubborn. Carol Krinsky, who knew Bunshaft personally, said, "There probably wasn't much chance for even LBJ to have overwhelmed" him.[61]

As Roy White, who was also there, recognized, Bunshaft was getting "the full treatment," which almost always concluded with a visit to Johnson's preserved boyhood home in Johnson City, where LBJ liked to regale people with his life story.[62] Bunshaft recalled:

> And that house, and the interior, and the Victrola and stuff! He's about my age, see, and it was just like the house I was raised in. . . . Then they had some drinks, and he started talking about what he wanted to accomplish in this building and all that. He really talked. . . . He was very interesting, very intense, and he was talking to me. . . . We listened, for a couple of hours.[63]

The subject was the library, but not, as might be expected, the architecture. Instead, the president spoke at length about how his legacy might be presented in the museum. After staying for a late dinner and receiving some inscribed books from the president about his life, Bunshaft left. A few days later, LBJ told Heath to hire him.[64]

The Presentation

Bunshaft immediately began devoting time to the project, having understood the president's urgency. By late January 1966, Bunshaft and Brooks, in collaboration with the University of Texas, had worked out a detailed program for the building, which listed how many thousands of square feet would be devoted to each purpose—including 35,000 for the document archive, 3,000 for the research room, 1,000 for a vault for security-classified documents, 30,000 for the museum exhibit, and 12,000 for an auditorium.[65] Their ambitious schedule envisioned a final design by the end of the summer of 1966 and the initiation of construction before the end of 1967. LBJ, who wanted the library to open in 1969, asked what could be done to hurry the project along.

Bunshaft, working with drafters, engineers, and model-makers at SOM, prepared detailed plans, slides, and models, which he presented at the White House on 12 May 1966 to Lady Bird Johnson, with Heath, Brooks, White, and others in attendance. For any architectural project, this is a moment of tension, when an attempt is made to sell an architectural rendering that has been worked on for months. Sometimes the presentation is greeted with enthusiastic approval, at other times there are demands for substantial changes, and once in a while it happens that an entire plan is scrapped. The architect can even lose the commission. Bunshaft had been making these kinds of presentations for decades and had an impressive record of success, but Mrs. Johnson turned out to be one of his tougher critics. Her initial reaction to his design was that it was "monolithic, massive, unrelieved, and forbidding" and added that the ramp leading up to the building "is abrasive to me."[66]

Bunshaft grimly stated that changes could be made to his initial design, but emphasized that for architectural planning to continue, approval for the overall concept was needed. Two hours into the meeting, LBJ strode into the theater and said, "Mr. Bunshaft, I only have five minutes." The nor-

Gordon Bunshaft explains the plan of the library to LBJ in the White House. Photo, Yoichi Okamoto, courtesy Lyndon Baines Johnson Library.

mally unflappable architect, used to having at least an hour to present his designs, was taken aback:

> God, I ran him back and forth between these two things [the plans and the models], and he stayed about fifteen minutes. I didn't ever figure out how he could understand what I was talking about. This is a complex building, if you see it, especially on drawings. . . . He didn't say a word whether he liked it or not. He left, and Mrs. Johnson said, "Well, we'll have to do a lot of thinking and talking about this."[67]

To help his cause, Bunshaft discussed the design with Frank Stanton, the president of the CBS television network. He hoped that Stanton would encourage LBJ to approve the plan, and, if necessary, explain it to the president. On Tuesday, when the Johnsons had dinner with the Stantons, however, LBJ described the building in great detail to Mrs. Stanton, clearly having absorbed a thorough understanding of the design. In fact, by the time of the dinner, Johnson had already approved the plan without any changes. The usually staid Bunshaft was almost giddy when he heard, saying in a telephone conversation shortly after he was told, "I hear . . . that the President was pleased and that he had approved the design, and of course I was on cloud nine. [laughter] Well, one, that he was pleased, and two, that he had made his decision so quickly. . . . I'll kill myself to make it wonderful. [laughter]."[68]

The Design

Lady Bird Johnson was right to call Bunshaft's design "monolithic," but that is its strength. Brooks and Heath had told Bunshaft not to produce architecture that was in any way "decoratorish," as his competitors did, and he complied.[69] As Bunshaft said, "The President was really a virile man, and he ought to have a vigorous, male building. And we have got a vigorous, male building."[70] The Johnson Library, as built, closely followed the designs that Bunshaft presented and Johnson approved. The complex of structures symbolizes Lyndon Johnson's personality as well as his presidency.

Driving down Red River Street toward downtown Austin, visitors see the Lyndon Baines Johnson Library on the right, rising on the crest of a hill. The Texas sun makes the tan of the travertine building appear bright, almost incandescent. It is an eight-story structure with side walls that flare slightly at the top and reach toward the upper cantilevered floor, which juts out over the sides. Bunshaft explained this cantilevered level with a second refined model shown to President Johnson in September 1966. The architect called attention to "the floating appearance of the entire upper floor."[71] Windows three feet high wrap around the seventh floor, which, when lit at night, makes the eighth floor almost seem like a flying saucer on a landing pad. The design of the library itself appears to be based, in part, on Bunshaft's American Republic Life Insurance Company Headquarters building of 1965 in Des Moines, Iowa, which also has eight main floors, blank walls on the sides, balconies with recessed glazing across the facades, and tapered walls organized around an interior court. Bunshaft took these elements and elevated them into the realm of the symbolic, creating for the Johnson Library an architectural image of a space-age bureaucracy of the imperial ex-presidency.

After parking their cars, visitors walk beneath the long three-story facade of Sid Richardson Hall, which houses the LBJ School of Public Affairs.[72] Dark glass windows recessed within a grid of concrete bays rise above a pedestrian walkway for the length of a city block.[73] As Leon Moed, the architect who was SOM's job captain for the library, said, "In terms of composition, the School of Public Affairs next to it gives the Library a backdrop and frames the plaza."[74] The surfaces of the School of Public Affairs are a concrete aggregate of Texas stone, which contrasts with the rich surface of the travertine that faces the library just beyond.

As visitors emerge from the School of Public Affairs, the library looms above. On the right, three square reflecting pools divide the plaza between the library and the School of Public Affairs, while on the sloping hill, a large circular fountain sends a jet of water more than 20 feet into the air, creating waves that lap over the flared basin. The plaza is enclosed by walls capped with a simple but elegant balustrade whose pattern is repeated in the balconies found on both sides of the library's second floor.[75]

Bunshaft chose to orient the complex overlooking the hillside to the south rather than to integrate it with the rest of the campus, which concerned Mrs. Johnson.[76] Bunshaft made the entrance to the library face away from other campus buildings and secluded it in a spacious park, as he usually sited his suburban office buildings. He did not create a relationship between this and other campus buildings, as Mrs. Johnson had seen at Yale.

The entire library sits on a raised plaza platform. Approaching the building from the fountain side, visitors need to use the ramp that Lady Bird found "abrasive" to reach the library. The ramp slopes laterally up the side of the platform, providing an indirect line of approach as well as creating a sense of dynamism. The sloped platform as well as the ramped stairway recall some aspects of the ancient ziggurat at Ur, which seems appropriate. As one art historian has written, "Ziggurats towering above the flat plain proclaimed the wealth, prestige, and stability of a city's rulers . . . and functioned symbolically, too, as lofty bridges between the earth and the heavens—a meeting place for humans and their gods."[76] The Johnson Library might be seen as a modern reinterpretation of this concept, an attempt to create a sacred space where Johnson might become part of America's civil religion.[78] It is meant for the meeting of citizen and president—or at least the president's memory as preserved in the archive and interpreted in the Johnson Library's museum.

There may be other historical references in Bunshaft's design as well. At least two journalists referred to pyramids in reviewing the building, an Egyptian architectural form closely connected to the pharaohs,[79] but it more closely resembles ancient Egyptian pylon temples. The library has more than a passing resemblance to one side of a pylon in its shape, as both have steeply sloping sides that rise almost vertically. Egyptian pylons vary in height, but some are more than 80 feet tall, as is the library. In addition, pylons were capped with carved cornices that projected beyond their edges and provided a strong visual termination, similar to the way the library's cantilevered top floor concludes the building emphatically. And a pylon temple has more in common with the Johnson Library than does a pyramid. The pyramids were burying places for pharaohs who were gods, but otherwise there was not much going on inside them. Pylon-fronted temples, in contrast—like the Johnson Library—have priests (employees) dedicated to serving deities through rites and ceremonies. An archivist at the Johnson Library, tending its millions of documents for years, keeps the deeds of a modern-day leader alive.

Bunshaft himself said, "Architects are really influenced by what they have seen and lived with all their lives. . . . When you sit down to design something . . . they come out in different forms just like dreams."[80] Bunshaft traveled extensively and loved to flip through books with architectural illustrations.[81] Some of his inspirations for the Johnson Library may have come from such sources as Mesopotamia, Egypt, and even Japan, where he traveled in 1960. For instance, the facade of the library in outline closely resembles a Shinto torii gate, such as the one at Ise.[82]

Finally, Bunshaft's decision to clad the Johnson Library entirely in Italian travertine evoked Imperial Rome. Bunshaft himself said: "Most of the wonderful buildings I have seen from antiquity were built out of one material. That gave them unity. Prior to the Johnson Library, architects made the exterior out of one material, the interior out of another. I made it all of travertine."[83] Whether or not most ancient buildings were made of a single material, the travertine suggests ancient Rome, which enhances the building's "monumental impression."[84]

After choosing him, Lyndon Johnson said, "I understand Bunshaft's expensive."[85] Bunshaft's passion for high quality is found in many elements of the building, including in the texture, color, and cut of the library's beautiful marble, which he personally selected in Italy.[86] Because of the cheapness of Italian labor at the time, however, the travertine not only fit within the building's budget, but was less costly than some alternatives.[87] Travertine, usually formed of calcite depositions in hot springs, is distinguished by fine bands of similar color rather than strong contrasts. This makes for a subtle surface marked by textural relief. Bunshaft used the linear patterns in the stone to provide visual interest throughout the library. Travertine panels the height of each floor, with vertical bands, run the length of the building. At the transitions between floors, Bunshaft laid in narrow panels with horizontal striations. The alternating horizontal and vertical bands in Bunshaft's design make the stone surface seem woven and at the same time illustrate the modernist architectural idea that form should reflect structure.

The whole exterior, in spite of its bold and heavy forms, is enhanced by precision and complexity. The walls at each end of the building flare out at the base and taper elegantly to the top where the profile of the wall is closed by a rectangular form. Massive post-tensioned girders, cantilevered 16 feet beyond the walls, close the 90-foot-long hall inside. Contained within the ends of each girder are nine polished circular steel caps that create a frieze-like effect, reminiscent of a Greek temple, beneath the eighth floor.[88]

Visitors enter the Johnson Library at a broad foyer lined with dark glass. The reception desk is a large oval made from dark leather and travertine, highlighted by the bronze wall paneling behind it. Throughout the public floors, bronze fittings accent the travertine, creating an interplay of lustrous tans and browns. Originally, visitors would walk past elegant inset display cases of bronze and glass, designed in a linear, minimalist style.[89] Visitors would enter through the door and look down the hallway with nothing to interrupt the gaze until the eyes came to rest on a clamshell display case positioned near the stairs, which provided a visual pause before drawing them to the staircase and the Great Hall.

Entering the Great Hall is meant to be, and is, an architectural epiphany. Pei attempted to create a similar experience in the Kennedy Library, with its giant flag draped in a glass tower, but it fails to impress to the same degree. The Johnson Library's Great Hall of Achievement, in contrast, creates a palpable sense of awe. On each side of the first floor, thick bands of travertine form the ceremonial staircase, which rises to the second floor, where visitors look up and see what Lady Bird Johnson wanted them to see—four floors of the archives displayed behind glass but enlivened by color. Forty-four thousand two hundred archival boxes in red buckram embossed with a gold Presidential Seal surmount a mural that features several images of Lyndon Johnson.

The mural, by photographer Naomi Savage, was created by abstracting photographs and etching them into bronze-colored magnesium sheets that form a 50-foot frieze. Lady Bird Johnson, who had admired the Thomas Hart Benton mural at the Truman Library, probably encouraged the commissioning of a work of art for her husband's library. But while Harry Truman insisted on being excluded from his library's mural, at the Johnson Library the mural is all about Johnson. It first pictures a young Johnson with one of his first political mentors, Franklin Delano Roosevelt, when they met in 1937. Just as in photos that Johnson used for his political campaigns at the time, the person between LBJ and FDR has been removed.[90] Succeeding photographs picture Johnson with presidents Truman, Eisenhower, and Kennedy. The final panel depicts Lyndon Johnson alone as president. Echoing the title of one of biographer Robert A. Caro's books, the photo-mural is an illustration of Johnson's "path to power."[91]

Planning the Johnson Library's Initial Exhibits

From January 1968 through January 1969, extensive planning meetings at the White House were devoted to the exhibits for the Johnson Library. Lady Bird Johnson participated actively in all of them. Other people who attended included Bunshaft, Brooks, Arthur Drexler (head of the Department of Architecture and Design, Museum of Modern Art), Dr. Wayne Grover (director of the National Archives), Horace Busby, Jack Valenti (a former Johnson aide and head of the Motion Picture Association of America), and sometimes the president himself. Minutes of these meetings illustrate how the Johnson Library would, consciously or not, represent Lyndon Johnson's imperial presidency.

At the 28 January 1968 meeting, Drexler began by presenting a scale model of the design concept, stating that the first floor should be "detailed and intimate," while the Great Hall would be "devoted to the President's achievements, ideals, and aspirations."[92] Mrs. Johnson, voicing one of her abiding concerns, wondered if there would somehow be space for a replica or partial replica of a White House room, perhaps one to display her daughters' wedding gowns. Lady Bird had seen the hugely popular exhibits of first ladies' gowns within replicated White House rooms in the Smithsonian, and she had also seen how popular the Oval Office replica was at the Truman Library. Clearly, however, she had already run into resistance to this idea from Bunshaft, who did not want his modernist design corrupted by re-creations of period rooms.

Bunshaft did not respond to her requests for a replica at this or other meetings, but instead gave a vivid description of the Great Hall. He said that even though it was an entirely different architectural style, his room would have the same appeal to visitors as the architecture of the White House because of its dignity and elegance. He stated that he did not want the displays in the Great Hall to be "jazzy," because he feared that might detract from the monumental architectural effect.[93] In fact, he and SOM had designed elegant display cases that included a 20-foot-long glass rectangle, with bronze fittings and subsidiary boxes for viewing smaller displays or audiovisual materials. These "were purposely made permanent," because Bunshaft "did not trust future display people and what they might do."[94] He wanted the cases fixed and placed in a symmetrical pattern so that they would harmonize with, rather than detract from, the architecture.

Toward the end of this meeting, President Johnson entered and talked about subjects that he hoped could be displayed in the library. Referring to the Treaty Room, where the meetings were held, he recalled the twenty-three treaties negotiated with foreign governments in the previous year, including a nuclear nonproliferation treaty. He then spoke of American leadership in aiding family planning in India and said that during the recent drought there "no one died" because of wheat furnished by the United States. He spoke of U.S. involvement throughout the world, including in such countries as Mexico, Pakistan, the Philippines, and Laos, emphasizing that "all roads lead to Washington."[95] Busby expanded on the president's theme, saying that the library's displays ought to focus on the president and the world and dramatize "what Johnson will be remembered for—keeping the world together."[96]

Busby, apparently feeling that the meetings were not creating a strong overall concept for the exhibits, wrote a memo, dated 26 February 1968, on concepts for the Johnson Library:

> At the outset, it is important to be clear on objectives. We do not seek or
> desire the end to be—
> —A shrine or a sepulcher.

—A show or a spectacular.

We do seek and desire that the end shall be—

—A quietly eloquent and enduring statement which engages its audiences to say to them: The people of the United States have created a great office; it is theirs—what the people are, the office is; what the office is, they are.

Busby acknowledged that Johnson's presidency had been "a time of testing—for the people, for their nation . . . and to the cause of all mankind in the world."[97]

This was the closest reference in the library planning documents to the Vietnam War and to the protests against it that were gripping the United States and the world at the time. But one thing that Busby's memo said that the library should not be—"a shrine"—is in fact what it was meant to be—and became—while the "show" he worried about was already under development in the films planned for the library. Furthermore, Busby's idea that the American people and the office of the presidency were one and the same strains credulity. One of the effects of the presidential library, and especially of the Johnson Library, is to elevate the individual president as well as the office above the average citizen by attempting to inspire awe and reverence. A degree of self-delusion was expressed at times by Busby and others in planning the Johnson Library.

Given the issues and events swirling around the White House during these months, such as protests against the Vietnam War and the assassinations of Martin Luther King, Jr., and Robert Kennedy, the amount of time devoted to these meetings is surprising. For instance, on Sunday, 23 June 1968, a meeting lasted from 2:30 until 5:45. The transcript for this meeting is fifty-five single-spaced pages long.[98] At this meeting President Johnson stated that he had reviewed a film of one of his recent speeches that might be used in the library. He thought his voice "didn't sound right" and wondered "if we could do a retake of the words" so that it would sound "better."[99] Mrs. Johnson agreed, but a participant at the meeting said it should not be changed because "it's history."[100] Jack Valenti agreed that it was important not to appear to be too "self-serving."[101]

During her visits to presidential libraries in 1965, Lady Bird Johnson had expressed a desire that "there should be a melding of both library and museum, a melding from which they would both profit and become more alive."[102] By the time they were planning the exhibits, however, Mrs. Johnson came to believe that the archival and museum functions were largely distinct. The summary minutes of one meeting state: "Mrs. Johnson said she wanted very much to appeal to the people who will come to the Library as tourists rather than to gear to the scholar."[103] To find out what actually appealed to tourists, the planners commissioned a survey that was mailed to presidential library visitors to identify what they most enjoyed and what they might like to see. About 600 surveys were mailed out and approximately 300 were returned.[104] The survey asked which presidential libraries respondents had visited and whether the visitor had "much interest," "little interest," or "no opinion" about specific displays, including some potential displays for the Johnson Library. The survey asked about such things as the drafts of important presidential messages, gifts from foreign visitors, Luci and Lynda Johnson's wedding gowns, civil rights, Social Security, and foreign aid.

Some of the results confirmed the obvious, while others were surprising. For instance, a strong interest was expressed in seeing gifts from foreign heads of state, historical documents, the president's desk, and office furnishings. Mrs. Johnson noted, however, that these responses reflected what visitors had actually seen at existing presidential libraries.[105] On the subject of her daughters' gowns there was a sharp split: 39 percent expressed much interest in them, and 46 percent expressed very little, probably reflecting gender differences in reception—also seen in the first ladies exhibits in the Smithsonian. Mrs. Johnson seemed hurt, stating, "I am inclined not to believe that."[106] Very few were interested in seeing an exhibit about Social Security, prompting Mrs. Johnson to say, "That is kind of discouraging. . . . [I] guess they've swallowed and digested that so long ago that they take it for granted."[107] A high level of interest was expressed in Mrs. Johnson's efforts at civic improvement, which had resulted in accomplishments such as the 1965 Highway Beautification Act. When this was pointed out to her, she replied, "Imagine that, by golly. As much as civil rights and almost as much as outer space."[108]

The survey indicated that visitors wanted to see a replica of some part of the White House, preferably the Oval Office. Jack Valenti, unaware of Mrs. Johnson's long struggle with Bunshaft for a White House replica, asked her, "Is there going to be any place in this Library for a replica of the President's Office?" Lady Bird replied, "Oh, Jack, why didn't you ask that question two years ago. . . . You see, we have this hall which has an enormous ceiling, but otherwise our ceilings are about nine feet," and so would not be able to fit the high ceilings needed for an accurate replica of a White House room. Valenti replied that that was unfortunate, because the Oval Office "is the one thing in the White House that they [the public] are very much impressed with . . . [but] if you can't do it, I would drop the subject."[109] But Lady Bird would not drop the subject. Although discussions continued in the meetings for an evocation of various White House rooms through huge transparencies that would be lit from behind—which were in fact eventually installed in the library—Mrs. Johnson had one final weapon to deploy in her battle with Bunshaft.

Bunshaft remembered that whenever Lady Bird brought up White House replicas, he tried to discourage her and thought he had succeeded. Then, on 10 October 1968, just before 9:00 P.M., he received a call from President Johnson in the White House:

> LBJ: Gordon, our folks have been out looking at these libraries, and uh, is there no way in the world we can reconstitute as nearly as possible the president's office in the library?
> BUNSHAFT: Well, we haven't thought of it, but it's possible.
> LBJ: I hate to build me a little one out there to the side and say, "This is the way the President's office looked. And here's his desk, and here's his chair, here's his FDR picture. . . . " Now that is the most attractive thing, they tell me, to the people who go and hear Mr. Truman discussing where he sat in this office. . . . Lady Bird said, "Well, we have a trouble. . . . We just played hell not doing it." And now we got a bunch of can't-do philosophy.

Bunshaft resisted giving President Johnson an absolute commitment to build an Oval Office replica, but LBJ made a case for the replica and finally got Bunshaft to agree:

> LBJ: You see, relatively few people come in the president's office, but all of them want to see where the president works. . . . That's one of the basic things! And it's gonna be remembered and impressive on em' a lot more than some book up there in a shelf. . . .
> BUNSHAFT: . . . Goodness me, if that's what you'd like, we'll make every effort.
> LBJ: I'd rather have that than anything else about the building.
> BUNSHAFT: I gather that all right! . . .
> LBJ: You do it. Thank you. I know you can.

As soon as Bunshaft got off the phone with the president, he called Max Brooks, who knew Johnson well and apologized for not warning Bunshaft that the president might contact him about the replica. Brooks added, "I understand he [Johnson] wants to use this office."[110]

The seven-eighths Oval Office replica was installed in lieu of the contemporary office that had been planned for Johnson on the eighth floor of the library. To create a ceiling that approached the correct height for the reduced replica, a bubblelike projection was built onto the roof. But the idea of Johnson using the replica disturbed Bunshaft. At a meeting on 8 January 1969 of the now officially named Lyndon B. Johnson Library Audio-Visual Committee, Brooks reviewed the plans, including the reduced replica. Mrs. Johnson said she was "delighted," while Bunshaft was not. As he said, "I just wonder about visiting dignitaries seeing him in the exact environment that he is in now, in Texas. . . . I have been wondering whether some people may not criticize."[111] Mrs. Johnson replied, "I hope to walk out of here on the 20th [of January 1969] and quit worrying about who is going to criticize." Bunshaft said, "Wonderful." But he continued to think it might be "a terrible thing, with visitors coming to see the President now that he has retired . . . like some man who won't leave, you know, who is carrying on. . . . The press would crucify him for hanging on to something that wasn't his."[112]

President Johnson Weighs In

In the weeks before the 1968 election in which Richard Nixon won a narrow victory over Hubert Humphrey, Johnson was engaged in an intense effort to end the Vietnam War. Days before the election, Johnson was shocked to learn that Richard Nixon's campaign had sabotaged the negotiations by promising the South Vietnamese government a better deal from a Nixon administration.[113] Johnson still hoped that before his administration ended on 20 January he could salvage the peace process. He decided against revealing Nixon's "treason," because he felt it might lead to a constitutional crisis.[114] In this environment, a meeting of the Johnson Library Audio-Visual Committee was held in the White House on the morning of 9 November 1968, the notes of which were not declassified until 2004.[115]

The committee reviewed impressive transparencies that were being created of various White House rooms and heard Mrs. Johnson's commentary from her experience in the White House. The East Room, she said, "is a cold room without something going on in it. Yet so much goes on in it, from press conferences, to bill signings, balls for kings, receptions for Prime Ministers, and also weddings."[116] There followed a lively discussion, in which Mrs. Johnson spoke the most but also listened at length.

There was extensive discussion about how to create a film for the Johnson Library to summarize the president's life and career.[117] Mrs. Johnson said to the committee that the president would certainly cooperate with television networks if they made a film for broadcast that could later be used for the library. Harry Middleton, a Johnson speechwriter who later became director of the Johnson Library, asked, "Mrs. Johnson, who would have the final control of [the] film?"[118] When he heard that the network would control the content, Middleton said, "I see the Johnson years . . . in terms of accomplishments. . . . Someone making a film . . . might go light on accomplishments."[119]

President Johnson joined the meeting and was briefed on ideas for making a documentary, "The Johnson Years."[120] President Johnson asked, "How much of my time would it take?" He was told that it would take at least an hour. Johnson replied, "I think it is a good idea. . . . I would set aside five hours if you want to."[121] For a short while there continued to be a give and take, as the president asked questions and received answers.

Soon, however, he launched into a monologue full of ideas for films for the library. He thought that they could be projected in the library and at the Johnson School of Public Affairs to show "the advances we have made in space, health, conservation, education, and so forth."[122] What Johnson said—in more than twenty single-spaced transcript pages, a few of which will be quoted here—helps to illustrate one of the themes in this chapter and the book: that presidential libraries reflect the imperial presidency and the presidential egos that go along with the modern office. President Johnson seemed to be visualizing his life as a dramatic film narrative, almost as good as those created by Hollywood, and wondering if this narrative could be preserved and made into a vivid re-creation for the Johnson Library. He began by thinking about the charts he had seen that showed the progress made during his term in office:

> Some of them are rather dramatic—the charts. We looked at them last night just in the fields of conservation and recreation. . . . There are some very

exciting stories. . . . Four or five things that everybody the world over would want to know something about and let them be seen for the first time.

We had signed a communiqué with [Nguyen van] Thieu on the peace proposal. After we got ready to go with it, he backed out because of influences in the United States. [Here Johnson was referring to the Nixon campaign's sabotage of the peace process.] . . . It would almost rock the nation if it was done now, but afterwards, when you go through this, it is going to be an exciting story, particularly if the thing ultimately works out as we expect it to.

I would say you can count on me for five hours. You just tell me where you want it, one in the office, one hour in the West Hall, one hour in the East Room, you plan it out. Give it some thought. Talk to . . . Harry Middleton. . . . Then, if you will outline to me through some producer or some person who understands television, to do whatever we can do, I think it would be good.[123]

The president then launched into a discussion of the various lucrative offers he had received for his memoirs, which would be written using the archives of the Johnson Library. One had come from Holt, Rinehart, and Winston, one of whose senior officers, Frank Stanton (also president of CBS), was at the meeting. Stanton said, "Inasmuch as I control Holt, I think I should not be listening."[124] The president assured him that it did not matter. (Holt, Rinehart, and Winston did, in fact, publish Johnson's memoirs.) Johnson continued:

You would be better for that than anybody else, because you know our eccentricities better than anybody else for twenty-five years. The thing I want to do with the money is send the kids to school. If we pay $5,000 per person and you get x-thousand you will send 100 or 150 [to the LBJ School of Public Affairs]. . . . So, the main thing I want is the people who work with me out there [in Austin] every day in the television, and in the writing, and in the research. Aside from my own people, I will have two or three competent people working with me. We will have all the files. . . . It is a very interesting story that nobody has ever heard. I want a person that I like and trust or that you think would be good for me, or someone who has some interest in me, besides the television. Whether you have ten or twenty extra kids going to school—if I am mad as hell every day with people working with me—it is not that important.[125]

Johnson continued:

> If you think one hour is enough, fine, but I will not be too rigid about it.
> . . . But here I will be busy with the budget and the State of the Union,
> besides the peace thing.
>
> But I will make that commitment to five hours. . . . Sitting there in the
> Oval Room at the President's desk, I think would make it effective . . .
> and then maybe Secretary [of State Dean] Rusk and Secretary [of Defense
> Clark] Clifford sitting there.[126]

Johnson turned from this cinematic mise-en-scène to financing for his library and for the Johnson School of Public Affairs. He was excited about the plans to get funding for scholarships from private foundations, which he saw as a way to break the deadlock of the Ivy Leagues on the federal government. He said that Arthur Krim, a Hollywood executive and Democratic fund-raiser, had told him that fund-raising was going well: "He hopes that our work can bring that up to $25 million, and in five years we have that locked in with investment. We will turn out 200 students a year, ad infinitum."

The president then started talking about some documentaries that were under way for the library with his twelve cabinet officers. He had told his cabinet officers to focus more on the future than on the past, and he was excited about what he had heard thus far:

> [Secretary of the Interior Morris] Udall started by saying this country has
> been in existence for 188 years, and during that time we have added 178
> parks. But, during the last five years we have added 146 of those parks. . . .
> [T]he [next] President is going to be confronted with these problems, oil
> shale, pollution. . . .
>
> Housing is so exciting. We have all these charts of the homes we
> are opening in Austin on Thanksgiving. We have ten big companies in
> America competing with each other on building us a $5000 home. Nobody
> has ever heard of a $5000 home. . . . When we open it we will have a real
> home, but it shows how we will have 26 million homes. . . .
>
> All of these things. Here are the indications of our effectiveness of our
> new bombing the last four days in Laos: . . . "On October 20th not a single
> truck passed. . . . Indicating the enemy has most serious difficulties." . . .
> [T]he enemy is not negotiating from a position of military strength. . . .

Then we have the Middle East. There are things there that have never been told before. . . . I asked [Secretary of Defense Robert] McNamara where the fleet was. I picked up the phone and asked the location. They were 300 miles away. . . . I said, "turn them around put their nose right into it." . . . [T]he Hotline message went over and the next message [from the Soviet Union] . . . was a much more conciliatory message. . . .

Another illustration is the Turkish fleet . . . we turned it around from an automobile coming from Georgetown and told them if they did not turn it around it would be no good. We told them that on a telephone in an unsecured line. The world doesn't know about it. The Turks know about it, and they have not liked it.[127]

Johnson was spinning in a dizzying way through his entire administration, including recent events, in search of things that might be portrayed in the Johnson Library.

He came back to his current obsession, the bombing halt and peace negotiations for the Vietnam War, and imagined it as a library documentary:

On this bombing halt we go around the room and . . . we have exact quotations from each member of the Joint Chiefs of Staff. We start with the Chairman, Westmoreland, and go around and each one of them expresses it in his own words. . . .

Then I sent for General Abrams and I said, "I want to know what you recommend to do." He was the only one who I thought handled it appropriately. He said, "It is not for me to tell the Commander in Chief what to do, but it is up to me to tell you what I would do as his Field Commander." He said, "As your Field Commander I would heartily recommend you do it." . . . .

In each one of the areas of the world you have some very dramatic, exciting things that people don't know anything about. Some is appropriate.[128]

One can only imagine what his audience felt in listening as President Johnson revealed still-classified events he had participated in as president that might someday make dramatic museum exhibits.

Johnson then shifted from foreign affairs back to his environmental legacy:

Here is just a little sample. This is in this century. When we put that in red, white, and blue in a nice chart form, you can see what it does. . . .

Theodore Roosevelt put in 19 [National Parks]. . . . Hoover, you see, didn't do much. Franklin Roosevelt, people knew he really got with it in this period. Truman came back down and Eisenhower about the same, and Kennedy here. Look at this. . . . This is the first period when we have put more back into the public domain than we have taken out. Does that tell you anything?[129]

The president answered his own question, "I think that it is a tribute to pretty good management." He then went on to review how his administration had appropriated more for the American Indian, reclamation projects, and the industrial water supply than his predecessors. He said that an impressive record of achievement had been recorded by his cabinet, which included reducing poverty by seven million people. He spoke of meeting a sixty-seven-year-old coal miner in West Virginia, who said, "This is the greatest day of my life. . . . I . . . shook hands with the President of the United States."[130]

Johnson then expressed his frustration that his administration's achievements were not recognized:

They say we have a problem communicating, and we certainly do. When you look at the ten biggest bills in the Nation's history, one of them was the housing bill this year. We scheduled two different public appearances by the President in front of new housing offices. We had everybody from the Chief Justice to the Mayor's office. We never got one minute [of media attention]. Rufus "Catfish" Mayfield paraded with a sign that said the President was a no-good bum, and he got all the attention.

That bill provides an expenditure of over $1 trillion. Nobody can conceive of it. [Secretary of Housing and Urban Development] Joe Califano wouldn't tell the figure because he is afraid that if Congress figures that is the legitimate estimate, they will not make the appropriation for it. . . . This housing story is a dramatic thing. Every person in this country wants some day to own their own home, and they have never had the opportunity to do it. Now we have a bill that will provide 26 million homes.[131]

Lady Bird Johnson finally interrupted to say, "How can we afford it, the taxpayers?" Johnson assured her that private enterprise and insurance would cover most of the cost. Johnson then mentioned a conversation he had with a woman in his hometown of Johnson City who lived in a federally subsidized apartment: "I said, 'How do you like it here?' She said, 'It is the most wonderful thing that ever happened to me in my life.'"[132]

After reviewing some of the good things that had happened because of his Great Society programs, Johnson expressed his fears that incoming President Nixon probably would not continue on this path. He lamented, "How he can pull away from this, I don't know."[133] His strangest story was one in which he heard from a government employee about how Social Security was helping to send kids to college:

> I said how? He said, if Pat dies out there in Vietnam, little Lyn can go to college until he is 22 years old. I didn't know that. But Pat's Social Security outfit takes care of that kid until he is 22 years old for education. . . . This is what really touches you about government.[134]

What Really Touches You about Government

David Halberstam writes that Johnson was "a study in political psychopathology."[135] One of his aides described him as "manic-depressive," and one of his biographers writes that a few aspects of his presidency raise "questions about his judgment and capacity to make rational . . . decisions."[136] At the least, sections of this Johnson monologue suggest narcissism. To be fair, the subject being discussed was how to make vivid and real the exhibits at the Johnson Library, which were, by definition, centered on him and his administration. The Johnson Library, like other presidential libraries, is a site for narcissistic spectacles of governance, for the institutionalization of presidential egos. This is one of the themes of this book: that the imperial presidency combined with the psychology of individual presidents leads to the particular qualities of their commemoration in presidential libraries.

In Johnson's case he wanted his presidential library to demonstrate how—from the environment, to housing, to health care, to transportation (all of which he covered in his monologue)—his federal government positively touched the lives of people. In his most disturbing vignette he acknowledged how the Vietnam War affected people's lives as well, but even there he managed to see how government could help the surviving children of deceased veterans. Perhaps fearing that in the judgment of history the Vietnam War would overshadow his domestic accomplishments, Johnson, even while hoping he could end the war, described in detail all of the ways he had tried to improve people's lives. But Johnson's epic vision that many of the most dramatic events of his presidency, including some that were still classified, could somehow be re-created in the library would not be completely realized.

On 22 May 1971, the $18-million Lyndon Baines Johnson Library complex was dedicated in a nationally televised ceremony, during which Johnson said, "It's all here: the story of our time—with the bark off. There is no record of a mistake, nothing critical, ugly or unpleasant that is not included in the files."[137] However, the museum exhibits almost completely ignored the ongoing Vietnam War. One reviewer wrote that he thought "quite a bit of bark was still in place."[138] Although the library had more audiovisual presentations, including films playing on several television screens, than any other presidential library at that time, almost all focused on the positive achievements of the Great Society.

In addition to the documentaries, the library's initial exhibits focused on subjects like presidential gifts, life in the White House, and Johnson's accomplishments. The gifts, displayed in SOM's bronze and glass cases, included a Venetian glass candelabra, a Gelede mask from Senegal, a carved ivory tusk from South Vietnam, and a diamond-encrusted sword given by King Hassan II of Morocco. The glamour of White House life was also illustrated by displays of Luci and Lynda Johnson's wedding dresses, as well as by the pictures of White House rooms that Lady Bird Johnson had approved. Artifacts that illustrated Johnson's accomplishments included a moon rock representing his support of the Apollo program, handwritten drafts of speeches, and scores of photos taken at every stage of his career. As Newsweek observed, "Inside the Library the visage of LBJ is as ubiquitous as Chairman Mao's in Peking."[139]

The displays did not impress reviewers as much as the architecture did. In addition to being likened to a pyramid, it was called "a one-man Valhalla."[140] Newsweek wrote that it was "as outsized and imposing as the man whose name it bears . . . the big daddy of all U.S. presidential libraries."[141] As Ada Louise Huxtable, architectural critic of the New York Times, wrote, "It puts Mr. Johnson in the same class as some Popes and Kings who were equally receptive clients for architects with equally large ideas. . . . This will be a hard one to top."[142]

On the eighth floor of the building, Johnson could work in his Oval Office replica. He did not have to enter the building the way tourists and scholars did—but could arrive via helicopter onto the specially constructed pad on the roof of the building, from which a private stairway led down to his suite. Behind the Oval Office replica is perhaps the single most beautiful room in the building. The Great Hall is much bigger, grander, and more awe inspiring, but Johnson's spacious living and dining room decorated with stylish modernist furniture is more luxuriously elegant. A large Japanese screen made of dark wood decorated with golden herons provides the backdrop for the large dining set with yellow upholstered chairs. Over the dining table and living area, recessed lights form, respectively, oval and circular patterns, while a glass case in the living area displays delicate Asian porcelain and other objets d'art. The whole room is finished with full-length windows that look over the eighth-floor balcony, from which the view across the campus and beyond to Austin is, as Bunshaft said, "quite fabulous."[143]

Perhaps the most remarkable single feature of Johnson's suite is found in the bathroom. The bathroom itself is a marble and chrome space with a bright green carpet; next to the toilet it appears there was once a telephone or intercom, now removed. Inside the large travertine shower is the feature that probably elicits exclamations from most of those lucky enough to receive a tour of this area, which is still closed to the general public. In the shower are four industrial-strength showerheads to spray Johnson's body, similar to those LBJ had had installed in his White House bathroom. They perplexed President Richard Nixon in his first days in the White House because "the thing was like a fire hose; it almost knocked him down the first time he turned it on."[144] As Johnson showered and dried himself off, mirrors on the walls and ceiling would have reflected back to him his own image, multiplied.

Outside the bathroom, and adjacent to the Oval Office replica, is a small study, which has a recliner, a telephone, and a drinks table. It seems undersized for Johnson, but probable evidence that he actually used it is found in the television setup: three small identical Sony color television sets provided Johnson with the television-viewing experience that he preferred—the ability to watch three stations simultaneously. It is awkward to move from this room into the Oval Office. A door right behind the Oval Office desk allowed Johnson entry. As one employee of the presidential library system said, "Johnson could emerge from the door behind his desk into the replica to surprise visitors, almost like the Wizard of Oz coming out from behind the curtains."[145] Johnson could request to be undisturbed when he worked in the replica, but he would also sometimes meet distinguished visitors or even schoolchildren there.

Inside the replica, just as inside Johnson's real Oval Office, is a custom-made three-screen curved television console, but it is not the exact one that he used in the White House. The huge television console that Johnson used in the real Oval Office would not fit in the seven-eighths-size replica and so is stored in the library's basement. As it happened, however, Johnson did not use the replica often. In the real White House, the Oval Office was a nexus of activity where major decisions were made. At times Johnson would personally select the bombing targets in Vietnam and then be able to watch the results on all three network television news programs. The replica, in contrast, must have seemed comparatively lifeless.

Johnson spent much more of his four years in retirement at his ranch than at the library. A massive heart attack ended his life on 22 January 1973, just days before the Vietnam War itself came to a close. The Great Hall in Johnson's library, although perhaps not consciously designed for it, functioned beautifully to display his flag-draped casket as thousands poured through the building to pay their final respects. Johnson had always been obsessed with the attendance figures at the library, and so on this day the director of the library and former aide Harry Middleton had a count made. When asked why, Middleton replied, "Because, I know that somewhere, sometime, President Johnson is going to ask me."[146]

Democratic Access, Architectural Problems, and Symbolic Power

Two and a half years after Johnson's death, Pulitzer Prize–winning author Robert Caro first walked into the building and looked at the archives that loomed above him. Although his biography of Lyndon Johnson was based not just on the materials in the archives, but also on extensive interviews and other research, in a sense Lyndon Johnson was right—in the archives, if you spent enough years digging and reading, the story could be told with the bark off. Johnson probably believed that, on balance, the story of achievement that would emerge from the archives would be more good than bad, but in the 2,555 pages of Caro's biography that have appeared so far, the balance sometimes tips the other way. The library, a shrine to Johnson's presidential ego, has ended up providing the material that in some places may even shock his critics. This material has been provided to Caro in a professional manner, in spite of the hostility that Harry Middleton, director of the Johnson Library from 1971 to 2001, sometimes expressed toward Caro's books.[147] In his acknowledgments, Caro thanks many people at the Johnson Library who spent decades assisting him, including senior archivist Claudia Anderson, who also assisted in the research for this chapter. As Caro writes, "She knows—she has made it her business to know—the archival material in her charge as thoroughly as it is possible for a single human being to know those thousands of boxes of documents. And she wants historians—and through them history and the world—to know that material."[148]

Anderson has worked at the Johnson Library since spring 1969, when she was twenty-one years old, just before her graduation from the University of Texas at Austin.[149] At that time, Bunshaft's building was still under construction, and Johnson's papers and the library's staff were located in the federal building in downtown Austin. It was on the top floor of the federal building that Johnson worked with his aides and staff writers on his memoirs. She recalled that during her life she had seen a few celebrities in person, and they almost always seemed smaller and less impressive in real life than on television. But when President Johnson came down to the ground level of the federal building where papers were stored, she was impressed that he seemed much bigger in life than on television. Once Johnson gave a pep talk for some of the library's staff that Anderson described as "a monologue," but one that she found "inspiring." Over the more than three decades that she has worked at the Johnson Library, she has thought often of the building and its symbolic relationship to President Johnson. To her, "the building captures something of LBJ's personality and presence, particularly a feeling of strength."[150]

Overall, Anderson likes the building, but also described some problems with it. Specifically, the archivists were initially expected to work on floors near the stacks without windows and without toilets.[151] This would not only have been inefficient, as it would have required trips to other floors that did have restrooms, but also would have made for a claustrophobic work environment. Before the library was dedicated, however, the library's administration decided to use the seventh floor with the high band of windows (that help to create the floating effect at night for the floor above) as the office area for the archival staff. But Bunshaft made no provision on this floor to prevent the deep window ledges from becoming landing and nesting places for birds and bats, as well as for the insects and droppings associated with them, which were not only aesthetically displeasing but posed a potential threat to archival materials.[152] Covers over the supports for the eighth floor above had to be sealed to keep out the bats. Electrified wire was also placed around the edge of the ledge to keep away pigeons, which had been nesting there. How to keep windows at this level clean in a cost-efficient manner was not considered in Bunshaft's design. For many years the windows were cleaned infrequently because it was necessary to build expensive scaffolding up to the seventh floor to get to them. Now, however, window-cleaning techniques using belts and pulleys allow cleaners to move along the ledges, and the windows are cleaned more frequently.

For the archival offices—as well as for the entire library—Bunshaft and his staff designed elegant furniture, including desks, bookcases, and tables, as well as book carts for transporting document boxes to researchers. But the book carts were essentially unusable because their overly tight tolerances made it almost impossible to fit them into the specially designed book lift. The carts were also too low, causing archivists to stoop so much that their backs ached. Ultimately, Bunshaft's carts were replaced with more accommodating conventional ones. Bunshaft, a master of the bold architectural concept as well as of intricate architectural details was, like some other high-profile architects, not always as good at working through all of the practical problems of his designs.[153]

Only a few years after the Johnson Library was finished, some of the beautiful slabs of travertine on the exterior of the building, which Bunshaft had personally selected, began to loosen. There was a danger that pieces might even crash down onto the plaza, potentially threatening the lives of the tourists and scholars drawn to the building. Ada Huxtable, the *New York Times* architectural critic who had praised the building just two years before, wrote in an article that criticized the architectural egotism of all presidential libraries: "There may be some poetic or philosophical justice in the fact that the Johnson Library is cracking up shortly after it was built, showing the vulnerability of an overblown concept and the morality of contractors. . . . Here is a building whose joints we personally admired, notable for a Pharaonic air of permanence, falling apart at the seams."[154] This problem was not actually Bunshaft's fault. The contractor did not follow his specifications for attaching the travertine to the building. The contractor used gypsum plaster mortar instead of cement mortar, as well as inferior metal pins that did not meet Bunshaft's design specifications.[155] It took almost two decades to solve the problem with the travertine, and when I first visited the building in the mid-1990s, there were still wooden gates and scaffolding around the building, to prevent human injury and to effect repairs.[156]

But today, visitors walking toward the building will not be aware of any of these problems, almost all of which have been remedied. Although the original displays avoided the Vietnam War, new exhibits installed in the mid-1990s deal not only with the war but also with the political and cultural reaction to it. Visitors today are likely to be impressed by the insight into this period of American history revealed by the exhibits, as well as by the power of the building's design, which somehow combines grace and power, clothing the imperial presidency and Johnson's psychology in an expressive form.[157]

Architect Leon Moed, who worked for five years on the building with Bunshaft, sums up its meaning using an explicitly religious architectural metaphor: "The building reflects the aura of the presidency, and the power of the office, even more than it reflects Lyndon Johnson as an individual. It was done purposefully to express the dignity, formality, and awesomeness of the presidency. . . . As visitors enter the Great Hall, it is like walking into a cathedral of the presidency." Moed gave significant credit to Lady Bird Johnson for the success of the building. As he said, "Lady Bird was really the client for all intents and purposes. LBJ trusted her, and she rolled up her shirt-sleeves and got down to work. . . . Lady Bird was extraordinary. She was a knowledgeable client and she anchored the project."

Mrs. Johnson has also helped to anchor the library in other ways in the many years since its completion, allowing the release of as many materials as possible, including President Johnson's secret White House tapes that he thought should be sealed until 2023.[158] In doing so, Lady Bird Johnson has helped create an institution of symbolic power and democratic access that at the same time expresses the political and psychological realities of the imperial presidency.

4 Celebrity and Power
The Commemoration of First Ladies

In Henry James's novel *The Portrait of a Lady*, Madame Merle, a scheming older woman, says to the main character, Isabel Archer, "What do you call one's self? Where does it begin? Where does it end? It overflows into everything that belongs to us—and then it flows back again. I know that a large part of myself is in the dresses I choose to wear." Isabel Archer replies, "My clothes may express the dress maker, but they don't express me. To begin with, it's not my own choice that I wear them; they are imposed upon me by society."[1] These quotations address an important truth—that whether we choose our clothing or have it imposed on us, or some combination of the two, our sartorial signs are bound up with our identities, roles, and cultural values. As the saying goes, "Clothes make the man"—and the woman. In keeping with this idea, the commemoration of first ladies begins with dresses.

At the Smithsonian, the commemoration of first ladies stretches back to the early twentieth century, and these displays eventually had an impact on first ladies displays in presidential libraries. Helen Taft lent her inaugural gown to the museum in 1912, establishing the tradition of first ladies giving their dresses to the nation. Since then other first ladies and their descendants have donated many gowns to the Smithsonian. Today, the "nation's attic" has more than forty such dresses. First exhibited in the Smithsonian's Arts and Industries Building in 1914, six years before women got the right to vote, first ladies' dresses were immediately popular. They are now on display at the National Museum of American History and are among the most popular exhibits at the Smithsonian, competing effectively with the Mercury capsule in the Air and Space Museum and the Tyrannosaurus Rex skeleton in the Natural History Museum.

First ladies have fascinated the nation since its beginning.[2] For instance, the *National Intelligencer* and other newspapers covered Dolley Madison's activities extensively, including her bravery in saving George Washington's

Helen Herron Taft's gown, in the 1915 *Catalog of American Historical Costumes, Including Those of the Mistresses of the White House as Shown in the United States National Museum.*

portrait hours before the British army burned the White House in 1814.[3] In almost all presidential monuments in Washington, D.C., however, first ladies are absent, despite the crucial role they often played in their husbands' careers. Part of what fascinates us and—for some—generates anxiety about first ladies is their power. Powerful first ladies, such as Edith Wilson, Eleanor Roosevelt, Nancy Reagan, and Hillary Clinton, have all aroused controversy. What is at stake in the commemoration of first ladies is the expression as well as repression of women's power in the United States. As Edith Mayo, retired curator of the Smithsonian's current exhibit, said to me, "First ladies structure the image and politics of the White House through their social roles."[4] Such social roles require their mastery of clothing, of sartorial signs. Clothing is sometimes considered a minor art, but it has received significant attention from anthropologists, and as the displays at the Smithsonian show, first ladies' dresses are both beautiful objects and key parts of their identities. The first ladies' dresses functioned as social and political signs that demonstrated how for first ladies the domestic and personal became national and political.

Ultimately, however, limiting the memorialization of first ladies in the Smithsonian almost exclusively to dresses, as was done from 1914 to 1987, was problematic. If clothes helped to make the man in this period, it was in terms of providing crucial finishing touches to acknowledged power and accomplishments. However, for first ladies, clothes threatened to overwhelm and obscure their accomplishments and keep their roles strictly circumscribed. Displaying first ladies' dresses, without also displaying their accomplishments and power, risked reducing women to ciphers of vanity and narcissism that portrayed women bodily but neglected their minds, their power, and their continuing and increasing participation in political life.

Anthropology and the Reception of the First Ladies Displays

Understanding the institutional context is crucial to understanding the exhibitions of the first ladies. From its founding in 1881 through the 1930s, the Smithsonian's National Museum featured ethnological displays that were pervaded by prevailing racist anthropological notions. While academic anthropology, under the leadership of Franz Boas and others, moved increasingly toward a nonracist view of human cultures in the early twentieth century,[5] the Smithsonian continued to display outmoded hierarchies of race.[6] The first volume of the lavish Smithsonian Scientific Series (1934), for example, contained an illustration of a mannequin of an Australian aborigine, who was "classed among the lowest races of man."[7] Smithsonian displays portrayed Native Americans as midway between savagery and civilization, while the first ladies exhibit, "the most popular exhibit in this division, indeed one of the most popular in the whole Museum," was placed near displays of "mechanical technology," which represented the apex of humanity.[8] These elegantly dressed mannequins, holding books, sitting on chairs, or standing beside tables, were members of this most elevated and modern group of humans.

Social Darwinism, which influenced the early displays of first ladies' gowns, was popularized in many of the world's fairs held in the late nineteenth and early twentieth centuries in Europe and the United States, including Chicago's Columbian Exposition of 1893.[9] Many Smithsonian employees were involved in setting up anthropological displays at world's fairs and saw them as testing grounds for future museum exhibits in Washington, D.C. For example, the assistant secretary of the Smithsonian, G. Brown Goode, wrote in 1890 that the upcoming Chicago exhibition would display "the steps of progress of civilization and its arts in successive centuries, and in all lands up to the present time."[10] At the Chicago World's Fair, as at other world's fairs, displays of non-Western cultures provided exotic counterpoints to the displays of technology, industry, and arts of Europe and the United States.[11] The idea was presented, both in world's fairs and in ethnographic museum exhibits like the Smithsonian's, that gradations between savagery and civilization existed and could be displayed.[12] This message was clearly received by at least some of the many millions who attended the fair. For instance, an 1893 article in the *Chicago Tribune* stated that "an opportunity was afforded [at the Chicago World's Fair] to the scientific mind to descend the spiral of evolution, tracing humanity in its highest phases down almost to its animalistic origins."[13]

As Curtis Hinsley writes, "Chicago marked the critical change in technique and arrangement. Under [Smithsonian curator W. H.] Holmes's direction the Smithsonian's exhibits displayed an impressive number of life-size, realistic groups of North American aborigines. . . . [T]he theme was environment, but the new element was the group, and the concept changed the displays from pieces of sculpture to 'pictures from life.'"[14] From the late nineteenth century to the mid-twentieth century the Smithsonian often displayed ethnological artifacts in glass cases arranged by type and region, usually moving from "the simplest types" and proceeding to "the most perfect and elaborate objects of the same class which human effort has produced."[15]

Smithsonian anthropologists had been collecting clothing and regalia from around the world, which was being used to form a collection documenting present-day life as well as to preserve evidence of the past. Some of these costumes appeared in the figural habitat groups Smithsonian anthropologists were designing for display in public expositions. But the interests of the anthropology department were not the only sources for the display of costumes. Clothing had also been displayed in the London Universal Exposition of 1854, the International Health Exhibition in London in 1884, and the Paris Universal Exposition of 1889.[16]

Hoes and James

Within this framework two members of high society of Washington, D.C., Cassie Mason Myers Julian-James and Rose Gouverneur Hoes, volunteered in 1912 to create what would become one of the most popular displays in the Smithsonian. In the museum's archives and in the exhibition catalogs written by Hoes and James, the story of the exhibition of the gowns of the mistresses of the White House unfolds. These materials tell us about changes in exhibition practices over time, about the gender politics of the early exhibitions, and about the attractions of dress displays as they were laid out at the Smithsonian. James's account of how the collection of first ladies' clothing came about illuminates how these outfits functioned as an expression of American women's history, as well as their relationship to the Smithsonian's Department of Anthropology:

> One very stormy day my mother . . . was not feeling well. Thinking how
> I could amuse her, we talked of a trunk filled with beautiful things that
> belonged to my grandmother. . . . In looking over the costumes we
> thought we would pack away a complete outfit belonging to each one
> of us, making three generations, as the collection would then cover the
> century from eighteen hundred to nineteen hundred. . . . The United
> States National Museum . . . urged me to place its contents on exhibition.
> . . . Mrs. Rose Gouverneur Hoes became interested, and as she was the
> great granddaughter of President Monroe, possessing . . . the dress of her
> grandmother, the idea of collecting the costumes of the ladies of the White
> House came to us. The problem of mounting the dresses soon became an
> important question. Wax figures would not do, and Mr. W. H. Holmes, the
> head curator of the Department of Anthropology, suggested plaster. . . .
> It was decided . . . that the same face should be used for each figure. The

result has been most satisfactory. . . . We were told that we could never fill a hall, but in a short time we accomplished the impossible.[17]

It was, at the time, difficult to insert women's history into the almost completely all-male displays of the Smithsonian, but James and Hoes did it in part through an appeal to high civilizations of the past. The plaster of paris figures for the exhibition were ivory white, recalling ancient Greek and Roman statuary. Hoes sought the first White House dresses for the exhibition at a Dolley Madison charity breakfast in Washington, D.C., where she received promises of five gowns from Mrs. Taft and other presidential descendants. Hoes wrote that she was "determined to get a dress of every first lady before I pass on. . . . [F]ifty years from now, I hope the collection . . . will rank with the best in any part of the country and will be the most popular exhibit in the museum."[18]

As first conceived and executed, the display encompassed the history of upper-class American clothing, with the gowns of the mistresses of the White House receiving special prominence. As Hoes explained, "It is not an exhibition of the dresses of the wives of the Presidents, but the gowns of the mistresses of the White House," because "if it were the former there would be many vacancies in this long line of historical costumes."[19] Hoes was indicating that the role of the first lady was so important that, for a widower or bachelor president, a surrogate first lady almost always filled the role. For example, the niece of bachelor president James Buchanan, Harriet Lane Johnston, acted as White House hostess during her uncle's term. As a result, Johnston's elegant dress was on display to ensure there was not a stylistic gap in the dresses of the 1850s.

The collection of first lady materials, always identified by the full name (including maiden name) of the owner, ranged from Martha Dandridge Custis Washington's receipted dressmaker's bill, to lemon-colored slippers worn by Abigail Smith Adams, to a monogrammed white satin fan of Sarah Angelica Singleton Van Buren, to a chair with sphinx-headed arms owned by Elizabeth Kortwright Monroe.[20] Fifteen of the dresses were from first ladies when the display first opened, and more were added annually as the Costume Committee led by James and Hoes actively acquired more of the first ladies' dresses, which constituted the highlight of the collection.

From the first, there was relatively little male clothing on display. Examples included a military uniform worn by George Washington before he was president, the court dress of James Monroe while a special envoy to

Rose Gouverneur Hoes (left) and Cassie Mason-Myers Julian James (right) dress one of the plaster of paris first ladies mannequins. Photo, Smithsonian Institution, c. 1916.

the court of Napoleon Bonaparte, a variety of breeches, an undershirt and a waistcoat worn by Thomas Jefferson, and a uniform of Andrew Jackson.[21] Washington designed his own visually impressive uniforms, but for the most part men's formal wear changed slowly compared to that of women, had less variety and color, and consequently aroused less interest.[22] In addition, most of the art and architecture of Washington, D.C., already commemorated powerful American men. For these reasons, the examples of male dress were far overshadowed by the clothing of the White House mistresses.[23]

In some ways these exhibits of first ladies and their personal objects evoked dioramas, although a more accurate term for this kind of display is habitat group, a display genre that does not include a painted backdrop.[24] In keeping with the idea of the habitat group, the curators attempted to pose the first ladies in their environment of upper-class refinement. For example, the mannequin of Dorothy Paine Todd Madison, in her yellow satin brocade dress draped over a white satin petticoat embroidered with flowers, stood next to a mahogany chair, holding a copy of Milton's *Paradise Lost*. Other first ladies were also shown posed in different arrangements, whether seated by a coaster table (Martha Washington) or standing beside music books (President Monroe's daughter, Maria Hester Monroe Gouverneur).[25] The mistresses of the White House were displayed as educated and refined women at ease in social settings, in marked contrast with ethnological dioramas that showed non-Western people engaged in manual work.

An article written by Garret P. Serviss of the *San Antonio Light* portrayed the displays of White House gowns as being at the top of the hierarchy of cultures in the Smithsonian: "Dress Gauges Civilization: . . . You take the measure of a tribe, a people, a race, a nation, when you see how it dresses its women, or rather, how they interpret its civilization by the dress which they choose for themselves."[26] James's description in the exhibition's first catalog as "giving to the public a most valuable collection of historic costumes of the great women of our country of whom we are so justly proud" helped place these displays of notable American women at the pinnacle of civilization.[27] James and Hoes were proud of these women because their class and position virtually assured them of being exemplars of taste and morality. These elegant costumes functioned as indexical signs of the character of the women who wore them.

Serviss's newspaper account contrasted the differing ways in which women and men responded to the exhibition:

I have observed that, while some of the women visitors to this exhibition inspect the historic dresses with appreciative glances, some with an air of charitable criticism, some with unsophisticated surprise and admiration, and some with intent looks and thoughtful pauses which suggest the gathering and memorizing of valuable hints, the men generally have the furtive and half-ashamed look of members of their sex who have been dragged into a modiste's shop. Most of them escape as soon as they can; some step just inside for a moment, glance around in a startled way, and hurry off as if they had been on the verge of a great impropriety. A few stay and look at the faces and figures, ignoring the gowns which are the sole object of the exhibition. Even masculine indifference, however, is piqued a little by . . . Dolly Madison's captivating gesture as she holds out a time-stained copy of "Paradise Lost," opened at one of Adam's solemn love-makings to Eve. . . . It is not what the men wore, but what the women wore that best indicates the quality and degree of past civilizations.[28]

Serviss's colorful account makes some important points about the gendered reception of the displays. For instance, he notes the levels at which women were engaged, whether from wanting to observe the dresses for their own use or from fascination with outmoded fashions. Men, as Serviss observed, sometimes fled the exhibit and seemed less interested in the gowns. Most likely, it was not just that the costumes were uninteresting to men, but more importantly that taking a public interest in women's clothing might be seen as threatening to their masculinity. But for Serviss, the dresses were worthy of careful study by both men and women because they were markers of civilization. His account chastises the men he observed for paying attention to the ladies wearing the gowns, while largely ignoring the dresses themselves. Were the dresses or the first ladies being commemorated?

Secretary of the Smithsonian Charles D. Walcott appreciated the work of James and Hoes, in part because their wide social connections among upper-class women made them extremely effective at obtaining dresses with which families were frequently reluctant to part. For instance, the gown worn by Helen Herron Taft at the inauguration of her husband on 4 March 1909 was the object of much negotiation. Mrs. Taft offered to lend her gown, but the museum wanted it permanently. Helen Taft wrote that she felt "provoked" but eventually agreed to donate the gown, in part as a result of diplomatically worded appeals from Hoes and James.[29] Following this example, later first ladies gave their inaugural gowns to the Smithsonian.

Hoes wrote that "so many of the Museum costumes have been obtained with much difficulty. . . . [I]t has meant so much urging, and in some instances influence." She continued:

> This was certainly true of Abigail Powers Fillmore. . . . Mrs. Frances Hubbard Larkin . . . came to Washington for a visit [and] brought along with her a gown she had owned for many years worn by Mrs. Fillmore while living in the White House. Her idea was to pass it over to the Museum, but she weakened. She had so much sentiment in regard to the dress that . . . three times she brought the costume to Washington, and each time she took it back again. She could not make up her mind to part with it. . . . [T]he Costume Committee . . . took up the matter through correspondence, and in the end Mrs. Larkin most generously gave the dress to the United States National Museum.[30]

For many upper-class women, ownership of a gown, and especially a first lady's gown, maintained a family's connection to a material trace of American history, an American woman's history at the height of political power and patronage. A few women, to Hoes's despair, had little concern for the historic materials passed down to them and allowed their first ladies' dresses to be seriously damaged or even destroyed.[31]

James and Hoes presented the social face of upper-class American history through clothing. As Hoes wrote, "This striking assemblage of gowns and court-dresses worn by Presidents' wives, ancient Knickerbocker dames, wives of diplomats, and social leaders of the past, forms a brilliant, unique, epoch marking, kaleidoscopic mass of form and color that makes of this exhibition a realistic illustrated diary of a hundred years of changing styles."[32] But out of this broader collection, Hoes and James, and the public, from the beginning, had a special fascination for the first ladies. Their dresses, representing the pinnacle of American power and style, were highlighted, and over the next few decades the gowns and accessories from other ladies were removed.[33]

Without the effort of James and Hoes, it probably would have been several more decades before the first ladies were commemorated at the national level, and they probably never would have been commemorated in quite as grand a style with such a complete collection of first ladies' gowns. Without these women's work over many years the Smithsonian might have been largely deprived of one of its most popular exhibits.

Attendance figures were important for the Smithsonian, as evidenced by the emphasis placed on these statistics in the Smithsonian's annual report.[34] The institution's popularity ensured continued congressional funding. The immediate success of the first ladies collection was an obvious boon to the museum, but because two volunteer women with their own agendas had curated it, tension arose between James and Hoes, on the one hand, and the all-male senior museum staff, on the other. Until the early 1900s, volunteers sometimes outnumbered the professional staff. Beginning in 1900, however, Secretary Walcott placed an emphasis on professionalizing the staff and curtailing the input of volunteers over whom the Smithsonian's administration had limited control.[35]

Hoes and James solicited objects, helped design display cases and mannequins, wrote labels, picked up and received loans and gifts to the exhibit, and repaired and mounted the dresses on the mannequins, even bringing in their own family possessions to complete the ensembles.[36] In short, they did everything a professional curator would have done, and more. In their minds, they owned this tremendously successful exhibit.[37] By 1915, Hoes, with the encouragement of James, and to the consternation of some of the Smithsonian's professional staff, had independently published a catalog of the exhibit, complete with photographs of the first ladies mannequins. She offered it for sale in the museum to earn at least a small amount of recognition and compensation.[38] Upon publication of the catalog, Hoes removed most of her identifying labels in the exhibit cases, which the curator of the History Division correctly saw as an attempt to make visitors purchase the catalog; otherwise they would have no idea who owned items in the cases, or even which mannequin represented which first lady.[39] The dissension was noted by W. H. Holmes, who wrote that the "collection is repudiated by the Curator of History," Theodore Belote, who referred to it as the "so-called Period Costumes Collection."[40] In 1916, Hoes proposed installing her own portrait in the costume gallery "as a memorial," further irritating the curator. However, the senior staff acceded to her request.[41]

In 1918, James asked Walcott for a letter of thanks to be sent to Hoes and suggested that she herself would no longer work on the exhibition, in part because she felt unappreciated. Walcott sent the requested letter of thanks and told James and Hoes that the Smithsonian would take control of the exhibition. This angered James, who immediately wrote to Walcott:

> We have no idea of giving up a trust reposed in us by many friends and acquaintances by passing over, as your letter suggests, to the officials of the United States Museum, the Costume exhibition. I simply asked you to send Mrs. Hoes a word of appreciation in acknowledgement of her splendid work as neither of us has ever received a line of commendation. . . . [W]e feel that it might be well to break up the collection, returning the costumes and heirlooms now on exhibition, lent on our representation and our responsibility to their owners. It seems to us the only way out of the situation. I have however taken the liberty of sending your letter to my lawyer . . . who may see fit to talk the matter over with you.[42]

Walcott wrote a polite but firm response: "The Museum is exceedingly grateful to Mrs. James and Mrs. Hoes . . . [but] the material thus assembled does not constitute an independent exhibition. . . . [I]t is subject to the rules and regulations that govern the acceptance and care of all historical material received by the Museum."[43]

However, as James and Hoes pointed out, many of the objects had been lent rather than given and so were not actually owned by the Smithsonian. Over a period of several years, the Smithsonian wrote letters to secure ownership of as many of the dresses and objects originally owned by first ladies as possible. This, predictably, was a source of further irritation for James and Hoes.[44] However, they had no choice but to eventually accept that the exhibition was owned by the Smithsonian. In 1922, James died, but Hoes continued working on the collection for ten more years, writing two more editions of her catalog, each larger than the last, reflecting the growing number of first ladies' gowns in the collection.

The Deterioration of the Dresses and the Arrival of Margaret Brown Klapthor

By the time of Hoes's death in 1933, the museum had been wrestling for some time with the disturbing reality that some of the dresses on display, so lovingly collected by James and Hoes, were being damaged by the way they were exhibited. The first ladies' dresses, as displayed in the 1910s, were lit largely by sunlight streaming through the windows, often causing irreparable damage.[45] As early as 1916, two years after the gowns were placed on display, visitors and curators noticed that sun exposure was damaging some of the dresses, and the Smithsonian took modest measures to protect them. To last more than a few decades, the gowns required very low-light display conditions and periodic environmentally controlled dark storage. At this point, lightweight curtains were put over the windows and skylights, which only slightly diminished the sunlight.[46] This slowed but did not stop the deterioration.

An example was Helen Herron Taft's inaugural ball gown, an Empire-style dress made by the Frances Smith Company of New York City in early 1909.[47] The dress has a delicate lace bodice with a long narrow skirt and rounded train of white silk chiffon. The chiffon was decorated in Tokyo with waving lines of goldenrod embroidered with white and silver threads and crystal beads. The dress is exquisite (see photo, p. 106). Over time the delicate fabric, made brittle by exposure to the sun's ultraviolet rays, was slowly pulled by the weight of the heavy embroidery until it ripped to shreds. In 1921, Theodore Belote, the curator so often annoyed by James and Hoes, reported that "visitors are criticizing the present installation of the Presidential gown presented by Mrs. Taft . . . [because there are] noticeably long rents . . . torn in various portions of the fabric. . . . [U]nless something can be done this process will continue until the dress is seriously injured."[48] Hoes proposed that the gown be stitched around the embroidery to a new petticoat beneath, and evidently this repair was made.[49]

The costume collection featuring the gowns of the mistresses of the White House, with sunlight streaming into the gallery, damaging the objects on display. Photo, Smithsonian Institution, 1930s.

In 1943, Margaret Brown, who had earned a bachelor's degree in history from the University of Maryland,[50] joined the Smithsonian as a "scientific aid" and began to work on the first ladies collection. In spite of the earlier repairs, the Taft dress and others had continued to deteriorate. Brown wrote the year after she was hired that "naturally we are perturbed about the deterioration of this dress because the loss of any one of the dresses would mean that our collection is no longer complete."[51] Brown and the museum had the fabric of Taft's gown analyzed by a private firm, which concluded, "It is a source of great regret to us that we are unable to recommend any procedure which will have a reasonable chance of arresting the deterioration and at the same time not practically destroy the garment itself."[52] Finally, Brown decided to have a professional seamstress re-stitch the gown with fifteen yards of matching pure silk chiffon, making the dress a mélange of the authentic and the reconstructed.[53] The obsession with preserving these gowns was laudable, but the vast effort put into these examples of fragile upper-class clothing may also have prevented the formation of a larger discussion and display of the role of women in political culture. All of the concern about gowns helped reduce first ladies to their clothes, limiting them, and in a sense women in general, to an extremely circumscribed role, politically.

Reinventing the First Ladies Exhibit

Brown eventually became the curator of the first ladies collection, which she oversaw for forty years. By the early 1950s, a photograph of the exhibit shows mannequins standing together in a larger case reminiscent of a department store display. Brown would sometimes take distinguished guests on personal tours of the collection. For instance, in 1954 Mamie Eisenhower wrote, "Dear Miss Brown, Thank you so much for your graciousness in conducting Her Majesty, the Queen Mother, and me through the Smithsonian on Thursday. It was a delightful experience for both of us to see the first ladies dresses and to have you tell us so many interesting anecdotes about them."[54] Mamie Eisenhower's patronage increased Margaret Brown's clout within the Smithsonian.[55]

During this time, the Smithsonian was embarking on an ambitious Exhibits Modernization Program to update displays throughout the museum and make them more visually impressive.[56] The new First Ladies Hall, which Brown made one of the stars of this program, benefited from the fact that serious architectural problems were being dealt with at the White House during the late 1940s and early 1950s. The White House, as noted in an earlier chapter, was then near structural collapse and was almost completely rebuilt. It essentially became a replica of itself during Truman's term, with most of its original architectural innards either removed or destroyed.[57] The Smithsonian was able to salvage some of the White House's most significant architectural details, such as nine ornate fireplace mantles, including one from the East Room.[58] The Smithsonian's staff also examined the traces of earlier wallpaper designs hidden under layers of lathe and stucco. These materials and knowledge were used by Margaret Brown to direct the construction of a series of highly realistic period rooms "which give the viewer an opportunity to see the dresses in the type of surroundings in which they were originally worn."[59] Through this strategy Brown took the displays of the first ladies to higher levels of visibility and popularity. In the new hall, one end of the East Room was reconstructed as the location of several twentieth-century first ladies' gowns. Details included the carved mantel with its large gilt mirror, Corinthian pilasters, gold furniture, a custom Steinway piano, and paneling—all of which came from the White House.[60]

In May 1955, the internal newsletter *The Smithsonian Torch* featured a cover story on the new First Ladies Hall, entitled "Hustle and Bustles":

> One by one, Margaret Brown's first ladies have been trundled from their cramped cases . . . to their palatial new homes in the remodeled First Ladies Hall, scheduled to open with appropriate fanfare at 9 P.M. on Tuesday, May 24 . . . [a] gala day in Smithsonian history. Mrs. Eisenhower has accepted an invitation to be a guest at the occasion, which will honor her and the other First Ladies, their families, and their descendants. The pink silk inaugural dress the present first lady has given to the collection will be on public display for the first time.

By tradition, previous first ladies' gowns were displayed only after their husbands had left office, but with Mamie Eisenhower's renowned pink inaugural ball gown that tradition was broken. The gown was a sure draw because of her popularity and celebrated fondness for clothes in an era when women were embracing fashion after the Depression and World War II. In contrast to the publicity-shy Bess Truman, Mamie Eisenhower reveled in public attention. Her celebrity was linked to her husband's position, but it flourished because of her style. When Brown changed the Smithsonian's policy and put Mamie's pink rhinestone-encrusted gown on display in the replicated end of the East Room, she was relying on Mamie's celebrity to draw people to the new exhibit.

At the gala opening, Mamie Eisenhower, accompanied by the president, threw a special master switch that lit up the rooms of the new hall. Smithsonian secretary Leonard Carmichael said, "The hall which Mrs. Eisenhower opened is designed to display, in a way that teaches American History, the gowns of the first ladies of the White House. . . . It symbolizes the growth of our country step by step from General Washington to General Eisenhower."[61] It also symbolized the growth of the new consumer economy of the 1950s, for like most museum displays it told viewers as much about the era in which it was created as the one it portrayed.

Karal Ann Marling, in her study, "Mamie Eisenhower's New Look," analyzes Mamie's dress and its representations as part of the burgeoning of a consumer culture of televised looking, consuming, and imagining in the 1950s.[62] The new hall, although not discussed by Marling, fits in with her analysis of the ways in which Mamie's fashion reflected and was amplified by American visual culture of the time. Set amid the sumptuous details of the presidential rooms and relics, the beautiful gowns echoed a consumer-oriented fashion show.[63] Indeed, the fashion-show quality of the gowns could be seen less than a year before the new hall opened, when a benefit fashion show featuring designer Philip Robertson's modern reinterpretations of the Smithsonian's first ladies' gowns were for sale at Martha Washington's granddaughter's historic home.[64] Just as at this fashion show, visitors to the new exhibit could wander through the spaces admiring the gowns and their luxurious environments. Both the fashion show and the museum exhibit encouraged conspicuous consumption.

Brown's First Ladies Hall owed something to the work of James and Hoes in its celebration of the celebrity of the first ladies through their gowns, but its elaborate period rooms went far beyond the group format of the initial first ladies displays. Brown's exhibit was a visual feast for visitors that drew upon the increasing mass-media visibility of first ladies, but it was also indirectly tied to contemporary consumerism. It was not that viewers for the most part wanted to decorate their houses as exact copies of these rooms or wear exact copies of the first ladies' dresses, but in a broader sense, the display of lavish upper-class spending on clothing and interior design dovetailed with middle-class consumerism in the postwar era.[65] It enveloped visitors in lavish settings that encouraged conspicuous consumption. In the prosperous 1950s, it was not merely the wealthy who could aspire to fashion and opulence. The economy's health depended on middle-class consumers outfitting themselves and their homes extravagantly. But the history that the gowns addressed was the history of elites—and contrasted with, as much as it complemented, middle-class consumer culture. Few in the middle class could afford one of Mamie's rhinestone-encrusted gowns.

The period rooms were peopled with the same mannequins that had appeared in earlier displays, now often reoriented into conversational groups. For instance, the mannequin of Dolley Madison, previously holding a copy of *Paradise Lost*, was reoriented to gesture (without a book) toward Martha Washington and Abigail Adams. These were imaginary groupings of first ladies who actually rarely socialized with one another and sometimes did not even like one another, often because they and their husbands represented different political parties. Seeing these first ladies harmoniously speaking, when in fact they were sometimes bitter competitors—or occasionally had never even met because they lived in the White House in entirely different decades—was a remarkable and pleasant fiction. It created a fantasy world where upper-class manners and morals trumped time, partisan attachments, and personality differences.

In the hall, Brown also included a small narrative diorama representing one of the most heroic events in the history of first ladies. Here, Dolley Madison was shown standing in the large Oval Room, directing a servant to pack up the red velvet curtains as the British army approached and prepared to burn the capital in 1814. President James Madison had left Dolley in the White House as he went with a small army contingent to try to ascertain the invading British army's intentions. Dolley Madison was urged by many to abandon the White House as the British drew closer, but wrote, "I confess that I was so unfeminine as to be free of fear, and willing to remain in the Castle. If [only] I could have a cannon through every window."[66] Finally, hours before the British arrived, she had the portrait of George Washington stripped from its frame and the expensive red velvet curtains in the Oval Room removed, which is the event shown in the diorama, so that they could be taken to safety. She fled shortly before the British torched the White House. Her steely resolve made her the subject of laudatory articles, illustrations, and even poetry by her contemporaries.[67] The diorama honored this example of White House interior design, in which Dolley Madison played a part in terms of its initial design, as well as in terms of the salvation of a few relics from it. More importantly, it celebrated Dolley Madison's bravery.[68] Her acts of cultural salvage were paralleled by those of the Smithsonian, where Margaret Brown was salvaging materials from the White House to create replicated rooms, as well as saving dresses.

The new Smithsonian period rooms in the First Ladies Hall shared similarities with the commemoration of George and Martha Washington at Mount Vernon—both preserved and re-created domestic spaces where visitors could marvel nostalgically at the architecture of American political power. At the Smithsonian, the rooms presented the social face of presidential power through the lens of women's social roles. These beautiful rooms were a locus of feminine authority visible in the refinement of the decor and in the gracious poses of the first ladies who oversaw them. The First Ladies Hall recognized the power of women within the White House, in part through the absence of men in the displays—except for the presidential portraits on the walls—and implied that these women had significant, if hidden, effects on history. The exhibits celebrated the spaces of balls and receptions, teas and socials, where repartee and gracious discussion furthered the politics of every administration. Their sphere of power, however,

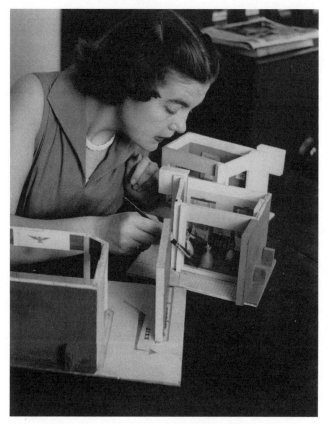

Margaret Brown Klapthor preparing a model of the First Ladies
Hall, 1950s. Photo, Smithsonian Institution.

was still limited to the domestic sphere, even if the house in question was
the White House. Being a first lady meant in a sense being married to the
White House, which was reinforced by the displays.

Margaret Brown, now Margaret Brown Klapthor—she had married Frank
Klapthor, the curator of the Daughters of the American Revolution Museum
in Washington, D.C., in 1956[69]—continually reworked the displays, changing poses, accessories, and furniture to improve them. In 1962, the first
ladies mannequins themselves were made more lifelike, complementing
the opulence of the displays.[70] From the beginning, the first ladies figures
had individualized hairstyles drawn from old prints and photographs, but
now instead of being ivory-white the mannequins were painted with pink
flesh tones, colored hair, ruby lips, and rouged cheeks. Their eyes were emphatically lined with long dark lashes that did not look much like photo-

By 1964, the mannequins had been painted with naturalistic flesh tones and hair color, as well as given heavy eyelashes, a style popular during the period. Photo, Smithsonian Institution.

graphs and paintings of nineteenth-century first ladies but more resembled models found in 1960s fashion magazines. Perhaps the new glamour of the mannequins was influenced by the most glamorous first lady ever—Jacqueline Bouvier Kennedy. Kennedy helped design her own white silk inaugural ball gown with silver-embroidered bodice and matching full-length cape, which was added to the collection in the same year that the mannequins were painted.[71]

In 1964, the collection was transferred from the Smithsonian's late-nine-teenth-century Arts and Industries building to the entirely new National Museum of History and Technology (later the National Museum of American History), where the replicated rooms were rebuilt and made larger and even more opulent. For example, the East Room, previously represented by a small section of the room with one fireplace, was now re-created as a much larger section of the room with two fireplaces separated by three large gold-curtained windows framed by pilasters. The new hall featured the diorama, seven rooms, each populated by the mannequins of three to eight first ladies, and an eighth room, which contained historic furnish-ings. As Klapthor wrote, "Since each room setting contains dresses repre-

The expanded replica of the East Room of the White House on display in the First Ladies Hall in the new Museum of National History and Technology, 1964. Photo, Smithsonian Institution.

senting a span of several administrations, it has been necessary to select a style of background and furnishings typical of a certain period or a single administration. . . . Thus, the hall reflects changing styles of interior decoration as well as changes in fashion since 1789."[72] On exhibit were two rooms from the Executive Mansion in Philadelphia that was used before the White House was completed (representing the years 1787–1809), as well as six rooms from the White House, including the Music Room (1809–1829), a Reception Room (1829–1845), a Victorian Parlor (1845–1869), two versions of the Blue Room (1869–1893 and 1893–1921), and finally the largest room of all, the East Room, representing the most recent first ladies dating from 1921 to 1965. The earliest rooms were based largely on meticulous reproductions of written descriptions of the curious styles of the past, such as a nineteenth-century text that told of "white [wall]paper sprinkled with gold stars and a gilt border" that was re-created for the Reception Room.[73]

As head of the Political History division, Klapthor also oversaw the burgeoning collection of political artifacts, relics, and memorabilia in the Smithsonian, from a couch owned by President Adams to Lincoln's writing desk. As she worked with these materials, displaying some of them in the period rooms in the First Ladies Hall, she began to study and collect White

House dinner china as well. In the 1965 catalog to the first ladies exhibition, a piece of presidential china was included in each section, from a cup from Martha Washington's china, to a service plate used from the Wilson through Hoover administrations. Klapthor spent years identifying pieces of china used in the White House and writing what is still the leading book on the subject.[74] The first ladies' gowns and the china emphasized the social character of first ladies' lives, allowing visitors to imagine themselves among the objects and symbols of national power.

While the visual material in the exhibits was rich, the textual information about the lives and roles of the first ladies was limited. As curator Edith Mayo, Klapthor's successor, said, "Margaret Klapthor lovingly tended that collection and brought it to a very high level of visibility. But beautiful as it was, the political and social history of the First Ladies was not seriously addressed. The exhibit essentially consisted of giant dolls in a giant doll house." People loved these dolls, however, and their popularity should be taken seriously. Dolls tend to be dismissed as children's playthings. But for both children and adults, dolls can be used for what anthropologists call "serious play." Elizabeth Cameron analyzes how dolls are used in play and ritual in several African cultures, but she also comments on dolls in western cultures: "Playing with dolls . . . is serious business. . . . While the average parent views these figures as relatively inconsequential objects, it is becoming increasingly clear to social scientists that they can be active in establishing value systems and constructing identities."[75]

In the Smithsonian's vast archives, where for many years museum staff were required to record and copy every piece of correspondence received, as well as their replies, I read four of the twenty-six thick correspondence files about the first ladies exhibit for the year 1976. The sheer volume of correspondence about the first ladies exhibit is a strong testament not just to its popularity but to how personally some viewers engaged with the exhibit. There was a great variety of letters about the first ladies, but the single greatest subject of inquiry—nine letters—was for information on the first ladies' gowns for use in creating handmade dresses for personal collections of dolls of the first ladies. Such doll collections even appeared in at least three presidential libraries.[76] One of these letters, dated 20 August 1976, sent from a woman in Kenmore, New York, is typical:[77]

> I am a doll collector and as part of my collection I have dressed 40 dolls copying the dresses of the First Ladies as displayed in your lovely exhibit

in the Smithsonian. . . . Mrs. Monroe . . . and Mrs. Ford are the only two I
have to do in order to complete the collection. I understand that you have
recently accepted a dress from Mrs. Ford. It certainly would be so helpful
if you could send me a description of the dress so that I could begin
working on my doll of Mrs. Ford. It would be helpful if you could include
the color and type of material, or if you would have time also a sketch of
the style as well as a description.

Margaret Klapthor had sent to this particular woman (most of the requests
were from women, but I did find a similar request from a man) photos
and the information required to sew an accurate doll-sized replica of Betty
Bloomer Ford's inaugural dress.

Ford records in her memoirs that she thought she might be related to
Amelia Bloomer, and she certainly carried on in her footsteps politically
through her support of the Equal Rights Amendment. Amelia Bloomer
popularized the split skirt with pantaloons, which were more comfortable
and practical than the tight corsets and very long skirts of the nineteenth
century. Carol Mattingly writes, "Woman's gendered appearance, inscribed
by an elaborately ornamented and detailed wardrobe, not only defined her
femininity but also systematically and simultaneously distinguished her
place. That is, the cut and detail of her dress, often accompanied by the
specific style of her hair, signified her proper temporal location . . . as well
as social or class position." The Bloomer outfit was obviously political,
and first ladies' clothes are different from this kind of clothing. First ladies
generally wore elegant and very conservative styles, such as First Lady Julia Tyler's nineteenth-century dress with its flounced skirt supported over
a hoop armature.[78]

Although the styles of first ladies are elegant and conservative compared
to bloomers, these dresses also serve political aims. Part of the appeal of first
ladies is that they represent both power and, at the same time, the ultimate
in fashion and propriety. For example, Jackie Kennedy campaigned late in
one of her pregnancies in an ivory Givenchy ensemble with pillbox hat, and
her celebrity—enhanced by her fashion—helped her husband win one of
the closest elections in U.S. history. First ladies are often crucial to their
husbands' elections, have significant influence on their husbands while in
office, and sometimes have their own bases of political power. First ladies,
in part through their clothes, shape the social and political environment of
the White House and how it is perceived. Klapthor's displays of first ladies'

elegant gowns in beautifully re-created White House rooms may seem on the surface to be apolitical, but museum viewers knew that these women looked elegant while wielding power. Democratic first ladies stood next to Republican first ladies, and political issues were barely addressed in the exhibit's text, which instead stressed changing dress styles and anecdotes. But female power was always the subtext.

Even the faces of the first ladies were all alike. It was considered too expensive and complicated to create individualized faces for each mannequin. Even in the Smithsonian, the nation's museum, budgets are limited, and I found a letter from Klapthor to the Smithsonian's model lab complaining that despite having identical heads she could sometimes only get one mannequin a year to replace old ones and display new gowns, although—as she wrote—the first ladies displays constituted the most popular exhibition in the museum and therefore should have priority.[79] From the beginning, first ladies all had to have the same head, even if their hair and bodies were individualized. The head was chosen, presumably by James and Hoes, from a nineteenth-century marble sculpture by American artist Pierce Francis Connelly—owned by the Smithsonian and displayed in Klapthor's First Ladies Hall—of King Lear's daughter Cordelia.[80] At the end of Shakespeare's King Lear, Cordelia dies as a result of her virtue and honesty. The Smithsonian may or may not have intended to philosophize on Cordelia's character or meant to create a direct parallel with the virtue and self-sacrifice of the first ladies in relation to their husbands. Probably the sculpture of Cordelia was chosen because of her beauty and virtue.

The identical faces of the first ladies in the exhibit did not go unnoticed by visitors (see photo, p. 124). As Edith Mayo, who worked at the Smithsonian for twenty-five years, told me: "I can't tell you how many letters I answered from people who said, 'The Jackie mannequin looks more or less like Jackie, but you've got Mamie Eisenhower and the rest of them completely wrong.' . . . I must have written a thousand letters during my time there explaining the heads of our first ladies." Visitors wanted the first ladies mannequins to be individualized, as no doubt figures of the presidents would have been.[81] Making identical mannequins represented a refusal to recognize them as individual human beings which, as Erika Doss commented to me, "is tantamount to making them all Stepford First Wives."[82] If the Smithsonian was going to display giant dolls in a giant dollhouse, audiences wanted more lifelike dolls. The first ladies exhibit was, after all, one of the few places in the Smithsonian where women's history was addressed in any way. The celebrity of the first ladies, particularly the modern ones whose faces had appeared endlessly in the media, was remembered by visitors who wanted to see physical likenesses. Their power as celebrities was undermined by their representation as Cordelia, but if first ladies' individual identities were repressed they could not be completely contained, as evidenced by the many letters received by the Smithsonian about the mannequins.

In spite of this failure, Klapthor's exhibit remained the single most visited display at the museum year after year, decade after decade. In the late 1970s, for instance, the exhibit was so jammed with people that it became difficult for the Smithsonian's volunteer docents to circulate through the halls with their groups. As the internal *First Ladies Newsletter* put it, "Because of the great crowds in the Hall, it has been decided to suspend [formal] tours. . . . However, feel free to continue to come in on an informal basis if you like. You'll always be assured of an appreciative audience."[83]

Edith Mayo and Women's History

Margaret Brown Klapthor retired in 1983. Four years later, the Smithsonian took the exhibit off display, in part to facilitate replacement of the heating and air-conditioning systems. Despite the continuing popularity of the old displays, there was a desire to create something more historically contextualized and intellectually sophisticated.[84] Roger Kennedy, the director of the National Museum of American History at the time, said, "The dresses are a big yawn to high-style academics."[85] It is more likely that academics by the 1980s would have gasped in astonishment at the sight of first ladies reduced to dresses on identical mannequins. The exhibit was not so much a big yawn as a repression of women's history.[86] Fueled by feminist and postmodern critiques, scholars were actively writing and rewriting women's history to consider how women did participate in public and private life, and how they did so despite cultural values that isolated and repressed them.

In any case, Roger Kennedy considered a proposal to put the collection on tour to help pay for the new display. But the gowns were considered by many to be among the Smithsonian's crown jewels and far too fragile to put on tour. Klapthor was incensed at the idea: "It's like prostituting the first ladies' gowns, sending them out on the street to raise money."[87] Those opposed to sending the gowns on tour prevailed, which was fortunate because of their condition. The first comprehensive scientific assessment of the gowns was undertaken at this time, which divided them into three categories. About a third of the gowns were damaged beyond repair after decades of continual exhibition, and what remained of them had to be taken permanently off display. A second group was extremely delicate, but could be displayed in low-light conditions for relatively short periods of time. The final category consisted of the gowns that were sound enough to remain on display, as long as the lighting conditions remained extremely low—three or fewer foot-candles.[88]

The Smithsonian's new exhibit, curated by Edith Mayo, had a complicated history. She began work on it in 1990, and it opened in March 1992. But the Smithsonian called Mayo in only after it had gone through two failed scripts for the show. The first script was an in-depth academic analysis of the first ladies in historical context. As Mayo said, "It would have made a great book, but it didn't quite work as a popular exhibition." As a result, the senior Smithsonian staff decided to commission a second script, but it was also unsuccessful because it did not distinguish itself sufficiently from Klapthor's period room displays.[89] Finally, the director asked Mayo for her input, and she replied, "I think you need to politicize these women and put them in the context of women's history."

Mayo had worked at the Smithsonian for three years in the early 1960s before resigning to raise her children and get her master's degree in American studies at George Washington University. She returned to the Smithsonian in 1970, initially as one of Klapthor's assistants. As Mayo told me,

> Margaret did not have me work on the first ladies—that was very much her baby and she was very protective of it. Margaret did not really like my kind of social feminist history, but she allowed me to do it. I was always the person who was seen as doing this bizarre, radical stuff, but she took me under her wing and let me do it as long as my work was professional and nothing I did embarrassed the Smithsonian.[90]

Mayo worked on many exhibitions from the 1970s to the 1990s, including her own exhibition, *Parlor to Politics* (1990), which was an ambitious feminist analysis of women's history from domestic roles in the nineteenth century through the long struggle to gain women the right to vote in 1920. She was about to embark on a catalog for this exhibition, which was a cherished project, when she was asked to put it aside and take on the first ladies exhibit. Because of her interest in social and feminist history, ranging from civil rights to antiwar movements, some people at the Smithsonian wondered if she was the right person to treat such a popular and seemingly conventional subject. But complaints were being heard from visitors about the missing first ladies, which created pressure to get a new exhibit on display as soon as possible, and Mayo had a proven track record of assembling high quality exhibitions on tight budgets.[91]

One of Mayo's first big decisions involved Klapthor's elegant period rooms. Mayo considered rebuilding some of them in a different format, but a preliminary estimate for reconstructing the rooms came in at ten million dollars, and the budget for the entire exhibition was only one million dollars. As a result, the rooms, with their elegant wallpapers and tall, heavily curtained windows were all destroyed—a poignant event for many, including Klapthor and Mayo.[92] When one of the rooms was dismantled, a large leaded glass window cracked while workers were trying to get it out. This single window would have cost $10,000 to replace, illustrating to Mayo that they had no choice but to abandon the previous display strategy. Much of the period furniture for the rooms was placed in storage. As Mayo said to me,

> I knew it would be very awkward with Klapthor. It was her baby and I was going to have to tear it apart and start fresh. The problem with the old show was that it was a decorative-arts approach rather than a social-history approach. It was clear that if we didn't respond to the new thinking in academia about social history and women's history, the show would be an embarrassment.[93]

Only one re-created room was reconstructed—a large new space that evokes the East Room through its fireplace. However, to keep within the exhibition's budget, the windows and gold curtains were not rebuilt, and it is a much simplified—and rather inaccurate—replica known as the Ceremonial Court. The gowns of the most recent first ladies, those who were still remembered by many Smithsonian visitors, remained on display behind a wall of glass.

Mayo had only fifteen months from the time she started working on the show until it had to open, which in museum terms is a tight schedule for a major exhibition. She arranged to have it done like an assembly line, with everyone in her handpicked team working on different elements, such as a researcher working at the Library of Congress to gather information about particular first ladies and their objects.[94] The exhibition as a whole, however, was very much Mayo's. Klapthor was asked to review Mayo's preliminary script, and although she believed that "most of the things discussed in the area called political are really personal," overall she felt that "Edie has done a remarkable job considering the amount of time she had,"[95] which was high praise considering that Mayo was in charge of dismantling forty years of Klapthor's professional work. It is not surprising that Mayo, who was of a different generation, felt that the things that Klapthor labeled "personal" were in fact "political," since one of the hallmarks of the socially progressive movements of the 1960s and 1970s was that the personal is also political.

One of the problems faced by the Smithsonian was funding for the exhibit. Despite the popularity of the first ladies' gowns since 1914 and the desire of many to see displays of the first ladies returned to view, commercial sponsors for the new exhibit were difficult to find.[96] Probably corporate donors lacked interest because the new, politically engaged exhibition revealed some of the contested political, cultural, and social dimensions of the first ladies' roles. Chubb Insurance and *Good Housekeeping* magazine provided donations, but the bulk of the money for the exhibition was provided by the Smithsonian and raised by Friends of the First Ladies, a group of private individuals formed to support the new displays.[97]

The new exhibit was a dramatic departure. *First Ladies: Political Role and Public Image* completely reconceptualized the first ladies and displayed the gowns as only one part of a much broader examination of the roles of the first ladies. Previous exhibits had relied almost exclusively on the replicas combined with descriptions of the dresses and anecdotes about first ladies, but the new exhibit involved a significant amount of political analysis of their varied and changing roles. The activist first lady, once an aberration, had become more common since the 1950s when Klapthor's first replicated rooms went on display. In a sense, Mayo's exhibition reflected the changed world in which it was made. It was organized into two areas: Political Role and Public Image. Within Political Role, Mayo had six display areas: Inventing the First Ladies Role, The Nation's Hostess, Advocate for Social Causes, The President's Political Partner, Political Campaigner, and Widowhood and National Mourning. Under Public Image came The Partisan Press: The First Lady in Print; An Explosion of Images: The First Lady in Photographs; and Scrutiny vs. Control: The First Lady in the Twentieth Century.

As the subjects suggest, Mayo's exhibition represented a significant conceptual shift from the earlier displays, reflecting both the transformation of women's roles in American society and changed exhibition practices that focused on political context. Rather than glassed-in rooms that kept viewers at

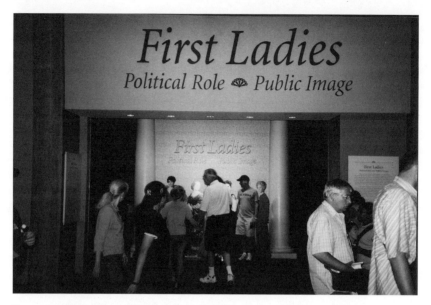

Entrance, First Ladies: Political Role and Public Image, with cut out life-size
photographs of first ladies, 1992. Photo courtesy Bess Reed.

more than an arm's length, the new exhibit used a larger number of smaller
glass cases, often mounted on the walls, so that visitors could get closer to
relics associated with the first ladies. Mayo also used longer texts to analyze
historical events and provide biographical information, as well as discuss
objects. Text panels and labels were interspersed with china, gowns, harps,
and visiting cards, as well as reproductions of historic prints and images.
Ensembles of images provided a range of ways for understanding and in-
terpreting the roles of first ladies. The exhibit discussed each first lady, in
part, through how she illuminated aspects of the role, and how the role had
changed over time.

I first entered the exhibit in summer 2003, several years after Mayo retired. At the entrance a large sign, "First Ladies: Political Role and Public
Image," is placed over a photographic life-size mural of six first ladies—including Grace Coolidge, Jackie Kennedy, and Nancy Reagan—framed by a
pair of faux Doric columns that evoke the White House. As visitors enter
the exhibit through an entry to the left side, they turn to see a wall adorned
with rows of oval portraits featuring the first ladies over and slightly ob-
scuring oval portraits of the presidents on a deep mauve wall. Usually, the
first ladies literally and figuratively stand behind the presidents, but here

Gallery display, Scrutiny vs. Control: The First Lady in the Twentieth Century, in the First Ladies Hall, designed by Edith Mayo. Photo courtesy Bess Reed.

they are moved in front of their husbands. Beside the portraits, a wall text discusses the first ladies' political role: "Many first ladies took on their new role with deep ambivalence. Notions of proper conduct for women made the role a contradiction. They were expected to be public, political wives in a society that denied women political power. . . . They often walked a fine line between supporting their husbands and avoiding the appearance of interfering with politics." Rather than celebratory history, Mayo's texts deal with ambivalences, contradictions, and the long history of the marginalization of women. The displays are no longer primarily about first ladies in beautiful dresses in opulent rooms; instead the exhibit attempts to reveal the profound tensions in first ladies' lives.

Other texts in the exhibition discuss how Martha Washington and Abigail Adams were involved in inventing the first ladies role, a role that was simultaneously "regal, but of the people." First ladies who have strayed too far on either side of this equation, as Mayo explains, frequently became controversial. The sense that these women were active agents of history rather than merely wives of the presidents was something Mayo wished to convey through her analysis. For instance, Setting the Scene: The First Lady as Social Partner and the Nation's Hostess states in part: "In Washington, parties and receptions have always set the stage for important political

First ladies' gowns and clothing on headless mannequins in low-light conditions in the new First Ladies Hall. Photo, Eric Long, Smithsonian Institution, 1994.

activity. First ladies have long used the elegant social setting of the White House as a backdrop for politics and diplomacy. Far from being just good hostesses, many politically adroit first ladies structured social occasions to benefit their husbands' political agendas." This message was always the hidden subtext of all exhibits about first ladies, but now was made explicit. And Mayo's analysis is backed up with case studies, such as how Mary Todd Lincoln was ridiculed for her extravagance in the White House, in part because she was seen as putting on airs when she was from rural Kentucky, while Julia Grant—while spending just as much on entertainment—cultivated a more relaxed and popular social image that benefited her husband politically.

The gowns were to a significant degree displaced by Mayo through her emphasis on the politics of women's history, but they are still an important part of the displays. Mayo and her team placed one group of gowns in the center of the exhibition in a winged display case. The gallery is of necessity dark because of the low-light conditions needed for preservation, and visitors peer into the shadowy cases to see what remains of the beautiful dresses that once graced the White House. A severely damaged gown lies on a table, too delicate even to hang on a mannequin, with a label explaining to visitors the fragile nature of these clothes and the problems involved in their restoration. Below the dresses, labels identify the gowns and their owners, note the changes in styles, and show details of the original colors—which have often faded with time and in any case are sometimes difficult to identify in the dim light.

The mannequins' heads, which had been problematic as Cordelia, were treated in an entirely different way in this section. They no longer have heads at all, which is unsettling. Aesthetically and politically it does not seem a good

The modern first lady mannequins with dresses, wigs, and autographs in the Ceremonial Court Gallery, which pays homage to the first ladies exhibition installed in the 1960s. Photo, Eric Long, Smithsonian Institution, 1993.

solution, although perhaps it was necessary to conform to the exhibition's budget. According to Mayo, the museum also considered this solution for even the more recent first ladies in the imperfectly replicated East Room:

> We tried that for the newer first ladies, but it was horrible. People knew these ladies, and it was as if we'd decapitated them. So instead we got these weird silver mannequins with silver hair. The mannequins were all silver so that, supposedly, the dress would stand out better, but it looked very strange to have all of these first ladies with identical strange silvery hair. Finally, we had the grand opening of the exhibit and Lynda Bird Johnson Robb came in, who was married to Senator Robb from Virginia. She said in a very loud voice—and she talks rather like her father LBJ— "Oh my Gawd! Now that Barbara Bush is in the White House ALL of the First Ladies have to have silver hair!" It was so quiet you could have heard a pin drop. And then everyone started laughing. Soon after that I got a memo saying that funds were available to immediately create appropriately colored hair for each mannequin. And that was what we did.[98]

The continued repression of the first ladies' individuality in the Smithsonian's mannequins is remarkable, even if it is in part due to budget constraints. In spite of the identical heads, or even lack of heads—the first ladies and their dresses continue to be quite popular, and today one can hear visitors marveling and sometimes exclaiming over the clothes of the past and the first ladies who wore them.

The new exhibit pays homage to the old displays in the Ceremonial Court, with each gown placed just behind oversized autograph cards bearing the signature of its first lady. The meaningful analysis found in the rest of the exhibition is somewhat downplayed and replaced by an appreciation for tradition and celebrity. The gowns and signatures emphasize how fashion and image are linked together to help create the first ladies for the public. The continued popularity of the first ladies commemoration through their dresses echoes the popularity of clothing exhibitions in other museums, like the black velvet dresses worn by the Supremes in the 1960s that are on exhibit at the Rock and Roll Hall of Fame in Cleveland, Ohio.[99] The attraction of clothing lies in the messages it bears, from glamour, to ideals of femininity, masculinity, status, sensuality, decorum, to tradition, but it is also a sign of how people create themselves and have, in turn, been created by their culture's markers of identity and status. Perhaps the attraction of clothing and adornment lies in its role as a form of symbolism to be deployed by the wearer, allowing people the ability to transform through style.

The first ladies exhibition currently draws a substantially larger audience than a far more expansive and expensive display (with major corporate sponsorship) that opened in the National Museum of American History in 2001, *The American Presidency: A Glorious Burden*. The corporate sponsors for this exhibit on the American presidency provided money for an audience survey, which ends with the suggestion that a similar survey should be taken of visitors to the first ladies gallery in order to discover the secret of this exhibit's enduring appeal.[100] In spite of this suggestion, this survey was not undertaken, and even today some Smithsonian employees are impressed, and a few even mystified, by its ability to continually draw the largest audiences in the museum. But perhaps the draw of the first ladies is not such a mystery. When I asked Edith Mayo about the continuing popularity of the first ladies at the Smithsonian, she told me,

> Everyone is, of course, fascinated by celebrities and stars, and first ladies are that throughout our history and today. But the deeper reason, I believe, is that women . . . in other exhibitions at the Smithsonian, or elsewhere, are not allowed to see themselves as actors in history. Women, especially, are starved for women's history. When I go and lecture on the first ladies

or other issues, women often ask me, "Why didn't we know this? Why weren't we taught this in school?" People in general are predisposed positively toward the institution of the first lady. And the exhibition attempts to give them access to how varied and complicated the job of first lady is.

Mayo closed her exhibition with a text panel, "First Ladies and Political Power." The last text that visitors to the new exhibit read as they exit ends as follows:

> How much will this change in the future? . . . What about being the husband of a president? When a woman is elected president will her husband give up his career? Society's expectations of women will continue to govern perceptions of the first ladies' roles—perhaps until the day when a "first man" enters the White House.

This text was written and submitted at the last minute by Mayo. Having worked at the Smithsonian for many years, she had seen how wall text could be edited down to pablum. She submitted it only when she knew that the deadline for getting it printed would prohibit the possibility of tinkering with it.

From 1914 through the early twenty-first century, there have been three generations of displays of first ladies at the Smithsonian. First, James and Hoes displayed the first ladies' dresses and their accessories in cases, which in its various forms lasted from 1914 to 1954. Second, Margaret Brown Klapthor designed period rooms used to exhibit the first ladies' dresses from 1955 until 1987. Finally, curator Edith Mayo reinterpreted the first ladies through a more directly political lens in her displays that debuted in 1992. This last exhibit seems likely to be on display with slight modifications for many more years. Each generation of display is connected to contemporary exhibition practices while reflecting changing women's roles.

James and Hoes focused on first ladies who lived largely within the limits of their time. This in part accounts for the popularity of their displays, for they made women's history a part of the Smithsonian through women's clothing, forming exhibits that were both normative and progressive. Since these clothes were linked to cultural conceptions of women's beauty and propriety and were examples of women's upper-class history rather than markers of working-class life or overt feminism—like Amelia Bloomer's

split skirt—the gowns were a way to commemorate women without pro-
voking controversy. The displays' continued popularity ensured that they
would remain central to the Smithsonian. Margaret Brown Klapthor's replicated rooms created a fantasy world of consumer fashion that combined
first ladies from different eras. The impact of these exhibits was so perva-
sive that at presidential libraries, where first ladies have since 1960 increasingly been allotted display space, their gowns and china have been featured
prominently, responding to the popularity of the Smithsonian's exhibits.

In *Portrait of a Lady*, Madame Merle, whom Henry James portrays as un-
usually perceptive even if devious, speaks a truth that could apply to the displays of the first ladies. She tells the young heroine, Isabelle Archer: "When
you have lived as long as I, you will see that every human being has his shell,
and that you must take the shell into account. By the shell I mean the whole
envelope of circumstances. There is no such thing as an isolated man or
woman; we are each of us made up of a cluster of appurtenances."[101] Appurtenances, such as the first ladies' dresses, are things that are secondary
to one's identity but still tell us a great deal about a person, his or her social
environment, and his or her experience. Henry James suggests that we ignore this at our peril. Thanks to Mayo's exhibit, this peril is avoided for first
ladies—for their dresses are for the first time not just presented but contextualized. Mere appurtenances become signs of experience and identity that
are properly recognized for how ambivalent and contradictory they are. In
Mayo's exhibit the contexts of the first ladies have been exposed. What was
previously considered personal has been made political.

In the final analysis, first ladies' dresses serve as signs of labor, for the
dresses lure tourists with a visual representation of work on two different
levels.[102] First ladies' dresses exhibit both the skilled labor of the seam-
stresses who made them and, more importantly, the efforts of the first ladies in forwarding the administration's policies through their social work.
In many ways, the first lady in her fine clothes has appeal because of her
work in stitching together the fabric of an administration and serving as a
sign of how the feminine is always and already enmeshed within the social
and political framework of the United States.

5 Reinventing the Presidential Library
The New Displays at the Truman Museum

The history presented in the museums of presidential libraries often lacks balance and critical perspective. This problem is rooted in the origins of each presidential library. A president, his family, and his supporters almost always exercise considerable control over a library for the first few decades of its existence, and in their desire to burnish presidential images they undermine the credibility of the institution. In the view of Larry Hackman, retired director of the Truman Library, "some presidential library museums are embarrassingly biased. There's a question as to whether taxpayers should be asked to support museums if they disregard historical objectivity."[1]

For example, the Roosevelt Library long avoided discussion of FDR's approval of the internment of Japanese-Americans during World War II, only adding a display about it in 1995.[2] The Eisenhower Library portrays Eisenhower as a supporter of civil rights, but the historical record is actually quite ambiguous. The Kennedy Library fails to address the extent of John F. Kennedy's infidelities and health problems. And the Johnson Library ignores the wiretapping of political adversaries, including Martin Luther King, Jr., and other opponents of the Vietnam War.

The museum displays at presidential libraries highlight the problem of the ownership of public history.[3] Who gets to decide how historical events are portrayed to the public? At presidential libraries, at least initially, the history presented in the museum is bought and paid for by interested parties. Historians certainly have a role, and many books have been written primarily through access to the archives at presidential libraries. However, less than 1 percent of the one-and-a-half-million people who visit presidential libraries each year use these archives.[4] Ninety-nine percent of visitors to presidential libraries are there for the museum displays, which at first

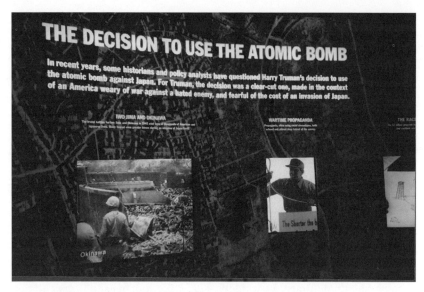

New displays at the Harry S. Truman Library, Independence, Missouri, 2001. Photo courtesy Bess Reed.

present a whitewashed and glamorized portrait of each president. It is not clear how many visitors believe the information presented in a presidential library museum, but it is an important question that has not and probably will not be tested through a rigorous and detailed government survey. The federal government's Reduction of Paperwork Act has meant that it is difficult for presidential libraries to survey their own visitors, even if they would like to.[5] Public reception of these varied displays, including visitors' confidence in the materials presented, has thus not been analyzed.[6]

The larger question of public history and public memory remains. Even though presidential libraries are public institutions that carry the imprint of the National Archives, those who pay for the initial displays, which often last for decades, largely control them. A president and his donors almost never want to see a display that addresses the problematic aspects of an administration, and as a result, almost nothing that might support unfavorable conclusions is found. The reinvention of the Truman Library—which broke away from this pattern—was made possible by the confluence of several forces, including an unusual financial windfall, the determination of the Truman Library's staff to react positively to change, and, most importantly, a recognition by the Truman Library's leadership that the presidential library was an institution in need of a fresh approach.

The Truman Library's new exhibition is, in my judgment, the best within the presidential library system at the present time. It would be difficult to decide where to begin an assessment of some of the system's museums, especially the more recent ones, because there is so little worthy of praise, as we will see below. The Truman Library's current presidential exhibition, by contrast, is so good that one can maintain a high respect for the professionalism of those responsible for its creation while at the same time highlighting its rare shortcomings. This chapter looks closely at the Truman Library's new displays, as well as at lessons that might be drawn from them that could benefit other presidential libraries. In doing so, it presents the first detailed review and analysis of an entire presidential library's museum, rather than merely an overview or critique of a few rooms. By way of setting the stage, it also examines some of what happens behind the scenes in creating exhibits at a mature presidential library.[7]

Problems at the Nixon and Reagan Libraries

A brief examination of the ways in which the scandals of the Nixon and Reagan administrations have been addressed in the two libraries illustrates the seriousness of the problem. Jon Wiener wrote a review of the Nixon Library shortly after it opened in 1990 that included this analysis of its Watergate exhibit:

> The "smoking gun" tape, recorded July 23, 1972, reveals that Nixon
> approved a plan to have the CIA tell the FBI to stop investigating Watergate.
> In the Nixon Library version, however, a narrator explains that what
> Nixon really said was, "the best thing to do is let the investigation proceed
> unhindered." . . . The Watergate room . . . doesn't mention Nixon's use of
> the FBI, CIA, and White House "plumbers" to harass, spy on, and punish
> those on the President's "enemies list." It doesn't mention the criminal
> convictions of Nixon's senior aides for carrying out these actions. . . . Most
> incredible of all, it doesn't mention that Gerald Ford pardoned Nixon for his
> crimes. Instead, the Watergate Affair is described the way Nixon has always
> described it: not as a systematic abuse of power, but as a single act, a second
> rate burglary carried out by overzealous underlings.[8]

Wiener went on to suggest that this historical rewriting was possible largely because the Nixon Library was a completely privately run and financed institution, unlike the other major presidential libraries that were built with private money but run by the National Archives of the federal government.[9]

When Nixon planned his presidential library in the 1980s, he wanted to avoid involvement with the National Archives that had control of his presidential papers and tapes, many of which detailed his crimes as president.[10] Congress had seized Nixon's materials in 1974 during the Watergate crisis and afterward passed a law that, beginning with Ronald Reagan, ended the tradition of making a president's official papers his personal property—a tradition that stretched back to George Washington. Roosevelt and his successors had voluntarily donated their presidential papers to their libraries. These presidents also had the legal—although unethical—option of destroying their papers, or at least keeping them forever private. But beginning with Nixon's presidency there was no longer a choice—either a president's papers would be controlled by the National Archives in or near the nation's capital or they would be administered in a National Archives–controlled presidential library.[11] As long as the Nixon Library was private, Nixon's presidential papers were administered elsewhere by the National Archives.

Wiener also observed that the Kennedy and Johnson libraries, run by the National Archives and Records Administration (NARA) of the federal government, "contain virtually no criticism of their subjects, but it's inconceivable that a National Archives–run Nixon Library would delete key portions of the Watergate tapes."[12] Wiener is right that a National Archives–administered presidential library would be unlikely to falsify evidence. Nonetheless, damaging evidence about a president has often been ignored in NARA-administered presidential libraries. Consequently, some of these museums are only marginally better than the one in the Nixon Library.[13]

Coverage of the Iran-Contra scandal at the Reagan Library's museum provides an apt example. Independent counsel Lawrence Walsh, appointed to investigate the Iran-Contra affair, stated in his final report that "the policies behind both the Iran and Contra operations were fully reviewed and developed at the highest levels of the Reagan Administration" and that many of these officials violated laws and executive orders by selling arms to Iran and then using the proceeds to fund an insurgency against the government of Nicaragua.[14] Fourteen Reagan administration officials were charged with criminal violations, and many of them were convicted, with the major exceptions being those pardoned by Reagan's vice president, George Bush, after he was elected president. In his final report, Walsh wrote, "It is important to emphasize that both the Iran and contra operations, separately, violated United States policy and law. The ignorance of the 'diversion' asserted by President Reagan and his Cabinet officers on the National Security Council in no way absolves them of responsibility."[15] The Iran-Contra affair involved, among other things, the trading of arms for hostages, in direct violation of the nation's stated policy on dealing with terrorists. Even though the Reagan Library's archives contain most of the surviving documents relating to the Iran-Contra affair, its museum displays do not, according to Reagan archivist Jennifer Sternaman, provide "any coverage" of the scandal.[16] Moreover, Reagan Library registrar Leslie Rankin confirmed that there are no plans to deal with it in the future.[17] That the Reagan Library's staff has felt that the Iran-Contra scandal could be left out of the museum's history of the Reagan administration is itself scandalous.

Completely sidestepping Iran-Contra and other serious issues, the Reagan Library focused on creating a display that used interactive CD-ROM technology, called Meet President Reagan. In this simulated meeting, one can ask questions about how President Reagan resolved problems such as the strike by air traffic controllers and then get videotaped replies that Reagan recorded after he left office. The videos suggest that every decision Reagan made during his years as president was correct.[18]

The Truman Library

When Larry Hackman, New York's state archivist, was selected by the National Archives to be the third director of the Truman Library in summer 1995, he decided to do things differently. One employee of the Truman Library reported to me that shortly after Hackman became director he said, "I don't care that much about Harry S. Truman, or about any particular president. I want to create museum exhibits that make people think, and that connect them with contemporary issues."[19] Some of the Truman Library's staff members, a few of whom began working there when Harry Truman himself came in on a regular basis, were shocked. Employees of the Truman Library, as at other presidential libraries, tended to have a proprietary relationship with their subject.

In the words of Raymond Geselbracht, an employee of the Truman Library since the early 1980s,

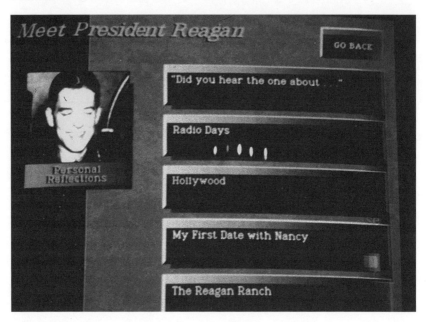

Meet President Reagan

GO BACK

"Did you hear the one about . . . "

Radio Days

Hollywood

My First Date with Nancy

The Reagan Ranch

Personal Reflections

Meet President Reagan, interactive CD-ROM display, Ronald Reagan Library, Simi Valley, California, 1995. Photo courtesy Bess Reed.

> Hackman turned everything upside down, which had to be done. . . . The very words "strategic plan," "proposal," and "manager" weren't really heard at the Truman Library until he came here. He gathered a group to work on the future of the Truman Library. . . . Larry had worked at the Kennedy Library, and had worked on an interactive project there, and he wanted to make a more ambitious version of that here. Larry said he wasn't even that interested in Truman per se.[20]

Hackman's arrival was a turning point for the Truman Library. Less concerned with promoting his subject's position in history than are most directors of presidential libraries, he wanted to present the Truman administration in a more complex and balanced way.

The biggest challenge that the Truman Library faced when Hackman arrived was its seriously outdated museum. The founding displays focused upon "the six jobs" of the president.[21] Truman, who was comparatively modest as presidents go, did not feel comfortable with the idea of exhibits that focused exclusively on himself and his presidency. Instead, he wanted to give visitors a civics lesson about the varied roles of the president, including the President as Commander in Chief, the President as Head of State,

Initial displays, Jobs of the President, Harry S. Truman Library, Independence, Missouri, 1958. Photo courtesy Harry S. Truman Library.

the President as Director of Foreign Policy, and the President as Legislative Leader.[22]

From the late 1950s until the mid-1970s, visitors entered the Truman Library's foyer and faced Benton's painting and then passed into the Oval Office replica. In the main gallery, the six jobs of the president were displayed in wall cases with large letters highlighting each theme. For example, "AS DIRECTOR OF FOREIGN POLICY THE PRESIDENT MUST DEVELOP PROGRAMS TO STRENGTHEN THE FREE WORLD AND SAFEGUARD THE SECURITY OF THE UNITED STATES." A photograph of Truman's secretary of state during his second term, Dean Acheson, accompanied the large text, while smaller photographs with explanatory labels illustrated a quotation from one of Truman's speeches. A few objects, such as state gifts emblematic of the roles featured in the display cases, were on exhibit.[23] One specially constructed two-story room featured an ornately carved table from the Philippines standing on a beautiful handwoven rug, both of which were given to President Truman in his role as head of state. For many decades, visitors admired this example of the lavish lifestyles of foreign leaders who interacted with President Truman.

After Truman's death in December 1972 and burial in the library's court-yard, the museum saw a need to reinvent itself. The display about the varied roles of the president did not sufficiently engage visitors, who were coming to honor the memory of Truman specifically more than the U.S. presidency in general. An exhibition focusing on a historical overview of Harry Truman's life and presidency was called for, but funding to support new exhibits was limited. In the words of Benedict Zobrist, director of the Truman Library from 1971 to 1994, "When I asked the federal government for support for new exhibits, they said to me, 'We'll keep a roof over your head, but when it comes to new displays you'll have to fund that yourself.'"[24] New displays were created, but they consisted largely of dry-mounted text and pictures. This low-cost fix was not seen by the Truman Library's staff as a long-term solution to the problems with their exhibits.

The necessity for older libraries to modernize themselves every twenty years or so was becoming apparent—to both NARA and the libraries themselves—during the 1980s. The libraries responded to the dilemma of their aging displays largely according to their resources, which were usually quite limited. Part of the problem was the way the libraries' displays were (and are) funded when first built. The early exhibits at the Truman Library and other presidential libraries were often shaped with oversight from foundation boards filled with presidential family members and support-ers. In part because of the National Archives' lack of experience in running museums, each foundation typically had fairly free reign to develop—along with a presidential library's director, curator, and usually outside firms—a library's initial exhibits. The outcome was an environment where historical accuracy and accountability were trumped by uncritical adulation. Sharon Fawcett, deputy director of the National Office of Presidential Libraries, has said that "as long as exhibits at presidential libraries are paid for by private money raised by a president and his supporters, the exhibits are going to be biased."[25]

These biased displays can be related to the life cycle of the presidential library. Essentially, a presidential library goes through at least three phases in its life: first, its founding and initial development (largely controlled by a president and his supporters); second, the organization and opening of its archives for use by scholars (largely controlled by the National Archives); and third, a period of maturity, when a presidential library must reinvent itself to remain relevant.[26] Zobrist described how he saw the life cycle of the presidential library playing out at the Truman:

One thing that I feel strongly about is that presidential libraries have a life to them. Phil Brooks, the original director, who served from 1957 to 1971, did a great job of founding the library and getting it going, but he was not as successful at acquiring additional papers and materials and getting them organized. Coming out of a strong archival background, my focus was really on acquiring materials for the archive, organizing them, and getting scholars to use them. Since I retired, Larry Hackman and others have worked on the museum and educational aspects.[27]

During the 1980s, the Truman's head curator, Clay Bauske, who was hired by Zobrist, knew that the museum displays needed to be changed. Bauske, who had done graduate work in American diplomatic history at the University of Michigan, began his professional career as the director of the Missouri State Museum in the state's capitol building in Jefferson City. When hired as curator in 1983, he recognized some problems common to most presidential libraries built before the 1980s:

> There is a generic problem shared by most presidential libraries in terms of their museum spaces. They are built by private foundations and turned over to the federal government, and the early presidential libraries didn't have much input from museum professionals in terms of their design. Our museum space is not only too small, but is composed of long rectangular rooms that do not particularly serve well as environments for effective displays.[28]

However, the funds needed to correct these structural problems, let alone create new exhibits, were simply not available.

This began to change on 10 December 1991 with the death of Greta Kempton, a painter and friend of Harry and Bess Truman. Kempton left almost all of her estate, a sum of nearly four million dollars, to the Truman Library Institute, the foundation that was established at the time of the creation of the Truman Library. One of the high points of Kempton's career had been painting the official White House portraits of the Trumans. In 1987 the Truman Library had a show, curated by Bauske, of this neglected painter's work, titled *Greta Kempton: Forty Years on Canvas*. Zobrist described how the show led to Kempton's gift:

> I think the show meant a lot to her, and through it she became interested in the Truman Library. After the show, whenever I visited her either in New York or on the phone, she would always ask what was going on at the

Truman. One time in New York she complained to me that she couldn't find a lawyer to draw up her will in a simple way. . . . I recommended . . . an attorney . . . [but] didn't think much more about it until she called me up one day and said, "Ben, I am leaving everything to the Library. And I also want you to take my paintings." . . . I said, "Greta, I hate to be inquisitive, but can you give me some rough idea of what you are talking about?" And she said, "Well, there are 80,000 shares of Exxon," and then she went on to list the tens of thousands of shares that she had in other big companies. I was stunned.[29]

As Bauske has recalled, "Since the 1980s we'd wanted to tell a more honest story of Harry S. Truman, and finally with Kempton's money as the seed, it looked like we might get the chance."[30]

Kempton's gift provided the impetus for the Truman Library Institute to try to raise more funds. However, by 1994, this fund-raising did not nearly suffice to cover the cost of the entire project, and the Truman Library's staff decided to start with a redo of the Oval Office exhibit. This remodeling corrected several inaccuracies in the replica to make it more closely match the actual Oval Office. It also reconstructed the space between Benton's painting and the replica. From 1957 to 1995, this space had been a hallway flanked by large storage closets. In the remodeling, the storage closets on both sides were removed to create a large display room centered on the original of Truman's "The Buck Stops Here!" sign. New interactive exhibits on the presidency placed Truman in historical context.

The Guggenheim Film

The other big project for this first stage of the reinvention of the Truman Library was a new film on Truman by Academy Award–winning documentary filmmaker Charles Guggenheim. The film was one of three that Guggenheim did for presidential libraries over two decades, including films for the Kennedy and Johnson libraries. It was meant to serve for visitors who knew little about Truman as a bridge to the library. The forty-five-minute film, which premiered in 1997, cost over half a million dollars.[31] It paired still photographs and film clips with the voice of David McCullough, author of a best-selling biography of Truman's life and a narrator for the documentary series *The American Experience.* Calm and reassuring, McCullough recounts the story of Truman's life from childhood through the presidency with an abbreviated documentary narrative that at times is almost like haiku:

> He was bright and inquisitive
> But had bad eyes.
> And avoided the playground.

And

> He earned a reputation as a builder—
> A man who got things done.
> Honestly.

And, finally, after the firing of General MacArthur, which diminished Truman's popularity, the abbreviated narration sees the upside:

> But his effort to avoid a Third World War
> And preserve the Constitution
> Had prevailed.

Some of the images are enlivened by Truman's own words, such as "Senator Barkley and I will win this election and make these Republicans like it. Don't you forget that!"

The film addresses a few difficulties in Truman's biography. For instance, in noting that the haberdashery Truman ran with his army buddy Eddie Jacobson went out of business, McCullough intones, "They failed." It ends with Truman's departure from office and his return to Independence, Missouri—the place of his retirement, his home, and his presidential library, which provides tourists a connection back to the place within which they are watching the film.

The Truman Library and the Truman Institute

Shortly after his appointment, and before the new Oval Office opened and the Guggenheim film premiered, Hackman distributed his initial assessment of the library to the Truman Library Institute's board.[32] He stated that the library needed "stronger direction" in order to become more effective as a museum, as an archive,[33] and as an educational resource. It was essential, Hackman believed, to create a closer partnership between the library and the affiliated Truman Library Institute: "The partners will need to adopt shared goals, set an ambitious but achievable agenda, identify effective strategies, and execute them in tandem with energy and purpose. If successful, the Library and the Institute will not only fulfill a worthy vision, but also establish a model for all other mature and maturing presidential libraries."[34] The issues that the institute and the library both needed to address were fund-raising, program development, and effective governance. From the outset, Hackman had a larger goal than merely remaking the Truman Library; he hoped to provide a model for the reinvention of the entire presidential library system.

An important element of this reform was to realize the full potential of the Truman Library Institute for funding purposes. This was crucial because NARA had already made it clear that the Truman Library would have to take the lead in raising the funds needed for any ambitious new exhibition. In fact, federal funding for presidential libraries slid significantly in the 1980s and the 1990s. For example, the number of permanent staff positions funded by the National Archives at the Truman Library fell by one-third during those two decades.[35] In short, the Truman Institute would have to play the primary role in paying for the library's reinvention.

When Hackman arrived, however, there were significant problems with the fund-raising drive, as well as with the management of the Truman Institute. For example, in 1995, a gala fund-raiser for the Truman Library in Washington, D.C., attended by President Bill Clinton, Vice President Al Gore, and many other political luminaries, raised $893,000. But expenses and fees incurred by various consultants and contractors hired to put on the event came to $791,000.[36] Net revenues generated by the event were only $102,000, one of several examples of how runaway expenses largely wiped out gifts to the Truman Library during this period. With an identified need of over twenty million dollars for the remaking of the Truman, this kind of mismanagement was a recipe for failure. In addition, most members of the board of directors of the Truman Institute were little involved. The board usually met only once a year, and its lunch period was often longer than the business meeting. During this time, a single member of the Truman Institute was serving as an appointed vice president, treasurer, and chair of several committees and was receiving a fee "to serve, in effect, as the Institute's part-time Executive Director."[37] Overall, the fund-raising effort and the institute were plagued by waste, disorganization, and a general lack of energy. Hackman worried that "these issues posed a very high risk of a public relations disaster."[38]

Hackman spent much of his first two years as director on reform efforts that included slimming down the Truman Institute's board and making it more active, hiring a new development team that would more effectively solicit funds without letting expenses run amuck, and reenergizing the Truman's staff to work toward the common goal of remaking the library. For instance, archivist Geselbracht and Hackman often took actual and prospective donors on personalized tours of the Truman Library's archival and artifact collections. Geselbracht showed them such things as documents relating to the Truman administration's creation of NATO and its decision to recognize the state of Israel. As Hackman wrote, "These special guests often remarked that during the Library's more than forty year history they had never been privileged to have this behind-the-scenes view of its holdings and operations."[39] These tours often concluded with Hackman showing donors a room-size model for the new exhibition on Truman's presidency.

This exhibition was being developed by Chermayeff and Geismar, a New York firm that had designed many well-known exhibitions since its founding in 1960, including the original exhibition at the Kennedy Library in Boston, which opened in 1979, as well as exhibitions at Ellis Island and the Statue of Liberty. The contract with the firm had been signed toward the end of Zobrist's directorship. Though pleased with the selection of Chermayeff and Geismar, Hackman was concerned about the size of the fees built into the contract.[40] Hackman renegotiated the Truman Library's contract to make it more equitable and also reformed the way all future contracts involving significant amounts of money would be agreed upon, insisting that they be reviewed by qualified financial analysts and lawyers.[41] A key point was that the revised contract allowed the library's director and staff, as well as the designers, to have final authority over the content of the exhibition. This contrasts with other presidential libraries where donors sometimes influence the content of the exhibitions.

Chermayeff and Geismar brought in one of their top new employees, Herman Eberhardt, to work on the project. Eberhardt, who had had graduate training in twentieth-century American history at Yale, worked, along with Tom Geismar, on the Truman Library's displays for more than six years. Eberhardt took lead responsibility for the content and Geismar took lead responsibility for exhibition design. Both recall that the exhibition was fundamentally a collaboration between their firm and the Truman Library's staff.[42] They presented a preliminary plan for the new displays around the time that Hackman arrived as director in 1995. At that time, however, the funding was not in place to implement it.

The Truman Library needed to raise vast sums of money—ultimately about $22 million—to fund its reinvention. Congress appropriated $8 million, stipulating that these funds would only be delivered if the Truman Library managed to raise $14 million.[43] This requirement turned out to be a blessing in disguise, because the Truman Library's development team could use this promise as a compelling closing pitch to large donors. In addition to private donors, Hackman and others personally lobbied Missouri governor Mel Carnahan and the Missouri legislature for $2 million in direct contributions as well as an additional $3.5 million in tax credits for Missouri corporations—such as Hallmark Corporation and H&R Block—that contributed to the Truman Library project. One board member made an early gift of $1 million that not only surprised the other members, but inspired others to also make substantial contributions.[44]

The single most compelling part of the Truman Library's pitch for money was its promise to develop the institution into a "classroom for democracy." The phrase came from former president Gerald Ford, who used it in his speech at the dedication of the George Bush Library in College Station, Texas. After the speech, Hackman and the Truman Institute decided to use Ford's phrase as a way of characterizing the central goal for the Truman Library's new exhibition.[45] Hackman believes that emphasizing the library's educational aspirations was such a powerful tool for fund-raising because

> everybody is interested in education. Everyone wants a way to improve the
> schools, because they represent the future. The way to remake the Truman
> from a funding standpoint was through education. . . . So I got together
> a focus group, which included an employee of the Rand Corporation,
> and some people from Kansas City to think about what would be a good
> educational experience, and we had a two-day retreat where we talked
> about it. Part of the aim was to see what got people excited, but also to see
> what might work.[46]

The retreat assembled a few of the Truman Library's staff members and some educators to discuss the institution's mission, educational programs, and future. After this meeting, Hackman came up with the idea of building a replica of the White House's West Wing in the library's basement. There, school groups could engage in decision-making games in which they addressed issues faced by Truman and his administration.

The Truman Library's New Exhibits

The library's new displays and educational program opened with great fanfare on 9 December 2001 with a rededication of the Truman Library. This rededication came with a significant name change. It was now the Truman Presidential Museum and Library in order to recognize that the vast majority of visitors came to the site for the museum.[47] According to Stacy Mc-Cullough, the Truman's marketing agent, "the Truman Museum has never before launched a big consumer campaign, and this is really an effort to convey a brand. What we are trying to do is develop a new and younger audience segment."[48] Marketing included a billboard campaign featuring giant photos of Truman with captions such as "meet the exercise nut who proposed America's first national health care plan," "meet the fisherman who landed a Jewish homeland," and, beneath a picture of Truman playing piano for movie star Lauren Bacall, "meet the pianist who played the last note of World War II."[49]

This last caption, not quite in good taste, was apparently a reminder that Truman had given the order for dropping two atomic bombs on Japan in August 1945. McCullough insisted that her advertising agency had not intended to give offense and said that the billboard referred to "the whole concept of [Truman ending World War II], not necessarily specifically just the bomb."[50] As Geselbracht said somberly,

> For some people the only thing that Truman is known for is the dropping of the atomic bomb. If there is one thing that has become clear to me in my fourteen years here [it] is that there will never be consensus about the use of the bomb. For some people, the dropping of the atomic bomb was unnecessary and immoral. Others, especially veterans who fought in the Second World War, are absolutely convinced that dropping the bomb on Hiroshima and Nagasaki saved their lives. So there is no way we were going to give an answer to that question. In our new exhibit we had to leave it to the individual viewer to decide by providing different sides of the issue.[51]

That, in essence, is what the Truman Library's exhibits provide that is lacking in nearly every other presidential library: a conviction that it is important to convey that history is contested ground. This message is announced at the outset of the exhibition with a remarkable text, worth quoting in full because it is so antithetical to the displays at most other presidential libraries:

The First Four Months Gallery in the Truman Library in Independence, Missouri.
Photo, Bruce Matthews, courtesy Harry S. Truman Library.

The years of Harry Truman's presidency are crowded with significant and controversial events. No single, universally accepted account of this period exists. Historians and non-experts alike bring a variety of perspectives to the study of these momentous times. Sifting through the same evidence, they often reach conflicting conclusions.

This exhibition presents one interpretation of the Truman presidency. There are other ways of looking at the subjects presented here. As you visit the galleries, you will encounter flipbooks that highlight some of these alternative views.

These differing viewpoints are reminders that the history of the Truman years is not settled. It is constantly being disputed, reviewed and revised. New research continually emerges to challenge accepted facts and alter the story. Much of this work is conducted here at the Truman Library.

The diverse voices in this exhibition also acknowledge an important truth: History never speaks with one voice. It is always under debate—a manuscript that is continually being revised, and is never complete.

This essay is a popular summary of some of the significant developments in the philosophy and theory of history since the late nineteenth century. From Friedrich Nietzsche's essay, "On the Uses and Disadvantages of History for Life," to the many books in the twentieth century, such as Hayden White's, that analyze historical representation critically, there has been a focus on illuminating the contingent and conflicted nature of history.[52] In other presidential libraries, the idea that the history on display is one interpretation among many is ignored.

Visitors may start their tour of the Truman Library's exhibition by viewing a thirteen-minute video—also by Charles Guggenheim[53]—about Truman's life before Roosevelt's death in April 1945. Or they may bypass the video and enter the exhibition with the introductory text. Nearby is a large photograph of Truman, with Bess at his side and his hand on a Bible, taking the oath of office under the large title, "Harry S. Truman: The Presidential Years." An array of front pages with explanatory texts highlights some of the many events during Truman's first four months in office, including the fall of Berlin, the surrender of Germany, the firebombing of Japanese cities, the taking of Okinawa, the signing of the UN charter, the Potsdam Conference, the dropping of the atomic bombs, and Japan's surrender.

The Decision to Use the Atomic Bomb

The first in-depth display is The Decision to Use the Atomic Bomb. This exhibit is oriented around the idea that there was a choice, and that military, moral, and cultural issues were all at stake. At other presidential libraries, major decisions by presidents are almost always presented as good, and the idea of giving visitors space and interpretive material to question a decision is for the most part unthinkable. The Truman exhibit on the bomb is a cacophony of voices—textual, visual, and aural. Graphic images displayed on four video monitors show the devastation from the firebombing of Japan, battles on Okinawa and Iwo Jima, propaganda using racial stereotypes, and the development of the atomic bomb. The Iwo Jima and Okinawa video includes images of soldiers' bodies and a lost child shivering as GIs approach with rifles. This tiny child's loss of family continues across the other screens, where images of firebombing evoke her plight on a wider scale. The role that racism might have played in the decision to drop the atomic bomb is also addressed in the video images of Japanese caricatures that were part of wartime propaganda. The words of Dwight D. Eisenhower are among those that question the decision: "I thought that our country should avoid shocking world opinion by the use of a weapon whose deployment was, I thought, no longer mandatory as a measure to save American lives. It was my belief that Japan was, at that very moment, seeking some way to surrender with a minimum loss of 'face.'"

Still, the largest text panel states, "For Truman, the decision was a clear-cut one, made in the context of an America weary of war against a hated enemy, and fearful of the cost of an invasion of Japan." The voices of veterans certain that their lives were saved by Truman's decision are heard through hidden speakers, emphasized by a White House military map with markings for a planned invasion of Japan involving the use of massive numbers of conventional forces. The display states that the three-month battle for Okinawa, which cost 12,000 American lives and about 100,000 Japanese lives, was seen by some as a preview in miniature of what the invasion of the Japanese mainland would have cost in human life. The display on the firebombing of Tokyo and other Japanese cities, which resulted in the deaths of hundreds of thousands, illustrates that indiscriminate killing of civilians was already a part of World War II on both sides. The exhibit implies that the moral line between killing massive numbers of civilians with firebombs and killing them with nuclear devices was not completely clear.

Thoughtful visitors with views on either side of the A-bomb debate might well exit the display with less, rather than more, certainty about their opinions. This, in part, was the purpose of the exhibit, as Herman Eberhardt of Chermayeff and Geismar noted:

> When people come to the museum they may not know that much about Truman, but they do know about the bomb and they probably have an opinion on it. . . . But a museum exhibit can't completely cover and address a subject as complicated and controversial as this in all its facets. What we tried to do was at least to frame the debate and give differing opinions from the time and now. We don't come to a conclusion, and we couldn't really. I hope viewers, when they see it, will be informed and provoked to learn more, and maybe some of them will leave the Truman Library and find one of the many books written on this period.[54]

Almost everyone involved in this exhibit—including Eberhardt, Hackman, Bauske, and Geselbracht—told me that the problems of the Enola Gay exhibit at the Smithsonian in the mid-1990s were often on their minds as they were working on the display about the bomb. The Smithsonian, which initially planned an exhibit that emphasized the devastating effects of the bomb on Japanese cities, and then attempted to integrate the pro-bombing viewpoint of veterans and the military, ended up by simply displaying the fuselage of the plane that dropped the first atomic bomb.[55] The Smithsonian's much-publicized failure made those at the Truman even more determined to mount, in their small space, a serious exhibit that at least touched on some of the key issues that the Smithsonian exhibit was prevented from addressing. They also wanted every part of the Truman's exhibition to be so thoroughly documented that it would survive any legitimate challenge that might be made to it.

The Truman Museum's treatment of the atomic bomb decision has provoked thousands of visitors into writing entries in this display's 8.5-x-11-inch comment books. Within two years of the exhibition's opening, fourteen such volumes were completely filled. The comments are occasionally small essays in themselves. They include the following remarks:

> The war had come to a point where the Japanese were viewed as evil incarnate. The decision to drop the bomb was reasonable under the circumstances (why did we drop two instead of one?). We probably would have defeated Japan, though, in a matter of months using conventional weapons.

> There was no good choice, but Pres. Truman made the best available choice. With courage and resolve, against the criticism of many, he made the tough but necessary choice to bring about as quick an end to the war as possible—God bless him.

> May God forgive this unmerciful man Harry Truman.

> Where are the pictures of the innocent Japanese civilians, women and children, who died the most horrific death on earth? The start of the Atomic Age is probably the biggest threat to human civilization.

> I was a P-38 fighter pilot getting ready to ship to Okinawa from Salinas, Calif. Harry saved my butt by dropping the A-bombs!

There are many more comments that support the use of the bomb than oppose it, but the comments of one seven-year-old sum up the ambivalence of a surprising number: "Yes and no because you shouldn't kill people but he was trying to stop the war."

Postwar America

The museum's next major display area is a perceptual, conceptual, and spatial break from the seriousness of The Decision to Use the Bomb. This area wraps visitors in a comforting sense of nostalgia as they look at a towering display of late 1940s and early 1950s records, a 1950-model television, a dinette set, and a refrigerator stocked with plastic food—all in front of giant photographs of the construction of postwar suburban houses, labor strikes, and advertising images of happy housewives. The old TV plays a loop of brief clips of early television programs such as *The Lone Ranger* and *You Bet Your Life with Groucho Marx*, interspersed with commercials for such things as Camel cigarettes.

Many of the texts detail problems in postwar life such as unemployment, inflation, strikes, women being pushed out of the workforce by the return of veterans, housing shortages, and racism. But the gravity of these issues tends to be undermined by the nostalgic images and artifacts on display that convey a sense of prosperity devoid of major problems. Only the most attentive of visitors would notice how one set of artifacts subtly confirms the wall text on racism:

> African-Americans and other minorities, in particular, were excluded from many benefits of the economic boom. In the 1940s, the U.S. was a nation thoroughly segregated by race. In the South, laws kept blacks from exercising political and economic power. Throughout the nation, discrimination barred blacks and Hispanics from well-paying jobs and excluded them from the new, all-white suburbs ringing many American cities. Instead, many were confined to inner-city ghettoes.

A tower display of hundreds of records, however, visually demonstrates that racial integration in music was ahead of that in American society as a whole. The display of records shows the variety of vocal artists—women and men, black and white—who hit the charts in the late 1940s and early 1950s, including Peggy Lee, Billie Holiday, Frank Sinatra, and Duke Ellington. As perhaps the biggest African American vocal star of the time, Nat King Cole, who had hits such as "The Christmas Song," "Mona Lisa," and "Unforgettable," is not shown, but that is a minor lapse in a display that shows the power of culture—in this case musical—to help pave the way for greater equality in other aspects of American life.

The Post-War America Gallery in the redesigned Harry S. Truman Library,
Independence, Missouri. Photo, Bruce Matthews, courtesy Harry S. Truman Library.

Europe 1947, and How the Cold War Began

The postwar room also contrasts strongly in form and content with the
one that immediately follows, Europe 1947, which is devoted to the devastating living conditions in postwar Europe. The cramped hallway–like display on Europe surrounds visitors with the noise of howling wind as they
view the re-creation of a hovel of the sort occupied by some Europeans during the first few years after the war. Under a smashed window frame, a bare
lightbulb illuminates a nearly bare cupboard and a table set for two with
gruel-filled bowls. This display effectively deflates the nostalgic bubble created by the previous exhibit, preparing visitors for the displays on the Marshall Plan to help rebuild Europe.

The Marshall Plan is dealt with in some detail in the next room, How
the Cold War Began. The exhibit includes a brief nine-screen video documentary outlining the Cold War's origins. The nearby wall text begins with
a fairly standard history of the beginning of the Cold War but ends with a
significant difference:

How the Cold War Began Gallery, Harry S. Truman Library, Independence, Missouri. Photo, Bruce Matthews, courtesy Harry S. Truman Library.

Events reached a crisis in 1947. Nearly bankrupt, Britain informed the United States that it could no longer aid Greece and Turkey, countries that were facing security threats. Greece was battling communist-led guerrillas, while Turkey faced direct Soviet pressures. Truman decided to act. In a dramatic speech to Congress on March 12, 1947, he unveiled the Truman Doctrine. It included a package of military and economic aid to Greece and Turkey. But Truman also made a broad pledge "to support free peoples resisting attempted subjugation by armed minorities or by outside pressures." Years later, critics argued this sweeping language helped guide the nation into a conflict in Vietnam that did not involve America's national security.

To anyone who has visited even a few presidential libraries, this last sentence is startling. Presidential libraries do not typically assign much responsibility to a president for problems in which he played a substantial role and sometimes give credit for positive developments that were largely

Suspended from the ceiling of the Truman Library, 594 metal airplanes symbolize
the average number of planes that landed each day in Berlin during the airlift. Photo,
Bruce Matthews, courtesy Harry S. Truman Library.

not of a president's making.[56] Here, the museum is placing at least a small
part of the blame for the Vietnam War—appropriately—on Truman's conduct and rhetoric during the beginning of the Cold War.

For the most part, however, these two galleries provide a relatively thorough and supportive interpretation of U.S. policy at the beginning of the
Cold War, including coverage of the Truman Doctrine, the creation of
NATO, and the Berlin Airlift, for an audience that may not be familiar with
the era. To a large degree, this room's purpose, like that of all the others
in the new Truman exhibition, is to make a period which is increasingly
remote seem real in visual terms—with large photographs, period documents, and film from the era. In this room, for visual interest, 594 small
metal airplanes are hung from the ceiling near cargo boxes to represent the
average daily number of flights that landed in West Berlin during the Soviet blockade. The "architects of containment" who were once household
names, such as Truman's secretary of state during his second term, Dean

Acheson, are profiled in a way that is comprehensible for those audience members who may not have heard of them.

A final element also sets this part of the exhibit off from those at other presidential libraries—a flip-book of "dissenting views." The book contains statements by contemporaries—such as Henry Wallace—as well as later historians who do not think that Truman handled the tensions with the Soviet Union as well as he might have. The introductory page of the flip-book states:

> Some historians question the wisdom of the President's actions during the early Cold War years. They argue that a less confrontational approach towards the Soviets—one which sought to understand the fears the Soviet Union had about its vulnerability to invasion from the West—might have prevented a long and costly confrontation that lasted decades. The President's critics say the tough, sweeping rhetoric of the Truman Doctrine needlessly heightened Cold War tensions. They maintain that Truman and his advisers took steps to ensure that the Soviet Union would reject the offer of Marshall Plan aid and that NATO prompted the Soviets to create the Warsaw Pact.

It is true that these opposing opinions are placed in a flip-book that is less likely to be read by visitors than the main text. Yet, the very fact that it exists—and there are similar flip-books in other rooms—shows that the Truman Library's exhibits go significantly beyond those found at other presidential libraries to provide visitors with historically relevant content—even where it might undermine the dominant narrative.

The Recognition of Israel and the First Decision Theater

The next display, on the recognition by the United States of the new state of Israel during the election year of 1948, helps to set up one of two Decision Theaters that together constitute one of the most innovative features of the Truman Library's museum. The display presents some of the pressures the president faced in this decision—political, personal, and strategic. The recognition of Israel was opposed by some of Truman's closest advisors, including George Marshall, secretary of state during Truman's first term, who said in a tense Oval Office meeting that he did not feel he could vote for Truman if he recognized Israel. Marshall felt that Truman might merely be searching for votes and that the action might be harmful to U.S. interests because of the hostility it would cause in oil-rich Arab states. The exhibit interprets Truman's decision as being motivated by familiarity with arguments for a Jewish state, knowledge of the horrors of the Holocaust and the plight of displaced European Jews, and the recommendations of his friend and former business partner, Eddie Jacobson, and his political advisor, Clark Clifford.

Presidential decision making is the subject of the first Decision Theater, which addresses Truman's decision to recognize Israel and his executive order to desegregate the armed forces. The Decision Theater contains four rows of seats, with each seat equipped with four keys to record visitors' votes. Once visitors are seated, the announcer states:

> How do presidents make decisions? People disagree about their motives. Issues are complex, and presidents face many conflicting considerations. . . . In your opinion, which factor most influences presidential decisions? 1. Interest groups/ public opinion, 2. Personal values, 3. Recommendations of policy advisers, 4. The long-term national interest. It's time to decide. Press a button to choose.

The announcer gives the result of the voting and then informs viewers that, to date, the most frequently selected answer to date has been the first, "the pressures of interest groups and public opinion."

Visitors then see film clips on the video monitor that contextualize the recognition of Israel, including scenes of the armed conflict between Arabs and Jews in Palestine in 1948, of Truman and his advisors, and of Dr. Chaim Weizmann, first president of Israel, with Prime Minister David Ben-Gurion. Visitors then get to select which of the four choices previously given they believe most influenced Truman's decision. The same process occurs for Truman's decision to desegregate the armed forces, with a disturbing description and photo illustrating the racial violence some African American veterans faced after World War II. Finally, the question is posed as to whether women should serve in combat positions in today's military. Visitors are again asked what factors would most influence their decision if they were president: public opinion, personal values, recommendations of policy advisors, or the long-term national interest. The announcer states that, to date, the second answer, personal values, has been selected most frequently.[57]

The Decision Theater makes visitors think more actively about at least three issues: First, what considerations entered into Truman's decision making? Second, how do the major decisions made by Truman still affect people today? And third, what related issues today are affected by presidential decisions? The first Decision Theater at the Truman Library contrasts sharply with the interactive media displays in other presidential libraries. For instance, the Carter and Reagan libraries use interactive technology to present these presidents' views without analyzing the divergent pressures and ideological concerns that shaped their decisions. What is innovative about the Truman Library's Decision Theater is not the technology—at other presidential libraries visitors press buttons as well—but the ways in which visitors are encouraged to see the complexities of presidential decision making and the problems inherent in it.

But this display's design could have done more to promote appreciation of decision making's complexities. Rather than forcing visitors to vote for a single option in each instance, it might have allowed them to make rank-ordered or weighted votes. After all, the main point of the theater is that a combination of factors almost always comes into play in a major presidential decision. On the one hand, the theater encourages a more sophisticated understanding of presidential decision making, but, on the other, it asks visitors for an oversimplified answer. Curator Bauske states that the theater does not quite work: "The first decision theater hasn't been entirely successful, because it's almost too straightforward. It has too much text, and some people get up and leave because it's too long."[58] Compared to the mind-numbing pro-administration interactive displays found in other presidential libraries, however, the Truman Library's first Decision Theater is a major advance.

Upset of the Century

The next section of the exhibition features the famous picture of the grinning president holding up the *Chicago Tribune* with its headline, "DEWEY DEFEATS TRUMAN." As the exhibit explains, because of Truman's firm anti-Soviet stance, he faced a revolt from the left of the Democratic Party led by Roosevelt's former vice president, Henry Wallace, who ran on the Progressive ticket. Because of Truman's support for civil rights he also faced a revolt from some white Southerners in the Democratic Party, led by Strom Thurmond, who ran as a Dixiecrat. Finally, he also faced a well-funded moderate

Republican, Thomas Dewey. As a result, in the 1948 presidential election nearly every commentator and poll predicted that Truman would lose. The exhibit features Truman's dogged whistle-stop train tour across much of the country, featuring audio phones on which visitors can press buttons to hear fragments of Truman's campaign speeches.

The exhibit shows as one of its many apparently authentic relics the folded and stained telegram that Truman received from the *Washington Post* after the election:

YOU ARE HEREBY INVITED TO ATTEND A 'CROW BANQUET' TO WHICH THIS NEWSPAPER PROPOSES TO INVITE NEWSPAPER EDITORIAL WRITERS, POLITICAL REPORTERS AND EDITORS. INCLUDING OUR OWN ALONG WITH THE POLLSTERS, RADIO COMMENTATORS AND COLUMNISTS FOR THE PURPOSE OF PROVIDING A REPAST APPROPRIATE TO THE APPETITE CREATED BY THE LATE ELECTIONS. THE MAIN COURSE WILL CONSIST OF BREAST OF TOUGH OLD CROW EN GLACE. . . . AS THE DEAN OF AMERICAN FORECASTERS (AND THE ONLY ACCURATE ONE) IT IS MUCH DESIRED THAT YOU SHARE WITH YOUR COLLEAGUES THE SECRE[T] OF YOUR ANALYTICAL SUCCESS. DRESS FOR GUEST OF HONOR, WHITE TIE: FOR OTHER[S]—SACK CLOTH.

The caption reports that Truman good-naturedly turned down the humorous invitation because he did not feel he needed to see people eat crow.

The small and worn telegram—like many of the other documents throughout the exhibition—helps this display evoke the authenticity of the history it interprets. It testifies to the many historical traces of Truman's presidency preserved in the library's archive. But like all the documents on display in the exhibition, it is a simulation and not the original document. Archivist Geselbracht described the process of watching an exhibit technician carefully duplicate archival originals by repeatedly folding carefully made replicas and then staining them with dyes, wearing corners until they became ragged, and tearing along worn fold lines—until they looked almost indistinguishable from the aged and worn originals. Even the staple marks in the corners were reproduced.[59] Viewers are often unaware that the documents exhibited are replicas for the simple reason that the exhibition neither announces nor explains this fact.

It is necessary to keep the originals in the archives, for they are too fragile for long-term display and they would fade and crumble. But the lack of clear labeling of these replicas is not reasonable. Several people involved in the exhibit thought there was an explanation that the documents are replicas in the exhibit, but Clay Bauske stated that this had somehow been neglected. Bauske admitted that it probably could and should be corrected.[60] Throughout the exhibit, in fact, there is a scarcity of actual period objects, which was intentional. As Larry Hackman said, "We wanted an exhibit that focused more on ideas and history than on artifacts."[61]

One of the few genuine artifacts in the exhibition, in addition to the Torah presented to Truman by Dr. Chaim Weizmann, is an oil painting by Norman Rockwell that was reproduced for the cover of the *Saturday Evening Post* for the issue dated 30 October 1948—just a week before the election. The original painting, measuring 38 by 37 inches, offers a kitchen scene of a middle-class postwar home. Accompanied by a dog, a cat, and a bird, a husband and wife in their twenties sit at the table with a small boy nearly two years old at their feet. The husband and wife are seated at a steel, chrome, and Formica dinette set similar to the one found earlier in the postwar section of the Truman Library's exhibit. The chair, a legless model that was a popularization of Bauhaus designs developed in Germany in the 1920s and 1930s, signals that this family is attuned to the modernist aesthetic popular after World War II.

The husband, ready to go to work in a dark suit and tie, leans aggressively forward—half out of his chair—and shouts at his wife while pointing at a picture of Thomas Dewey on what appears to be the front page of the *Chicago Tribune*. The wife, wearing a nightgown under a turquoise and white Japanese silk robe with magenta mules on her feet, holds her ground—her lower lip jutting out in silent determination—as she clasps a newspaper with a picture of Truman. She is literally digging her heels in "mulish" determination into the wide-eyed dog beneath her chair. The picture of Dewey points upward while the picture of Truman tilts down in what may be a reflection of the inaccurate expectations about the upcoming election. The toast in the toaster is ignored, as is their son who weeps on the ground next to his teddy bear. The teddy bear, the only figure to look out at the viewers, scratches its head at the tumult. Meanwhile, the pot on the stove (only a fragment of which is seen), with its corresponding knob turned on, is another punning indication of the near-boiling domestic situation. The painting has three informal titles, "Family Squabble," "Breakfast Table Political Argument," and "Dewey vs. Truman." It appears to be one of the first visual representations of one of the more important trends in American politics since 1940—the gender gap, the tendency of a greater percentage of women than men to support Democratic candidates.[62]

Second Term, the Cold War Turns Hot, Second Decision Theater

Truman's second term of office, as the exhibition makes clear, was even more difficult than his first. This display begins with the following introductory text, which indicates both how foreign affairs overwhelmed the Truman administration and also why this issue dominates every other topic in the exhibit:

> When he took the oath of office for his second term, Harry Truman had an ambitious agenda. He hoped to enact a broad program of domestic reforms including national health insurance, public housing, civil rights legislation and federal aid to education. However, little of what he called the Fair Deal was ever made law. Instead, his second term was dominated by events overseas that altered America's foreign policy and domestic life in fundamental ways. In Asia, the Cold War would heat up dramatically, raising anxieties and demanding sacrifices of Americans at home and on the battlefield.

The mention of how Congress thwarted Truman's domestic agenda, which largely set the Democratic Party's agenda for the next fifty years and beyond, remains that—a mention. The exhibit does not include an in-depth discussion of these policies or of the greater involvement that the federal government had in the economy—including the responsibility to try and maintain full employment—beginning with the Truman administration.

But the international developments upon which the exhibit focuses are convincingly portrayed as the most significant events of Truman's second term. As the exhibit labels it, the Truman administration faced "10 Fateful Months," starting in the fall of 1949, that were filled with events such as the Soviets ending the U.S. nuclear monopoly, the rise of Mao Tse-Tung to power in China, the Cold War arms buildup (including Truman's decision to develop the hydrogen bomb), the rise of McCarthyism, and, finally, the invasion of South Korea by North Korea in June 1950 that triggered the Korean War. During this time, anticommunist hysteria grew in the United States, as Hollywood movies such as *The Red Menace* and *Invasion: U.S.A.* were released, the posters of which are displayed in this gallery, while the Civil Defense Office created a booklet, also on display, about what to do "Just in Case Atom Bombs Fall." The Korean War, which is given special attention, claimed the lives of 54,000 Americans and more than a million Koreans and Chinese. As losses mounted, some protested Truman's leadership. Indeed, the exhibit reports, "late in the war, he received several bitter letters from parents of American soldiers killed in Korea. The parents enclosed medals earned by their sons as a protest against the war."

As the wall text says, Truman made two fateful decisions at the outset of the Korean War. First, he sought authorization from the United Nations to combat the invasion from North Korea, which resulted in the United States leading a fairly broad multinational coalition during the war. Second, Truman chose not to seek congressional authorization for the conflict. The absence of congressional approval was an aggrandizement of presidential power that does not get much attention in the main part of the exhibit. This criticism of Truman's entry into the Korean War is addressed in one of the flip-books of "opposing viewpoints." But the criticism of Truman for engaging the United States in a major war without congressional authorization is not a minority position or opposing viewpoint but the standard textbook treatment of the subject and should be treated that way in this exhibit's main text. For instance, Arthur M. Schlesinger, Jr., in his classic book The Imperial Presidency (1973), wrote, "By insisting that the presidential prerogative alone sufficed to meet the requirements of the Constitution, Truman . . . dramatically and dangerously enlarged the power of future Presidents to take the nation into a major war."[63]

However, the second Decision Theater, which immediately follows, is the hardest-hitting and most thought-provoking part of the entire exhibition. This theater deals with the tension between constitutionally guaranteed liberties and national security. The theater's design and content, which were finalized before the 9/11 terrorist attacks, are especially relevant in our era of heightened security concerns. The visitors, sitting in wooden chairs that mimic the seats in a Truman-era courtroom, face a glass wall behind which there are four tableaux: (from right to left) an ordinary parlor with chair, lamp, radio, and window with blinds that do not completely obscure the view beyond (which is provided by a video); a silhouetted Truman standing at his desk with its "The Buck Stops Here" sign and a view of the capitol's dome; a hearing table with microphone on it; and last, symbolizing the media, various printed materials, a video monitor, and a flash camera, which sometimes illuminates the visitors whose faces are reflected back in the glass.[64] The theater begins:

> Welcome, I'd like to thank you for coming here today. Now that you
> are seated, we would like to begin with a few brief questions about
> basic American rights. Do you agree that freedom of speech is a basic

constitutional right that must be protected? Please press blue for yes
or red for no. [VOTE] The majority of you agree that freedom of speech
is essential. But, do you think that, during a war, the media should be
permitted to broadcast military information, such as the location of troops
and ships? Press blue for yes or red for no. [VOTE]

The theater, using simple logic, gets viewers to see immediately a problem
with an absolute guarantee of freedom of speech. The theater explores how
far visitors are willing to restrict liberties in an attempt to achieve security:

Do you agree that you also have the constitutional right to be safe in your
home against unreasonable search and seizure. Please vote yes or no.
[VOTE] So, the majority of you agree that you have the right to privacy and
security in your own home. But, do you think the government should be
permitted to wiretap the home of anyone they suspect might be a terrorist
or spy? Please vote yes or no. [VOTE]

After each vote, the theater can give one of two responses, depending on the
tally. The highly likely responses for two of the questions are given above.
But as the program progresses, the choices become more difficult. Just as
the questions become more troubling, the spotlights, which have been
highlighting different views in the theater frame, begin to create disturbing
visual effects. The parlor chair, first presented as part of an ordinary home,
is picked out in relief, transforming it into a chair for an interrogation. The
lighting changes to make what appeared to be an idyllic scene into a space
of potential menace. This intensifies the emotional complexity of what
seemed at first to be a simple discussion of civics.

The tone of the narrator subtly changes along with the visual effects. This
segment of the program begins with the radio playing Winston Churchill's
famous "Iron Curtain" address:

RADIO [Churchill]: From Stettin in the Baltic to Trieste in the Adriatic, an
   Iron Curtain has descended across the continent. . . .
NARRATOR: It is the dawn of the Cold War, a time when the fear of
   Communist influence in government—of spies and subversion—is
   more widespread than ever before. . . . Republicans accuse the Truman
   administration of being "soft on Communism" and call for the
   president to purge the government of communists. . . . In response,
   President Truman issued an Executive Order, in March 1947, creating
   the first peacetime loyalty program in the history of the United States.

> The program required security checks for every government employee.
> . . . In early 1947, Loyalty Review Boards, in cooperation with the FBI,
> began interviewing government employees.

Suddenly a harsh white camera flash is projected onto the audience and they see starkly their own shocked reflections in the glass.

Audience members, perhaps having voted for security measures even if this meant curtailing liberties, suddenly face the result of their choice as they are interrogated:

> INTERROGATOR: Thank you for coming before this board. We appreciate
> your cooperation. We would like to ask you a few simple questions.
> 1. Are you a citizen of the United States? 2. Do you attend church? Do
> you attend regularly? 3. Have you or any member of your family ever
> belonged to an organization suspected of disloyalty to the United
> States? 4. Have you ever suspected any of your friends, neighbors, or
> coworkers of disloyalty to the United States? 5. Would you be willing to
> share those suspicions with the members of this board?

Part of what is disturbing about this Decision Theater is that previously for every question put to visitors a button needed to be pressed to record the answer, but as it suddenly shifts from more abstract questions of liberty and national security to an individual's personal behavior, some in the audience might wonder if they are expected to actually answer these questions. Of course, this is the one time the narrator does not request that buttons be pressed. The exhibition ends by returning to presidential decision making: "How should a president balance individual rights and national security issues? Even if the question is tough it must be asked."

America 1952, Leaving Office, Legacy Gallery

In drama, after the climax comes the denouement; similarly, after the powerful and unsettling second Decision Theater, the closing parts of the exhibition are relatively restrained. The next gallery is called America 1952, and its curved wall is covered in a panorama of more than 130 covers and pages from *Life* magazine from the early 1950s—with stories and photos ranging from a picture of Marilyn Monroe, to detective novelist Mickey Spillane, to stories on the 1952 presidential candidates Dwight Eisenhower and Adlai Stevenson. *Life* was where, in a famous editorial in 1941, Henry Luce proclaimed the dawn of "The American Century," and Truman was one of the presidents who represented part of a peak of American military, economic, political, and cultural power.[65] *Life* magazine, as Erika Doss has argued, attempted to fashion an image of a successful American middle class—whose ranks had been expanded by the policies of Roosevelt and Truman, policies often opposed by Luce. As Doss writes in the introduction to her book *Looking at* Life *Magazine*, "On the one hand, *Life* was a dynamic modernist hybrid of pictures, articles and ads; on the other, it was an arrogant mass cultural institution that supposed it could not only direct the terms of modern visuality, but also control them, thereby also directing and controlling its model of an American way of life."[66] The Truman exhibition's texts also look at *Life* critically, suggesting that the magazine both reflected and reinforced prevailing sexism and racism. Nonetheless, as with other parts of the exhibition, the textual critique is visually overwhelmed by the sense of nostalgia evoked by the images from *Life*. In this gallery two period songs are played. The "first lady of song," Ella Fitzgerald, is heard performing "Not for Me," alternating with Mel Torme's "Heart and Soul," creating a racially balanced musical environment.

The small Leaving Office Gallery admits that

> Harry Truman's popularity plummeted during his final years in office. The frustrations of Korea, the president's inability to enact much of his domestic program and scandals involving some of his staff led many to label him weak and ineffective. On the eve of his departure from office, his popularity rating in polls stood below 30 percent. In his farewell address to the nation he reviewed the accomplishments of his administration and made his case to history. He confidently predicted America would one day win the Cold War.

This is one of the few places in the museum where Truman's perceived lack of charm, at least in comparison with his popular predecessor, Franklin D. Roosevelt, is addressed. In smaller groups Truman could be charismatic, but as a politician in an emerging mass-media age, he sometimes seemed flat. Benedict Zobrist, who worked at and then directed the Truman Library from 1969 to 1994, said about meeting him, "I don't think it comes across in much of the newsreel footage of Truman, but one-on-one he struck me as an extremely dynamic individual. I knew right away the meaning of the word 'charisma' when I spoke with him."[67] The cumulative effect of the exhibits, however, in spite of being much more objective than those found at any other presidential library, would probably lead some visitors to feel some sense of mystification at the lack of appreciation for President Truman by his contemporaries. The structure of heroism generated by having an entire monument dedicated to one political leader makes it difficult to believe that many had a mixed evaluation of him. Overall, as former director Hackman said, "the new exhibits still perhaps do not emphasize sufficiently the cronyism and minor scandals in Truman's administration, or his perceived lack of charisma."[68]

The final gallery of the new Truman exhibits is a room that was newly constructed, at significant cost, largely to allow viewers to exit the exhibition and return to the entrance without having to retrace their steps. It is a spacious triangular room with a bronze statue of Truman that looks out into the courtyard of the Truman Library where Harry and Bess Truman's graves can be seen, along with an eternal flame donated by American Legion Post 21. The library insisted that the bronze statue by StudioEIS be exactly life size so that it would accurately reflect Truman's 5-foot, 9-inch height and not unduly heroize him, which is often the tradition in bronze memorial sculpture. It is supposed to be a reminder of Truman's human scale and even human frailties, and the figure does seem oddly diminished in the room. Yet overall there can be no doubt that one leaves the exhibition with a sense of the importance of the Truman administration in U.S. and world history. On that level, it is similar to other presidential libraries, but with a significant difference.

A majority of visitors to the Truman exhibition would likely emerge with an understanding not just of the positive achievements of Truman, but also of his troubled legacy. No other presidential library tries to give visitors such a deep understanding of the costs accompanying presidential choices. And even in the Legacy Gallery, where one would expect a heroic summing up of Truman's life, the short textual conclusions etched into glass panels provide further space for thought. For instance, one of them reads:

> Truman reversed the long American tradition of isolationism, leading the
> nation into unprecedented international military alliances and foreign
> aid programs. His plan to contain Communism guided foreign policy
> for decades, helped save Europe and contributed to the Soviet Union's
> collapse. It also led to controversial American military action in Asia, thus
> leaving a complex legacy.

By returning yet again to a reference to the Vietnam War, even in an oblique way, it is carrying through a theme found in the exhibit of tracing the roots of the problematic military involvement of the United States in Vietnam back to the Truman administration. In doing so, the exhibit continues to make visitors think rather than presenting them with propaganda for the seemingly never-ending campaigns of these presidents through their libraries to win the last and perhaps most important election of all—inclusion on the lists of the good and significant presidents of American history.

The reinvention of the Truman Library was made possible in part because of the presidential library system's decentralization. The Office of Presidential Libraries in the National Archives Building in Washington, D.C., exercised relatively little control over what was happening at the Truman Library and mainly provided encouragement from the sidelines. And so, in this case, decentralization and a lack of federal oversight for the process of creating public history worked. Some other presidential libraries, especially the older ones, also have good displays that do not insult visitors' intelligence. For example, the Herbert Hoover Library in West Branch, Iowa, includes a serious analysis of Hoover and the Great Depression, and the Lyndon Baines Johnson Library in Austin, Texas, attempts to deal with the Vietnam War. But decentralization has also allowed newer presidential libraries, such as the Reagan and Bush libraries, to create, without criticism or intervention, seriously flawed displays that have been visited by millions of people. When Sharon Fawcett, deputy director of the Office of Presidential Libraries, was extolling the potential educational value of all presidential libraries for schoolchildren at a meeting on the future of presidential libraries at Princeton University in 2004, I thought back to my visits to the Reagan Library. Although I would not mind my children visiting the Reagan Library, I would not want them to learn the history of the United States during the 1980s from its current displays.

What presidential libraries must do, but rarely do, is critically address presidential decisions in historical context rather than simply creating a Happy Meal version of presidential history. The McPresident that is packaged as a piece of public history at some presidential libraries needs to be replaced with history that leaves a president's mistakes as well as achievements intact, even if the former equal the latter. Some presidential choices— such as Truman's decision to drop the atomic bomb—need to be given context and enough arguments on each side for visitors to begin to make their own decisions, as well as see the problems with whatever decision might have been made.

Simply by existing, presidential libraries reify political leadership, and as a result they have a special responsibility to examine not just a president, but the larger historical and cultural environment, including issues such as race and class. In doing so they need to make sure that their images—including multimedia images—do not overwhelm the content of their text. Even in as good a museum as the Truman this can happen, such as in one of the Truman Library's displays dealing with women, where a fairly good text dealing with the problems women faced in the labor market after World War II is visually overwhelmed by advertising images of happy housewives. As national museums of history, which is what presidential libraries have the potential to be, presidential libraries must strive to present some of the complexity of our nation's political history.

It is not only the content that makes a museum succeed, however, but also what we might call its formal qualities. An exhibition becomes more effective when rooms with a variety of shapes, rich colors, and varied display techniques enliven it. Chermayeff and Geismar used all of these techniques, as well as others, at the Truman Library. They also layered different media, including newspaper front pages, *Life* magazine, newsreel footage, and TV programs, together with the voices of witnesses and participants in historical events. The simulated documents are also quite telling, although they need to be clearly labeled as replicas.

It has been suggested that many visitors to presidential libraries not only expect, but want, a completely celebratory portrayal. This view is an apologist's attempt to make the flaws of the system appear as virtues. But the sentences and essays written in the Truman Library's comment books—a total of fourteen volumes filled at each of the two stations where they are kept, prove that thought-provoking quality exhibits appeal to the public. A few quotes from visitors illustrate the wide range of views:

> What an excellent way to use multi-media to get the message across that there are tough questions we Americans need to ask and there are no quick answers.

> The exhibit is fair and balanced in my view. I have always regarded Harry Truman as one of our best presidents even though I voted for Tom Dewey in 1948.

> I like the different perspectives and the mix of audio, video, and text.

> I liked this museum. You get to see both sides of the issues.

Of course there are criticisms as well:

> Too much political correctness has crept into the library's exhibits, along with much Monday morning quarterbacking. Too much like the UN.

> Where is Bess in all of this? It's a shame that you have practically omitted her from this exhibit. As first lady she should be given respect in this exhibit as well.

Sometimes the comments are in dialogue with each other, such as this exchange on facing pages:

> I was a soldier in occupied Japan when Pres. Truman fired General MacArthur [in April 1951] for trying to win the Korean War! I was in MacArthur's honor guard, 20 miles long. This event has stuck in my craw ever since. As a 21 year old soldier, I didn't realize there was no "Declaration of War" by our Congress, that our forces were under United Nations Charter, which is another disaster for our nation. Now we have forces in Iraq with no "declaration of war"! God Forbid! Howard, Washington U.S.A.

> I disagree. I served under MacArthur in WWII. He had an excessive ego. He thought he could disobey orders of his commander in chief. And Harry did the right thing when he fired him—hey Howard, read your Constitution.

The thousands of comments clearly show that visitors seek quality of content and display in presidential library exhibits and that they are hungry for an opportunity to critically engage with history and politics as it is presented at the library. These comment books filled with pages of tightly wound or widely looping letters bring personal memory and human criticism back into the space of national public history, making it a space for dialogue between histories of leadership and personal experience.

CONCLUSION   Presidential Libraries and the Final Campaign

Lyndon Johnson's focus on the attendance figures for his presidential library illustrates the transformation of presidential commemoration since 1900. Johnson often asked the staff for admission statistics, and even considered opening the library at 7:00 A.M. and offering free doughnuts to boost attendance.[1] On 7 November 1971, he decided in advance on the number of people he wanted to come to his book signing at the library. As the ex-president signed stacks of his just-published memoirs, *The Vantage Point*, he surveyed the crowd. Photos of the event show that the library was jammed with people, but Johnson was still not satisfied. A library staff member was assigned to click a counter for every arrival through the library's entrance, but after an early rush the number of people entering dwindled.[2] For Johnson, however, it seemed that the size of the crowd was a measure of history's verdict on him, and he was not going to leave it to chance.

Suddenly the 6-foot-4 Texan got up and, towering over most of the people around him, headed for the library's exit. Johnson had been president from 1963 to 1969 and had, in the words of Robert A. Caro, "seemed at times to brood, big-eared, big-nosed, huge, over the entire American political landscape."[3] In retirement, Johnson still possessed enough presence to bring a substantial part of the crowd along with him as he walked out of the building. In the courtyard outside, the crowd following Johnson could look up at the towering exterior of the eight-story Johnson Library. But the former president was not looking at the building—he was rounding up additional people to come to the book signing. After gathering as many passersby as he could, Johnson led the now somewhat-larger crowd back through the entrance, where the staff member, following instructions precisely, clicked the counter for every person entering—including those who had left the building and reentered with the president. In the space of a few minutes, Johnson had significantly increased the attendance figure for the event.

President Johnson at his book signing at the Johnson Library, 1971. Photo, Frank Wolfe, courtesy Lyndon Baines Johnson Library.

However, a library supervisor realized that the number on the counter would still not satisfy Johnson.[4] The supervisor suggested the staff member take a fifteen-minute break. On leaving, the staff member could hear the counter clicking steadily, even though there were almost no new arrivals at this point. After the staff member returned and took over the counter again, a distinguished-looking elderly gentleman who had been standing nearby walked over. "I'm glad you're back on the job," he said. "That last man was not paying the slightest attention to what he was doing." This is an amusing story about Johnson's ego, as well as of a library supervisor's understandable desire to give Johnson the attendance figure he wanted; but in a larger sense the book signing was part of Johnson's last election, part of the final campaign that modern presidents launch after they leave office and that continues after their deaths.

This book has argued that there has been a shift in federal presidential commemoration—from monuments for exceptional presidents built in Washington, D.C., to self-commemoration for every president since Franklin Roosevelt through libraries located in their home states. These presidential libraries represent, as well as advocate, the imperial presidency in memorial form.

At the beginning of the twentieth century, the idea that a living ex-president would have a huge memorial building featuring a substantial museum, a vast archive with millions of items, and a staff dedicated to perpetuating that president's memory would have seemed un-American, but since 1941, self-commemoration has become an integral part of the modern presidency. As presidential historian Lewis Gould has written, "The modern presidency has evolved into a perennial campaign. . . . Achieving greatness and ranking high among presidents proved hypnotic temptations, once a chief executive sat in the White House."[5] Gould was addressing a president's time in office, but the perennial campaign continues in a similar way for ex-presidents and is centered largely on the presidential library. For this campaign, the library, either on its own or as part of an administratively independent post-presidential center, provides an impressive building in a cinematic setting from which to conduct a postpresidential career.

Presidential libraries have grown impressively since Roosevelt invented the institution. The FDR Library was originally a 40,000-square-foot building when it was completed in 1940 at a cost of $400,000.[6] In contrast, the William J. Clinton Presidential Center in Little Rock, Arkansas, completed in 2004 at a cost of more than $165 million, is a 152,000-square-foot complex of structures that includes the University of Arkansas Clinton School of Public Service.[7] Several factors contributed to the dramatic increase in the size and cost of presidential libraries during this six-decade period. The expansion of the powers of the presidency and its bureaucracy has meant a corresponding increase in the number of documents a presidency generates, as well as the archival storage space required for them. The Roosevelt archive holds approximately seventeen million pages of documents covering a twelve-year presidency, while the Clinton Library, covering an eight-year presidency, has more than seventy-six million pages, as well as millions of electronic records. The initial displays for the Roosevelt Library consisted largely of gifts and relics displayed on shelves and in glass cases. In contrast, the renowned firm that designed the Holocaust Museum exhibits in Washington, D.C., Ralph Appelbaum Associates, created elaborate interactive displays at the Clinton Library. Franklin Roosevelt wanted a building that would look almost like a home, albeit a mansion, and one that would blend in with other mansions in the area, while Clinton had the larger ambition to "have a building that was beautiful and architecturally significant that people would want to walk in 100 years from now."[8] Reaching out into space toward the Arkansas River as an architectural representa-

View of the William J. Clinton Library, Little Rock, Arkansas, designed by James Polshek and Associates. Photo, Benjamin Hufbauer.

tion of Clinton's 1996 campaign slogan to "build a bridge to the twenty-first century," this gleaming steel and glass building, designed by the acclaimed firm of James Polshek and Associates, conveys—like many other presidential libraries—the grandeur of the office it commemorates.

Roosevelt died in office and so did not get to use his library in retirement, but it is likely that he imagined writing his memoirs there, tending his collections, and greeting visitors. The Clinton Center, in contrast, not only has a school of public affairs in which Clinton will sometimes teach, but also will be the base from which he continues to carry out his philanthropic activities, including helping in the struggle against HIV/AIDS, working for racial and religious reconciliation, and fostering economic empowerment for the disadvantaged.[9] This privately funded work, which began before the Clinton Library opened, has helped to improve Clinton's favorability ratings in polls from a postpresidency low of 39 percent in March 2001 to 62 percent by June 2004.[10] As Clinton wrote in his memoirs, he had an important model: "Jimmy Carter had made a real difference in his post-presidential years, and I thought I could too."[11] .

Jimmy Carter, who was voted out of office in a landslide in 1980, provides the most remarkable example of a postpresidential career focused on a presidential center located alongside a presidential library. As a headline in the *New York Times* put it, "Reshaped Carter Image Tied to Library Opening."[12] The Carter Library, dedicated in 1986, is a series of four interconnected circular buildings, which includes the Carter Center, adjoining two man-made lakes and a traditional Japanese garden on a thirty-acre site in Atlanta, Georgia.[13] The Carter Library, like all presidential libraries, has an archive and museum, but Jimmy and Rosalynn Carter have directed almost all of their time and energy into the administratively separate and privately funded Carter Center, working on causes such as affordable housing for the poor, the eradication of Guinea worm disease from Africa, conflict mediation, and election monitoring.[14] His approval ratings soared after he left office, and in 2002 Carter was awarded the Nobel Peace Prize for his work.

The Carter Center was an important innovation that highlights something that the case studies in this book also demonstrate: the invention of the federal presidential library, as well as its most significant innovations, have been made at the presidential libraries for Democratic presidents. Roosevelt invented the federal presidential library, the Truman Library was the first to have a replicated Oval Office, the Johnson Library was the first to have a school of public affairs as well as distinguished architecture, and the Carter Library was the first to function as the headquarters for major philanthropic efforts. In general, presidential libraries for Republicans, even those as large and expensive as the Reagan and Bush libraries, have had fewer architectural and institutional innovations.

Although chance may have played a role, there were ideological reasons for this difference. Democrats since the 1930s have been more likely to believe in a role for the federal government in a variety of areas. This ideology helped Roosevelt, the father of the New Deal, to create a new deal for presidential commemoration that involved the federal government running a facility that was built with private funds. Once the institution was launched, Republicans, including even FDR's predecessor, Herbert Hoover, who loathed the New Deal, embraced the idea. The elevation of the Oval Office in the American imagination, which accelerated during the activist presidencies of Roosevelt and Truman, helped lead to its replication in the Truman Library. After the innovation of a replicated presidential room was developed it was subsequently used at the libraries of Republican presidents. President Kennedy decided in the early 1960s to affiliate his library with an academic institution, in part reflecting the large influence of academics in his administration. However, because the Johnson Library was completed first, it became the first to have a university linkage. In any case, it can be argued that Democratic presidents on average have had somewhat warmer relationships with academics than have Republicans. For instance, when the Reagan Library considered affiliating itself either with Stanford University or with the University of California at Irvine, protests were launched against the idea by professors and students at both institutions, which ultimately scuttled the plans.[15] Instead, the Reagan Library was built on a spectacular but isolated 29-acre hilltop site in Simi Valley, California. The Office of Presidential Libraries in Washington, D.C., however, now actively encourages the university model, and so the Reagan may be the last standalone library. Finally, the philanthropic programs launched from the Carter and Clinton libraries do not have close parallels in the libraries for Republican presidents, also seeming to reflect the differing ideologies of the political parties.[16]

Even the architectural style of a presidential library may sometimes reflect this partisan divide. The Johnson and Kennedy libraries are imposing buildings that look like what they are—archives and museums run by the federal government. The Reagan Library, designed by Stubbins Associates, in contrast, looks like a huge Mission-style hacienda. Its attractive red-tiled roofs, spacious courtyard, and low profile (made possible because a substantial part of the building is underground) almost give it the appearance of an imposing family mansion. This architectural style seems to fit with the ideology Ronald Reagan announced in his first inaugural address: "Government is not the solution to our problems; government is the problem."[17] Reagan wanted a greater emphasis on the family, religion, and private philanthropy to solve social problems. The irony, of course, is that the Reagan Library is a federal government program and bureaucracy. Reagan complained about those he called "welfare queens."[18] But presidents who have federal presidential libraries, whether Democrats or Republicans, are the kings of federal memorial welfare.

During Reagan's presidency, there was growing concern in Congress about the escalating operating costs of presidential libraries. In 1955, with just one library open, the cost to the federal government was only $64,000; but by 1985, with seven libraries, the cost had increased to $15 million. This was actually a minute fraction of the $946 billion federal budget for that year, but it annoyed some members of Congress who did not receive similar commemoration. Senator Lawton Chiles of Florida critiqued the "imperial former Presidency" and successfully championed the Presidential Libraries

Act of 1986, which attempted to limit the cost and size of presidential libraries.[19] The legislation required that an endowment to help pay for maintenance be privately raised for subsequent libraries, equal to 20 percent of their cost, and an attempt was made to limit the libraries to 70,000 square feet by significantly increasing the size of the required endowment for every thousand square feet over that limit. President Reagan agreed to sign the legislation only on the condition that his library, which ended up being 124,000 square feet, be exempt.[20] As the 152,000-square-foot Clinton Center demonstrates, however, this effort to limit size has not been successful. The Clinton Center fit within the law by turning over to the federal government the 69,000-square-foot archive and museum portion of the building, while retaining ownership of other elements of the complex, such as the Clinton Center, the Clinton's penthouse apartment, and the Clinton School of Public Affairs. The legislation not only failed to limit size but did not limit costs significantly because the required endowments were too small. By 2003 the presidential library system's budget had increased to $42 million a year.[21]

Driven by congressional irritation at the seemingly ever-larger presidential shrines, the 1986 act also suggested that a study be made of establishing, in place of the often glorifying museums in presidential libraries, a national "Museum of the Presidents," but one built and operated "exclusively with non-Federal funds."[22] It was an attempt to end federal presidential memorial welfare as Congress knew it, but the proposal had no basis in financial or psychological reality. A president and his supporters would be unlikely to, in fund-raising terms, "give until it hurts" to an institution honoring all presidents when they are primarily interested in a particular one. And the idea that such an institution could survive in perpetuity without federal funding was unlikely in the extreme. The imagined "Museum of the Presidents," if it had somehow been launched, probably would have been a small and unimpressive institution, which may have been exactly what Congress had in mind.

Even employees of the presidential library system, however, at times have wondered about its future. In August 1995 I met with the acting head of the Office of Presidential Libraries, Richard A. Jacobs, in his office in Washington, D.C. I asked about his thoughts on the future of the system. He replied, "I'm not sure we can continue to have individual presidential libraries. The public has a right to ask, 'Where are we going with this? A library for every president no matter how great or small?' We have to come to some kind of denouement, some kind of solution."²³ Jacobs suggested that instead of individual libraries a regional Presidential Archival Depository System, which he called PADS, might be developed. With PADS, as imagined by Jacobs, all the presidents from a particular area, such as the Southwest, would have a regional mega–presidential library that could be added to over time and which would have some economies of scale. This idea, although somewhat more realistic than the congressional proposal, has at this point also gone nowhere.

Raymond Geselbracht of the Truman Library told me that he had sometimes speculated about the future of the system:

> It's hard to see how it might come to an end, but I can perceive a
> couple of ways. The first is that there is a potential scandal in the way
> that presidential libraries are built. The sitting president raises private
> money for his library while still in office, often from foreign contributors
> and nationals, or extremely wealthy Americans. In exchange for these
> generous sums donated for the libraries, which currently the president
> does not need to reveal, contributors may receive access to the president
> that some people may deem inappropriate.²⁴

This happened at least on a small scale when, at the end of his presidency, Clinton gave what he called one of his "most controversial pardons" to Marc Rich, whose ex-wife had given $450,000 to the Clinton Library Foundation.²⁵ Rich had left the United States years earlier, shortly before being indicted on tax evasion and other charges related to his complex business deals. At the time of Clinton's pardon, Rich had repaid his back taxes and fines. But Clinton himself said that the pardon "wasn't worth the damage to my reputation."²⁶ He wrote in his memoirs, "I may have made a mistake, at least in the way I allowed the case to come to my attention, but I made the decision based on the merits."²⁷ In any event, if in the future a law is enacted to regulate the solicitation of funds for a presidential library by requiring complete transparency or forbidding a president from seeking funds for it while in office, it might become difficult to raise enough money to build a presidential library.

Geselbracht's second hypothesis for how additions to the presidential library system might cease was intriguing:

> It could be that a president some day will just decide that they are
> not interested in raising that kind of money for their own personal

glorification. They might instead just hand over their documents to the National Archives at the end of their term in office and say goodbye. Just as FDR started a precedent for presidential libraries by building the first one, some president in the future might end the process by simply refusing to build one.

Such a president would probably need to have a smaller ego than most modern presidents. Or perhaps he or she would need to be dead. Even then a president's supporters would almost certainly step in to fill the gap, as they did for President Kennedy. It seems unlikely that a president would voluntarily opt out of having one of the most powerful tools for the final campaign.

Executive Order 13233

On 1 November 2001, President George W. Bush asserted executive power over the release of materials from the archives at presidential libraries when he issued Executive Order 13233. This order gave sitting and former presidents the power to withhold the release of records at presidential libraries for any reason, including that they might be politically damaging. President Bush immediately used this power to block the release of tens of thousands of documents from the Reagan Library, apparently records involving his father or members of the Reagan administration who were also serving in the second Bush administration. The order, misleadingly titled "Further Implementation of the Presidential Records Act," contravenes in important ways the laws that previously governed presidential records.

As described in chapter three, presidential records starting with George Washington were considered the personal property of each president. As a result, some records were lost, deliberately destroyed, or unavailable for many decades after a presidential administration ended. Roosevelt modified this tradition by voluntarily giving his papers to his library, which became a branch of the National Archives. Subsequent presidents followed FDR's example, but presidential records remained the personal property of the president, and the possibility remained that they could be selectively destroyed for political reasons. In spring and summer 1974, as the Watergate crisis headed toward its climax, archivists in the Office of Presidential Libraries became concerned. Richard Jacobs described for me part of the process that ended the personal ownership of presidential papers, a process that Bush's Executive Order has, in some ways, partially reversed:

> In the early summer of 1974, there was some talk of Nixon possibly destroying tapes and documents. I remember driving to the Office of Presidential Libraries one day and asking myself, "What are we going to do about this? What are we going to do about these presidential papers?" When I got to the office I said to the archivist Mary Wallton Livingston, "Mary, I've got an idea: Why don't we try to set up a blue-ribbon commission on the presidential papers. Such a commission could cope with the problems of the private ownership of presidential documents, and suggest laws to change the situation." Mary said, "It'll never work." But I pressed, and together we wrote a detailed memo to the Archivist [of the United States] in June of '74. Mary was right in a sense, for after a month or so the memo came back, and it was clear that nothing was going to happen for the time being.
>
> Then in August, the day before Nixon resigned, the White House called our office, and asked about what the standard form was for a deed of gift of presidential papers. I asked when they needed it, and they said "One hour." We got to work, and somehow finished it in one hour. But shit, Nixon's lawyers looked at it and had all sorts of conditions, all sorts of changes that they wanted.

The mild-mannered Jacobs used an expletive because the conditions and changes that Nixon's lawyers wanted would have allowed Nixon to retain substantial control of the records and, if he chose, to destroy many of them. Few things upset an archivist more than the deliberate destruction of important records.

Congress decided to take the unprecedented step of seizing Nixon's materials, a step whose urgency was underlined when Nixon, after his resignation, negotiated an agreement with the government giving him the right to destroy the White House tapes, as well as withdraw documents from the collection. The remaining materials would then be given to the National Archives.[28] It was to override this agreement that Congress acted. Jacobs continued,

> Congressman John Bradamus [of Indiana] in the House called to say that Congress was serious about seizing Nixon's papers, and he asked to see the memo we'd written about making the presidents' papers national

property. Parts of the memo were inserted directly into the bill that eventually became law.

The Presidential Records and Materials Preservation Act of 1974, which seized Nixon's materials, was challenged by Nixon's attorneys for decades. As archivist of the United States, Robert Warner, wrote, "We were met with great resistance from Nixon's attorneys, who contested just about every move we made. When I left office in 1985, the Nixon papers were still closed."[29] Although the seizure was upheld by the Supreme Court, after Nixon's death his attorneys successfully sued the government for $18 million in compensation.

The Presidential Records Act (PRA) of 1978 permanently established the public ownership of all subsequent presidential records, starting with the Reagan administration.[30] President Carter, who signed the bill into law, voluntarily abided by its provisions. Among the requirements of the PRA was the stipulation that twelve years after a president leaves office many presidential records would be accessible, the major exceptions being those restricted for national security reasons, those directly involving the president in his role as head of his political party, and those personal in nature. A large release of Reagan administration records from the Reagan Library was scheduled to take place in 2001, twelve years after Reagan left office.

The release of many of these documents was first delayed by the Bush administration. Then, after 9/11, as part of a broad assertion of expansive executive power in the wake of the terrorist attacks, Executive Order 13233 was issued. It was condemned by a variety of groups, including the American Historical Association, the American Library Association, the Society of American Archivists, and others. The president of the Society of American Archivists, Steve Hensen, wrote to Congress in protest:

> I write to express the grave concern of the Society of American Archivists with respect to the President's recent Executive Order 13233 on Presidential Papers. . . . Our apprehension over this Executive Order is on several levels. First, it violates both the spirit and letter of existing U.S. law on access to presidential papers as clearly laid down in 44 U.S.C. 2201-2207. This law establishes the principle that presidential records are the property of the United States government and that the management and custody of, as well as access to, such records should be governed by the Archivist of the United States, and established archival principles. . . .

The Executive Order puts the responsibility for these decisions with the President, and indeed with any sitting President into the future. Access to the vital historical records of this nation should not be governed by executive decree; this is why the existing law was created.[31]

Many distinguished historians also strongly objected to the order, including Richard Reeves, who made an unusual personal protest to President Bush: "My reaction was to send him copies of my books on Presidents Kennedy and Nixon. I said that they might be worth something some day as artifacts because it would have been impossible to write them under his new order."[32]

Although legal challenges to the executive order face an uncertain future as of this writing, the outrage that greeted it in many quarters apparently influenced the Bush administration to reduce the number of documents that it was blocking from release, from tens of thousands to less than two thousand, although the exact number is in dispute. Deputy Director of the National Office of Presidential Libraries Sharon Fawcett, in a National Public Radio interview, tried to minimize the importance of the order by noting the relatively small number of documents affected,[33] but it is clear that the potential for the abuse of power exists and will persist. It is not an exaggeration to say that for some historians and archivists, Executive Order 13233 is one that will live in infamy.

Franklin Roosevelt's ideas about how the archive in a presidential library should function were distressingly similar to those of George W. Bush. As described in chapter three, while publicly advertising the openness of the Roosevelt Library archive, FDR secretly wanted to block the release of many documents even after his death. This was to happen through a Roosevelt-appointed committee with the power to prevent historians and others from seeing many politically sensitive records. The courts overturned Roosevelt's plan, but Bush's executive order has so far succeeded where FDR failed. By 2001, President Reagan was gravely ill and had not been in a condition to make decisions for several years, but Executive Order 13233 allowed the Reagan family to appoint representatives to decide whether material in the Reagan Library would be blocked from release. These records are still officially owned by the government and will be preserved, but if they do not see the light of day it is almost as if ownership had never passed from the president's hands, even in death.

During one of his 2004 campaign debates with Senator John Kerry, President Bush said that he believed in the judgments of history. Although Bush was reluctant to acknowledge mistakes during his term in office, he said, "History will look back and I am fully prepared to accept any mistakes that history judges to my administration. Because the president makes the decisions, the president has to take the responsibility."[34] But because of Bush's executive order, historians will probably not have access to the most sensitive material in the future George W. Bush library for many decades. Unless the order is overturned, the judgment of history will be delayed far beyond the time when Bush himself will be alive to take responsibility for it.

The Educational Potential of Presidential Libraries

Some presidential libraries have been plagued with biased displays, and now some face censorship of their records as well. There is the risk that most future presidential libraries will be high-tech temples of political propaganda, spreading across the memorial landscape of the nation. This is unfortunate, for the presidential library has already demonstrated that, at its best, it can be a balanced and engaging history museum as well as an accessible archive where the nation can learn from its history and hold its presidents and even the presidency itself accountable. The serious problems at some of the newer libraries should not obscure the potential that exists for this institution.

The Truman Library, like some other mature presidential libraries, has completely remade its permanent exhibit. The Truman's displays are particularly innovative because they engage visitors in a variety of ways with complex and controversial issues. At the same time that this new exhibit opened, the Truman Library also completed a new education facility, called the White House Decision Center. The Decision Center was the linchpin of the Truman's Classroom for Democracy fund-raising campaign. The campaign was effective, in part, because it promised to create an active and meaningful learning experience for students that used the facilities and archival resources of the library. By 2004, the Decision Center was operating near capacity, serving more than 5,000 eighth through twelfth-grade students a year.[35]

The White House Decision Center was constructed in an area of the Truman Library's lower level previously used for storage. Built to look like a section of the West Wing, the Decision Center has wide white hallways and spacious rooms painted light yellow and decorated with white wainscoting and trim. Period objects, such as an old radio set and a 1950s tele-phone, combined with presidential portraits lining the high-ceilinged halls and rooms, effectively evoke at least some of the atmosphere of the White House of Truman's era. There are not quite enough details and objects to give it the look and feel of a real working area in the White House, but over-all it has the feeling of a high-quality movie set.

Into this space, students come to play the roles of President Truman, his advisors, and members of his cabinet, such as the secretary of defense, while dealing with one of three crises: the North Korean invasion of South Korea in June of 1950, the 1948 Soviet blockade of Berlin, and civil rights and the desegregation of the military in 1948. The library has success-fully generated interest in the program by mailing information packets and videos, as well as providing speakers, to schools in the Kansas City metropolitan area and beyond. Teachers of history, sociology, debate, civ-ics, and language arts are those most likely to express interest, but teach-ers in other areas have participated as well. Before coming to the Decision Center, teachers and their students complete four hour-long preparatory "modules," which provide background information on the crisis selected as well as training in how to read primary documents. The modules also use role-playing to cover such topics as the responsibilities of a presidential advisor, the importance of information in decision making, the differences between decision making for individuals and for groups, the assessment of consequences and risks in the decision-making process, and the handling of a crisis in a democratic government.[36]

Students, in groups as large as sixty-four, enter the Decision Center at about 9:00 in the morning and take up their chosen roles.[37] The Decision Center has eight advisory rooms, and sessions divide into as many as eight groups of eight, with all the presidents in one room, all the secretaries of defense in another room, and so on. For a full capacity session, eight stu-dents play President Harry or Harriet Truman. The sessions in the Decision Center, which last approximately five hours, are divided into three phases. First, the crisis is explored by each group of students through primary source documents—the students work together to analyze these documents and decide what information needs to be communicated to the public. A press briefing, held in the Decision Center's large and elaborate pressroom, is con-ducted by the press secretary. This person outlines the crisis and fields ques-tions from students acting as members of the White House Press Corps, referring some questions to members of the cabinet who are standing by.

Second, the presidents meet with their advisors, who present policy options and make recommendations to the president. Finally, the president chooses a course of action. Because of time limitations, only one president, chosen by the presidents as a group, can announce a decision at the second press conference in the afternoon. In one session videotaped by the library, a President Harriet Truman answered a hostile question from a member of the press who accused her administration of being soft on the Soviets and allowing the takeover of Eastern European countries. The student playing the president defended her decision to aid Berlin without risking a wider conflict, but irritation at the reporter's question flashed across her face.

As this student said in a postsession interview, "I may have seemed confident, but I was really scared. Especially since the questions were just coming from everywhere, and they weren't planned, and I didn't know what was going to happen next."[38] Overall, student and teacher evaluations from the program have been enthusiastic. One student said, "It's a real rush. You get to go out there and make decisions." Another said, "The job they [presidential advisors] have is so much harder than what we just see on TV." One teacher felt that "more than anything it's changed how I look at some of these students." Another echoed this sentiment: "Some students especially don't seem to have much in the way of a conviction, then you really see what they believe." Another wrote that the White House Decision Center "provided my students with 'hands on' history. The past became the present, an interactive drama as my freshmen lived the push and pull of conflicting opinions within the halls of power . . . and dealt with the power of the press."[39]

Like the museum displays at the Truman upstairs, the White House Decision Center does not avoid difficult issues. For instance, the session on civil rights and desegregation in the military in 1948 deals in depth with racism as it existed at the highest levels of the federal government. The director of the Decision Center, Tom Heuertz, a social studies teacher for twenty-six years before being hired by the Truman Library, explained:

> The desegregation of the military is, I think, one of the more difficult decisions for students simply because it is hard for them to realize a world where segregation was the norm for much of America. I tell teachers that they will need to teach this negative side of America's past before the students come here. . . . We warn students that they will be reading 1940s-era documents that may be offensive, but that they must be able to see how some thought back then.[40]

Heuertz noted that several largely African American schools have selected the military desegregation decision and that these students and teachers "have been pleased and highly supportive in their evaluations."[41]

Teachers interested in the program usually need to obtain from their school or from students' parents the $10-per-student participation fee.[42] These fees cover only about 65 percent of the cost of the program, with the remainder made up with private funds from the Truman Institute. The Truman has applied for and received grants to allow some students in less prosperous districts to participate free of charge. Although the Office of Presidential Libraries has touted the program and it has received national press coverage, the program does not receive federal funding. The more than $1 million cost of building the White House Decision Center facility and developing the curriculum and the annual expense of more than $110,000 for the program, including staff salaries, has been paid for with privately raised money. Largely because of the challenges of funding, so far no other presidential library has created a similar program.

The curriculum for the White House Decision Center meets state and national standards for social studies. It sharpens students' skills involving cooperative group work, problem solving, communication, and leadership, while demanding that students gain access to knowledge of a historical crisis through copies of primary documents from the library's archive. Students are encouraged to dress professionally, and most do, some even wearing suits. Although it is a serious program, the main impression from the student responses is that for most of them it is fun. This is also true for the library's staff, who project genuine enthusiasm for their work. Outreach coordinator Judi O'Neill, a teacher for thirty years before she joined the program, works to spread information on the Decision Center and encourage teacher participation. As she said, "We believe in our product, which makes our job easier."[43]

For many students it seems almost a natural fit to step into roles in the West Wing because of how frequently they have seen it dramatized in films and television programs. As one student said, "It's very fun to play a role. It's kind of like 'West Wing' in a way." And ironically, while some elements of West Wing began to infiltrate the Truman Library, the TV show itself was dealing with the fictional Lassiter Presidential Library. In an episode titled "The Stormy Present," broadcast in January 2004, an ex-president spends much of his last years in the Oval Office replica in his presidential library. As his fictional wife says, "He'd come here to think. He took to eating here, and sleeping here," and eventually he dies in a bed in his Oval Office replica. With its banners proclaiming that the library is focused on "celebrating the promise of American leadership," the Lassiter Library is not only portrayed as an uncritical celebration of this fictional president's life, an all-too-real scenario, but it became this ex-president's obsessive plaything as well. President Bartlett, played by Martin Sheen, looks around Lassiter's Oval Office replica sadly. But as the Truman Library proves, presidential libraries do not have to be the toys of ex-presidents; they can be vital institutions that serve their regions and the nation.

The Final Campaign

In "The Stormy Present," President Lassiter has written a letter of final advice just before his death for President Jed Bartlett: "Jed—go see Lincoln and listen." The last scene of this *West Wing* episode shows President Bartlett standing between the columns of the Lincoln Memorial, looking up at the troubled face on the statue of the sixteenth president. The Lincoln Memorial remains the ultimate presidential memorial, whether in life or on television, and this book has made its own attempt to "see Lincoln and listen." It has also attempted to see subsequent presidential commemoration, on a variety of levels, and hear what it might tell us about power, the presidency, and the relationship of people to commemorative institutions.

One of the claims of this book is that presidential libraries have largely replaced monuments for presidents in the nation's capital. For instance, Dwight Eisenhower, heroic general of World War II and popular president, has no major monument in Washington, D.C., because instead he helped create a site with a museum, archive, and preserved house in his hometown. However, a few presidents may still be deemed so important that a library is not enough, and such was the case with Franklin Roosevelt. The FDR memorial, in the planning stages for decades and finally completed in 1997, rejected the neoclassical idiom with which Washington, Jefferson, and Lincoln were memorialized. It has different areas for each of FDR's terms and multiple bronze statues—of Eleanor Roosevelt and FDR's dog Fala, and two of Roosevelt himself. Its open-air rooms, laid out like galleries complete with wall texts, almost seem like a minimalist exhibit from a presidential library museum that has been turned to stone. It may be that the museumification of presidential commemoration found in the libraries has had an influence even here.

The Smithsonian has also recently played a role in the commemoration of presidents that may have been influenced by the museums in libraries, and certainly by the nearly century-long success of its own exhibits on first ladies analyzed in chapter four. In 2001, a major new exhibit, *The American Presidency: A Glorious Burden*, opened. In contrast to the first ladies exhibit, which had difficulty obtaining major corporate donors, this exhibit was sponsored by, among others, Sears Roebuck, Cisco Systems, and the History Channel. Some members of Congress once hoped that there could be a national museum for the presidents that functioned without federal funding, but the U.S. Congress swallowed its pride and contributed significantly to the commemoration of the executive branch in the Smithsonian, although earlier it had not deemed first ladies worthy of a similar appropriation. In any case, *A Glorious Burden* does not shy away from controversial issues. It even refers to crimes and impeachments associated with presidents, displaying the filing cabinet that once resided in Daniel Ellsberg's psychiatrist's office that was violently torn open by President Nixon's operatives.

But, as the national and international media attention focused on President Reagan's funeral at the hilltop site of the Reagan Library helps to show, presidential libraries are today where most of the action is in presidential commemoration. These institutions have become large and spectacular, so large that they have the potential to have a significant economic impact on the cities in which they are located. The Clinton Library, for instance, has become the catalyst for urban renewal and economic development in Little Rock. The library was built in an abandoned warehouse area, and it sparked a nearly $1-billion surge of private investment in this previously depressed section of town.[44] Land values in the area have more than doubled since the Clinton Library's location was announced.[45] A study of the library's impact suggested that it might draw as many as 300,000 visitors a year and provide a direct infusion of as much as $17 million a year into the local economy. There will probably never be a large Clinton memorial in Washington, D.C., but even if one was somehow built in the capital it would not have much impact, either commemoratively or economically. But in Little Rock, Clinton is the big guy on the block. As Skip Rutherford, president of the William J. Clinton Foundation said, in Little Rock "the impact is huge."[46]

The presidential egos involved in the creation of and represented by presidential libraries are also huge, as has been noted by the press. A 2002 overview of the presidential library system in the *Washington Post* was titled "Monumental Ambition," while a similar article in the *New York Times* two years later was called "Archive Architecture: Setting the Spin in Stone."[47] In general, however, these articles have fallen short in examining how presidential libraries vary in quality and in how they interact with their audiences. They fail to show that a few presidential libraries contain fine examples of public history and interact with their audiences in innovative ways. A library like the Truman is a temple that has also become a forum—a forum where students, tourists, citizens, archivists, and historians come together to gain a deeper understanding of the nation. In contrast, some presidential libraries are so celebratory that they verge on propaganda. These libraries immerse visitors in whitewashed presidential "heritage" rather than history. And these differences are not necessarily due to differences between the party affiliations of the presidents involved. Although this book has argued that the major innovations in the system have been made at the libraries for Democratic presidents, many high-quality programs exist at the libraries for Republican presidents. There are good museum exhibits at the Hoover and Ford libraries, a first-rate program to encourage high school and college students to use the archive at the Eisenhower Library, and a strong children's program at the Bush Library. There is a substantial group of presidential libraries whose quality is somewhere in between, and these are the ones whose development is most likely to be influenced over time by internal or external pressures, toward one direction or the other.

Whether high quality or uncritically celebratory, for a Republican or for a Democrat, however, the presidential library has become part of the cultural understanding of the modern presidency. This is evidenced in part by references to and depictions of presidential libraries, real and fictional, in television programs and movies, but even more by one of the most important ceremonies of the modern presidency in national life—the burial of a president at his library. Like earlier presidential memorials, presidential libraries endeavor to create sacred national sites. Roosevelt was a pioneer in this area, being the first president to plan for his library burial, joined eventually by Eleanor Roosevelt, and his choice set a precedent. Most succeeding presidents and first ladies are interred at presidential libraries.[48] Their burial sites help to confer an aura of the sacred on the libraries. In most states, the actual gravesite at a presidential library must be legally sanctified for burial.[49] The sacralization of the libraries through presidential burials locates the libraries in an ongoing dialogue between national mourning and celebration.

Reagan's death launched a nearly weeklong ceremony that began and ended at his library, major parts of which were televised live without commercial interruption as would happen with a major crisis. As for some other modern presidents, his body first lay in repose at the library, where tens of thousands of visitors paid their last respects. Then a similar ceremony took place in Washington, D.C., under the Capitol dome, and finally, his remains were brought back to California and laid to rest at sunset. The burial recalled his final communication to the American people when he had disclosed his Alzheimer's disease: "I now begin the journey that will lead me into the sunset of my life. I know that for America there will always be a bright dawn ahead."[50] Reagan, famous for his love of ceremony, pageantry, and photo opportunities, would almost certainly have been pleased at the cinematic quality of the event. Nancy Reagan, frail and grief-stricken as she said her final farewell at her husband's coffin, was said to have derived some strength from knowing that she was by his side for his last ceremony. She had been there by his side through all his political campaigns, and now she was helping to make sure that this phase of his final campaign would be a success.

A press release stated, "In lieu of flowers, Mrs. Reagan has asked that contributions be made to the Ronald Reagan Library Memorial Fund at www.reaganlibrary.com."[51] The Reagan Library also announced that a commemorative DVD of the funeral and burial proceedings would be produced in association with Merv Griffin Productions and warned, "There is an abundance of unauthorized and unlicensed product relating to the funeral proceedings. Please be advised that the Foundation is the sole licensee of President Reagan for the purpose of the use of his name, likeness, signature, or image on or in any products or merchandise."[52] This is quite similar to the branding and merchandising of other deceased celebrities, such as Elvis Presley, whose posthumous career development by Elvis Presley Enterprises, Incorporated, has been analyzed by Erika Doss.[53] Finally, the Reagan Library used a modified version of Reagan's campaign slogan from his 1984 reelection campaign, "Morning in America," for an exhibit that opened on 4 July 2004. The Reagan Library's *Mourning in America* display, a continuance of the final campaign that occurs after a presidential death, exhibited, among other items, the black velvet-draped catafalque used for the president's repose that was fashioned after one used for Lincoln, a selection of the vast number of letters and gifts sent to the library after Reagan's death, Reagan's favorite riding boots that had been placed backwards in the stirrups of the riderless horse led to the Capitol, and the flag presented to Mrs. Reagan that had been draped over the president's casket throughout the week's ceremonies.

The way library funerals appear from the inside is somewhat—although not entirely—different from how they appear on television. I asked head curator Dennis Medina of the Eisenhower Library about Eisenhower's funeral, which took place thirty-five years before Reagan's. Medina said,

> I happened to arrive for my first day of work at the Eisenhower Library the day of Eisenhower's death. Ike died about noon on March 28, 1969, and a few hours later the National Guard surrounded the entire complex. The White House Office of Protocol has detailed funeral plans on file for the president, as well as for all ex-presidents. Shortly after his death Eisenhower's funeral plan was implemented, and the Army and National Guard took over. By three o'clock in the afternoon there were soldiers with rifles at ten-foot intervals surrounding our entire site. All of the doors of the museum were locked and the eight employees were almost prisoners. Security was tight because President Richard Nixon was shortly to arrive to deliver Eisenhower's eulogy.
>
> A small crisis developed because the vault for Eisenhower's remains had not been cut in our Place of Meditation, and men were cutting through the marble around the clock. The Eisenhower Library, for a brief period, was in effect under martial law, with sharpshooters on the roof and soldiers everywhere. Soon the Library was packed with famous people, with crowds of the less famous outside. We felt very excited to honor Eisenhower for his qualities as a person, and for his service to his country. It was a solemn occasion, but also celebratory. For the Eisenhower family, of course, the event was more personal, and more personally sad.[54]

The funeral process Medina describes completed the Eisenhower Library, as other presidential libraries have been completed. As Medina states, it was a solemn but celebratory national occasion marking the end of a presidential life. The mobilization of the armed forces, the focus of national attention through the mass media, the eulogy of the sitting president, the gathering of the common and elite—all conferred a sacred quality on the site essential to its perpetuation as a site in America's civil religion.

The Place of Meditation within which Dwight and Mamie Eisenhower are entombed is based on military nondenominational chapels, with which General Eisenhower was familiar.[55] It is made of travertine marble, lighted during the day through abstract stained glass windows and at night with artificial lighting. A bell tower on the east facade ends in a sharp spire, while in front of the building a fountain runs perpetually and is dramatically lit at night. The Place of Meditation feels like a private space, and one built for the ages, as are all elements of all presidential libraries.

Robert Caro, who has worked for three decades on his biography of LBJ at the Johnson Library, calls them "America's pyramids . . . erected to the memory of the country's rulers."[56] Yet no commemoration lasts forever. Even the tombs and pyramids of ancient Egyptian pharaohs were often pillaged not long after they were constructed, although the priesthood in ancient Egypt maintained the pillaged monuments of some pharaohs for thousands of years.[57] As we saw in the chapter on the Roosevelt library, presidential libraries have a dynamic life cycle of their own.[58] A presidential library is born as the culmination of a huge fund-raising drive; first its museum is opened to tourists, and then its archive is opened to scholars. While the president is in living memory there is nostalgic interest from many people, who reminisce in presidential museums to gain a tourist experience linked to memories in their own lives. During this period there is immense work behind the scenes as archivists painstakingly catalog and organize presidential materials, which are slowly released for use by scholars, who then write histories and monographs. Often, just as tourist interest begins to wane, biographies that make use of the unprecedented scope of materials and access a presidential library provides are published. Some of these books, such as David McCullough's Pulitzer Prize–winning best seller, Truman, published in 1992, can even make an impact on contemporary political events.[59] And yet, eventually, the interest of both tourists and scholars slowly begins to subside. As Geselbracht said, "In the 1970s, the Truman Library had no problem attracting 250,000 tourists a year. And yet today—with better exhibits and better publicity—it is sometimes hard to get 150,000 visitors."[60] Geselbracht added that many people today have no living memory of Truman, and as time goes on an increasing number will not remember the Cold War. This loss of living memory motivated the redesign of the Truman Library's

museum exhibits that contextualized Truman and his era for a new generation of tourists for whom "President Truman seems as distant as George
Washington."[61]

French sociologist Maurice Halbwachs once wrote:

> There is scarcely a general notion that does not give society an occasion to
> focus its attention on this or that period of its history. This is evident when
> we deal with attempts on the part of society to know itself, to reflect on its
> institutions and structure, on its laws and mores. . . . The various groups
> that compose society are capable at every moment of reconstructing their
> past. But, as we have seen, they most frequently distort that past in the act
> of reconstructing it.[62]

Commemoration is an intercessor between death and societal memory. As
living memory of a president and first lady passes away, those who would
commemorate them must help them make the transformation into the
realms of history and societal memory, which is the object of the final campaign. Presidential libraries try to create the sense that their subjects, if not
immortal, are still relevant, and that visitors can acquire through a tourist
experience living memory of the dead. One of the most important goals of
a presidential library, using documents, displays, audio, film, educational
role-playing, and interactive video, is to transform presidential labor into
myth, giving it seemingly transcendent value.

Historian Catherine L. Albanese states:

> Whether looking to past or to future, under God or under the United
> States, deliberate or spontaneous, hypocritical or sincere, the civil religion
> revolved around what were considered memorable deeds that Americans
> had performed to initiate an age unknown before in history. Here, actions
> had to be striking to be seen; events had to make history to be meaningful.
> For people who did not like to dwell in the past, Americans were
> exceedingly anxious to achieve a past on a grand scale.[63]

Presidential libraries are major participants in the civil religion of the
United States. And presidents, in an attempt to construct their own pasts
on a grand scale have attempted to create a nearly propagandistic past.
Since Executive Order 13233, these libraries have more in common with the
imperial cult during the Roman Empire than they previously did. Outside of
Emperor Augustus's massive mausoleum were two pillars with an engraved
copy of his *Res Gestae*, or "Things Achieved," that he had written in detail

with the assistance of his aides.[64] The cult of the imperial presidency as envisioned by some presidents and their supporters has some parallels with the imperial cult, for the cult of the presidency they promote may increasingly become an attempt to sell uncritical acceptance of a president's self-proclaimed list of achievements and inspire veneration of an individual idol of the civil religion, rather than contemplation of national history. Larry Hackman, retired director of the Truman Library, said to me at a meeting on presidential libraries, almost in a whisper, "I don't like it when people say 'Truman's Library,' or 'Reagan's Library.' It is The Truman Library or The Reagan Library. These institutions are not owned by these individuals or their families." Or at least they should not be.

NOTES

Abbreviations Used for Archival Sources

FDRL Franklin D. Roosevelt Library
HSTL Harry S. Truman Library
LBJL Lyndon Baines Johnson Library
NARA National Archives and Records
      Administration
RG   Record Group

Introduction

1. Michael Kammen, In the Past Lane: Historical Perspectives on American Culture (New York: Oxford University Press, 1997), 214–224.

2. The Nixon Library was originally completely private in its funding and operation. As this book goes to press, the Nixon Library is in the process of being incorporated into the National Archives, which has promised to change the Watergate exhibit.

3. Transcript, Oral History, Gordon Bunshaft, 25 June 1969, LBJS.

4. These attendance figures are a rough average since 1990 and are from the "Office of Presidential Libraries Briefing Book" (Washington, D.C.: Office of Presidential Libraries, NARA, 2003).

5. Johnson Library.

6. These square footage estimates refer to these buildings as originally built. Recently the Lincoln Memorial has opened a small museum in its basement, increasing its square footage substantially, but this museum was not originally part of the Lincoln Memorial. Even with its new museum, the Lincoln Memorial is much smaller in floor space than the Johnson Library.

7. Some leaders of Congress, such as Sam Rayburn, have been able to get memorial libraries built. However, these are not federally run institutions.

8. Arthur M. Schlesinger, Jr., The Imperial Presidency, with a new epilogue by the author (Boston: Houghton Mifflin, 1989).

9. U.S. Constitution, art. 1, sec. 8.

10. Ibid., art. 2, sec. 2.

11. David McCullough, Truman (New York: Simon and Schuster, 1992), 775.

12. Ibid., 789.

13. Raymond Geselbracht, personal communication, 1995.

14. George Bush and Brent Scowcroft, A World Transformed (New York: Knopf, 1998).

15. Joseph A. Pika, John Anthony Maltese, and Norman C. Thomas, The Politics of the Presidency, 5th ed. (Washington, D.C.: Congressional Quarterly Press, 2002), 1.

16. Lewis Gould states that several of FDR's predecessors, including William McKinley, Theodore Roosevelt, and Woodrow Wilson, can also be considered modern presidents. But as Gould notes, FDR took several trends that had been developing regarding presidential power and celebrity to new levels. And these new levels of power, rather than being an aberration, held for all of FDR's successors, at least to some degree. The Modern American Presidency (Lawrence: University Press of Kansas, 2003), 79–99.

17. See chapter three.

18. See Percy Bysshe Shelley, Shelley's Poetry and Prose: Authoritative Texts, 2d

ed., ed. Donald H. Reiman and Neil Fraistat (New York: W. W. Norton, 2002), 109–110.

19. S. R. F. Price, *Rituals and Power: The Roman Imperial Cult in Asia Minor* (Cambridge: Cambridge University Press, 1984); Alastair Small, ed., "Subject and Ruler: The Cult of the Ruling Power in Classical Antiquity, Papers Presented at the University of Alberta on April 13–15, 1994," *Journal of Roman Archaeology* 17 (supp. series) (1996).

20. Jean-Jacques Rousseau, *The Social Contract and the First and Second Discourses*, ed. Susan Dunn (New Haven: Yale University Press, 2002), 253.

21. Robert N. Bellah, "Civil Religion in America," *Daedalus, Journal of the American Academy of Arts and Sciences* 96, no. 1 (Winter 1967): 8, 9, 13.

22. Catherine L. Albanese, *America: Religions and Religion*, 3d ed. (New York: Wadsworth Publishing, 1999), 447.

23. Among the many studies of civil religion are Leroy S. Rouner, ed., *Civil Religion and Political Theology* (Notre Dame, Ind.: University of Notre Dame Press, 1986); John F. Wilson, *Public Religion in American Culture* (Philadelphia: Temple University Press, 1979); Russell E. Richey and Donald G. Jones, eds., *American Civil Religion* (San Francisco: American Research University Press, 1990); and Catherine L. Albanese, *Sons of the Fathers: Civil Religion of the American Revolution* (Philadelphia: Temple University Press, 1976).

24. Marcela Cristi, From Civil to Political Religion: The Intersection of Culture, Religion and Politics (Waterloo, Ontario: Wilfred Laurier University Press, 2001), 3.

25. Albanese, *Sons of the Fathers*.

Prologue

1. Scott A. Sandage, "A Marble House Divided: The Lincoln Memorial, the Civil Rights Movement, and the Politics of Memory, 1939–1963," *Journal of American History* 80 (June 1993): 141.

2. Kirk Savage, "The Politics of Memory: Black Emancipation and the Civil War Monument," in *Commemorations: The Politics of National Identity*, ed. John R. Gillis (Princeton, N.J.: Princeton University Press, 1994), 140.

3. Christopher Alexander Thomas, *The Lincoln Memorial and American Life* (Princeton, N.J.: Princeton University Press, 2002), 128. Thomas writes, "In his Gettysburg Address, Lincoln referred, somewhat misleadingly, to liberty as the principle on which the United States was founded, yet he avoided emancipation and other controversies in his funeral oration over the dead."

4. George P. Fletcher, *Our Secret Constitution: How Lincoln Redefined American Democracy* (New York: Oxford University Press, 2001). See also Gary Wills, *Lincoln at Gettysburg: The Words That Remade America* (New York: Simon and Schuster, 1992), as well as Merrill D. Peterson, *Lincoln in American Memory* (New York: Oxford University Press, 1994).

5. Harry V. Jaffa, *A New Birth of Freedom: Abraham Lincoln and the Coming of the Civil War* (Lanham, Md.: Rowman and Littlefield, 2000), 73.

6. Ibid., 90.

7. Thomas, *The Lincoln Memorial*, 63–64.

8. Cortissoz to Henry Bacon, 6 April 1919, quoted in Sandage, "A Marble House Divided," 141.

9. Roy P. Blaser, ed., *The Collected Works of Abraham Lincoln* (New Brunswick, N.J.:

Rutgers University Press, 1953), vol. 4, 168–169.

10. "Speech at Independence Hall," 22 February 1861, p. 213, in *Abraham Lincoln, Speeches and Writings, 1859–1865*, ed. Don F. Fehrenbacher (New York: Library of America, 1989).

11. Jaffa, *New Birth of Freedom*, 21–29.

12. See Lincoln's support of woman's suffrage in 1832, when he was twenty-eight years old. Lincoln to the Editors of the *Sangamo Journal*, in *Abraham Lincoln, Selected Speeches and Writings*, ed. Don F. Fehrenbacher (New York: Vintage Books, 1992), 7.

13. Lincoln to Joshua Speed, 24 August 1855, in ibid., 105–106.

14. Quoted in Ronald C. White, Jr., *Lincoln's Greatest Speech: The Second Inaugural* (New York: Simon and Schuster, 2002), 190.

15. Lincoln to Thurlow Weed, 15 March 1865, in *Lincoln, Selected Speeches and Writings*, 451.

16. Jaffa, *New Birth of Freedom*, 290–291.

17. Ibid., 282–289.

18. Lincoln to Albert G. Hodges, 4 April 1864, in *Lincoln, Selected Speeches and Writings*, 419.

19. David Herbert Donald, *Lincoln* (New York: Simon and Schuster, 1995), 304.

20. As Michael Kammen argues, Lincoln's insistence on a "perpetual Union" was a "political fiction . . . [that] required a monumental distortion of collective memory . . . [because] it required an astonishing revision of historical reality in order to assert that the Union actually pre-existed the states." Ultimately, Kammen calls the idea of the perpetual Union both "mystical" and "ahistorical." Michael Kammen, *In the Past Lane: Historical*

Perspectives on American Culture (New York: Oxford University Press, 1997), 207–209.

21. See, for instance, Sandage, "A Marble House Divided," 141; and Christopher Alexander Thomas, "The Lincoln Memorial and Its Architect, Henry Bacon (1866–1924)" (Ph.D. diss., Yale University, 1990), 637–638.

22. Martin Luther King, Jr., *A Testament of Hope: the Essential Writings of Martin Luther King, Jr.*, edited by James M. Washington (San Francisco: Harper Collins, 1986), 217–220. See also Keith D. Miller, *The Voice of Deliverance: The Language of Martin Luther King, Jr.* (New York: The Free Press, 1992), 144-149.

23. Alessandro Falassi, "Festival: Definition and Morphology," in *Time Out of Time: Essays on the Festival*, ed. Alessandro Falassi (Albuquerque: University of New Mexico Press, 1987), 7.

24. Elbert Peets, quoted in Thomas, *The Lincoln Memorial*, 148.

25. Pierre Nora, "Between Memory and History: Les Lieux de Mémoire," *Representations* 26 (Spring 1989): 13.

26. Thomas, *Lincoln Memorial and Its Architect*, 217; see also Michael Richman, *Daniel Chester French, An American Sculptor* (Washington, D.C.: National Trust for Historic Preservation, 1976).

27. Lincoln, First Lincoln-Douglas Debate, in *Lincoln, Selected Speeches and Writings*, 149.

28. White, *Lincoln's Greatest Speech*, 199.

29. See Frederick Douglass, *Life and Times*, ed. Henry Louis Gates (New York: Library of America, 1994), 402.

30. Quoted in Thomas, *The Lincoln Memorial*, 356–357.

31. For a discussion of the importance of Lincoln's words, see also Robert N. Bellah, "Civil Religion in America,"

Daedalus, Journal of the American Academy of Arts and Sciences 96, no. 1 (Winter 1967): 9–12; and Richard V. Pierard and Robert D. Linder, *Civil Religion and the Presidency* (Grand Rapids, Mich.: Academy Books, 1988), 87–113.

32. I am indebted to Thomas's dissertation and book.

33. Thomas, *The Lincoln Memorial*, 14.

34. Ibid., 13–16.

35. As has already been noted, Pierre Nora has identified modern memory as increasingly relying upon "the materiality of the trace, the immediacy of the recording, the visibility of the image." Pierre Nora, "Between Memory and History," 13.

36. Patricia West, Domesticating History: The Political Origins of America's House Museums (Washington, D.C.: Smithsonian Institution Press, 1999).

37. Cortissoz to Bacon, 28 August 1911, quoted in Thomas, *The Lincoln Memorial*, 482.

Chapter 1. A Shift in Commeroration

1. This drawing is in the collections of the Roosevelt Library in Hyde Park, New York. FDR had considered building his own archive for some time. In 1934 he wrote to a Hyde Park neighbor that he wanted to build a "fireproof building in Hyde Park in which historical documents can be safely kept." FDR to Dr. Edward J. Wynkoop, 15 October 1934, Library File, FDRL.

2. FDR to Henry J. Tombs, 22 November 1937, Library File, FDRL.

3. Michael F. Reilly, *Reilly of the White House* (New York: Simon and Schuster, 1947), 170. Reilly was one of the Secret Service agents assigned to protect FDR;

he accompanied the president to Egypt during World War II.

4. For the earlier literature on the Roosevelt Library, which is very good but tends to be factual rather than interpretive, see especially Donald R. McCoy, "The Beginnings of the Franklin D. Roosevelt Library," *Prologue: Quarterly of the National Archives* (Fall 1975): 137–150; Frank L. Schick, with Renee Schick and Mark Carroll, *Records of the Presidency: Presidential Papers and Libraries from Washington to Reagan* (Phoenix, Ariz.: Oryx Press, 1989), 159–167; Geoffrey C. Ward, "Future Historians Will Curse as Well as Praise Me," *Smithsonian* 20, no. 9 (December 1989): 58–69; and Curt Smith, *Windows on the White House: The Story of Presidential Libraries* (South Bend, Ind.: Diamond Communications, 1997), 41–58.

5. Office of Presidential Libraries, NARA, Washington, D.C. Annual admissions to all presidential libraries generally total about 1.5 million visitors a year.

6. Some excellent examples of the literature on memory and commemoration include Pierre Nora, ed., *Realms of Memory: The Construction of the French Past*, trans. Arthur Goldhammer (New York: Columbia University Press, 1996–1998); John R. Gillis, ed., *Commemorations: The Politics of National Identity* (Princeton, N.J.: Princeton University Press, 1994); Kristin Ann Hass, *Carried to the Wall: American Memory and the Vietnam Veterans Memorial* (Berkeley: University of California Press, 1998); and Kirk Savage, *Standing Soldiers, Kneeling Slaves: Race, War, and Monument in Nineteenth-Century America* (Princeton, N.J.: Princeton University Press, 1997).

7. John Bodnar, *Remaking America: Public Memory, Commemoration, and*

Patriotism in the Twentieth Century
(Princeton, N.J.: Princeton University
Press, 1992), 14.

8. Presidential papers were privately
owned until the presidency of Richard
Nixon. In 1974, during the Watergate
crisis, Congress seized President Richard
Nixon's presidential papers, and the
Presidential Records Act of 1978 ended
the private ownership of presidential
papers. See Schick, Schick, and Carroll,
Records of the Presidency, 17, 242.

9. Washington to James McHenry, 3
April 1797, *George Washington, Writings* (New
York: Library of America, 1996), 993.

10. Washington, "Last Will and
Testament," ibid., 1029.

11. John D. Knowlton, "Properly
Arranged and So Correctly Recorded,"
American Archivist (July 1969): 372.

12. David Herbert Donald, *Lincoln* (New
York: Simon and Schuster: 1995), 14.

13. "Dedication of the Hayes
Memorial Library," *Ohio Archaeological
and Historical Quarterly* 25, no. 4 (October
1916): 401.

14. Donald W. Wilson, "Presidential
Libraries: Developing to Maturity,"
Presidential Studies Quarterly 21, no. 4 (Fall
1991): 771.

15. On Andrew Mellon, see Arthur M.
Schlesinger, Jr., *The Age of Roosevelt: The
Crisis of the Old Order* (Boston: Houghton
Mifflin, 1957), especially 62; and Burton
Hersh, *The Mellon Family: A Fortune in
History* (New York: William Morrow,
1978).

16. Emphasis in original. Geoffrey
C. Ward, *A First-Class Temperament: The
Emergence of Franklin Roosevelt* (New York:
Harper and Row, 1989), 752.

17. Hersh, *The Mellon Family*, 349.

18. In spite of his impressive
collection, Mellon was inarticulate on

the subject of art but would stare at his
canvases with such intensity that his aide
John Walker believed that a profound
connection existed between Mellon and
his paintings. John Walker, *Self-Portrait
with Donors: Confessions of a Collector*
(Boston: Little, Brown, 1974), 106.

19. Ibid., 132.

20. Homer Cummings to FDR, 15
January 1937, National Gallery File,
FDRL.

21. When I mentioned the probable
influence of the National Gallery on
FDR's creation of his library to Richard
A. Jacobs, then director of the Office of
Presidential Libraries in Washington,
D.C., he said that he had believed for
many years that Franklin Roosevelt got
the idea to create the first presidential
library largely from Andrew Mellon's
gift to the nation of the National
Gallery. Richard A. Jacobs, personal
communication, 18 August 1995.

22. Homer Cummings to FDR, 15
January 1937, National Gallery File, FDRL.

23. U.S. Statutes at Large, vol. 53, pt.
2 (1939), 1062–1066.

24. On Jefferson's admiration
for classical architecture, see Jack
McLaughlin, *Jefferson and Monticello: The
Biography of a Builder* (New York: Holt,
1990).

25. William Lescaze, "America
Is Outgrowing Imitation Greek
Architecture," *Magazine of Art* 37 (June
1937): 375.

26. *New York Times*, 8 April 1937, 2.

27. On FDR's relationship
with Tombs, see Ward, *A First-Class
Temperament*, especially 736.

28. Toombs to FDR, 13 November
1937, Library File, FDRL.

29. In this letter FDR wrote, "Before
you and I die we will have revived

Hudson River Dutch." FDR to Toombs, 22 November 1937, Library File, FDRL.

30. For the square footage of the Roosevelt Library, see Schick, Schick, and Carroll, *Records of the Presidency*, 254. Since its original construction the Roosevelt Library has been expanded to over 50,000 square feet. Other more recent presidential libraries, such as the Johnson and Reagan libraries, are well over 100,000 square feet.

31. FDR to Morison, 28 February 1938, Waldo Gifford Leland Papers, FDRL.

32. Morison to FDR, 11 March 1938, Library File, FDRL.

33. FDR to Keith Morgan, 25 May 1938, Library File, FDRL.

34. Journal of Robert D. W. Connor, 4 July 1938, Southern Historical Collection, University of North Carolina Library.

35. Schick, Schick, and Carroll, *Records of the Presidency*, 157.

36. FDR to Beard, 1 November 1938, Library File, FDRL. Other letters sent out that day were similar. Roosevelt got Professor Morison to assist him in drawing up the list of invitees.

37. Press Release, 10 December 1938, Library File, FDRL.

38. Ibid.

39. *New York Times*, 11 December 1938, 1.

40. *Chicago Tribune*, 13 December 1938, Library File, FDRL.

41. Minutes, First Meeting of the Executive Committee of the President's Records and Historical Collections, 17 December 1938, Library File, FDRL.

42. McCoy, "The Beginnings of the Franklin D. Roosevelt Library," 142.

43. Minutes, 17 December 1938, Library File, 2–3, FDRL.

44. Ibid., 3.

45. Ward, "Future Historians," 58–69.

46. Ibid.

47. U.S. Statutes at Large, vol. 53, pt. 2 (1939), 1062–1066.

48. *New York Times*, 20 November 1939.

49. Journal of Robert D. W. Connor, 7 April 1940, Southern Historical Collection, University of North Carolina Library; and Robert E. Sherwood, *Roosevelt and Hopkins: An Intimate History* (New York: Harper, 1948), 171–172.

50. Journal of Robert D. W. Connor, 30 June 1941, Southern Historical Collection, University of North Carolina Library.

51. FDR to Director of the Franklin D. Roosevelt Library, 16 July 1943, FDR Case File, RG 44, FDRL.

52. Judge Quintero's ruling was made in July 1947. See letter from National Archivist Solon J. Buck to Senator Owen Brewster, 25 July 1947, FDR Library Case File, RG 44, FDRL. Italics added.

53. Foreign researchers often come to the Roosevelt Library and its successors for access to documents that they are unable to obtain in their home countries. For an example, see Martin M. Teasley, "The Eisenhower Library at Thirty-Something," *Government Information Quarterly* 12, no. 1 (1995): 85; and Schick, Schick, and Carroll, *Records of the Presidency*.

54. See especially Dean MacCannell, *The Tourist: A New Theory of the Leisure Class*, 2d ed. (New York: Shocken Books, 1989), 2–14.

55. For a discussion of religious materials in the United States, see Colleen McDannell, *Material Christianity: Religion and Popular Culture in America* (New Haven, Conn.: Yale University Press, 1995).

56. See Walter J. Ong, *Orality and Literacy: The Technologizing of the Word* (London: Methuen, 1982): "The shift from

orality to literacy and on to electronic processing engages social, economic, political, religious, and other structures" (p. 3); and Marshall McLuhan, *Understanding Media: The Extensions of Man* (Cambridge, Mass.: MIT Press, 1994).

57. Donald M. Lowe, *History of Bourgeois Perception* (Chicago: University of Chicago Press, 1982), 2. See also James W. Carey, Communication as Culture: Essays on Media and Society (Boston: Unwin Hyman, 1988).

58. Lowe, *History of Bourgeois Perception*, 4.

59. This horseshoe is now in the archives of the Roosevelt Library.

60. For instance, see Werner Muensterberger, *Collecting, An Unruly Passion: Psychological Perspectives* (Princeton, N.J.: Princeton University Press, 1994), 10–12, 139; Russell W. Belk, *Collecting in a Consumer Society* (London: Routledge, 1995); Jean Baudrillard, *The System of Objects*, trans. James Benedict (New York: Verso, 1996); and John Elsner and Roger Cardinal, *The Cultures of Collecting* (Cambridge, Mass.: Harvard University Press, 1994).

61. Verne Newton, personal communication, 21 August 1995.

62. The number of films, sound recordings, and photographs of Roosevelt was substantially greater than that generated for any previous twentieth-century president. For instance, there are about 42,000 still pictures in the Hoover Library (which was built after the Roosevelt Library and based on its example) but over 134,000 still pictures in the FDR Library. Data from the Hoover and Roosevelt libraries.

63. Fred Shipman, "What Do You Know about the Franklin D. Roosevelt Library," 3, Library File, FDRL.

64. Data, Office of Presidential Libraries, Washington, D.C. Since 1994 admissions to the Roosevelt Library have increased.

65. Pierre Nora, ed., *Realms of Memory: The Construction of the French Past*, trans. Arthur Goldhammer, vol. 1, *Conflicts and Divisions*, "General Introduction: Between Memory and History" (New York: Columbia University Press, 1996–1998), 7.

66. This and all subsequent quotes of Verne Newton in this paragraph are Roosevelt Library Director Verne Newton, personal communication, 21 August 1995.

67. For a discussion of the life cycle of presidential libraries, see Wilson, "Presidential Libraries: Developing to Maturity."

68. An example is provided by Robert A. Caro's four-volume biography, *The Years of Lyndon Johnson* (New York: Knopf, 1982–2002), which has used materials in the Johnson Library to create a fascinating and disturbing account of the life of the thirty-sixth president.

69. Acknowledging changing demographic factors and technology, the library also teamed with nearby Marist College to create a searchable online finding-aid system and a digitized database featuring typed and facsimile versions of 13,000 documents from the archive.

70. William V. Roth, Jr., "Ex-Presidential Perks Are Way Out of Hand," *USA Today*, 28 March 1984.

71. Pierra Nora, "General Introduction: Between Memory and History," 8.

72. Jacques Derrida, *Archive Fever: A Freudian Impression*, trans. Eric Prenowitz (Chicago: University of Chicago Press, 1996), 91.

73. Presidential monuments in Washington, D.C., built before the advent of the presidential library represent the president alone. Since the invention of the presidential library, first ladies have been commemorated as keepers of the domestic environment of the White House and as policy advocates. This process of including the first lady within the commemorative and archival framework of presidential libraries culminated in 1972, when a new Eleanor Roosevelt Gallery was added to the FDR Library. The displays at the library include materials on her work as first lady as well as her work after FDR's death.

Chapter 2. Rhetoric of the Replica

1. I am grateful to Bess Reed, Sally and Karl Hufbauer, Alice Friedman, Carol Krinsky, Susan Ryan, Karen Chandler, Carol Mattingly, Ulrich Keller, Bruce Robertson, Ann Bermingham, Constance Penley, Raymond Geselbracht, Pat Dorsey, and Clay Bauske for assistance at various times with this chapter. Among the many useful studies of public memory are John R. Gillis, ed., *Commemorations: The Politics of National Identity* (Princeton, N.J.: Princeton University Press, 1994); and Kirk Savage, *Standing Soldiers, Kneeling Slaves: Race, War, and Monument in Nineteenth-Century America* (Princeton, N.J.: Princeton University Press, 1997), especially 4–8.

2. The Truman Library's Oval Office replica opened in 1957, and Benton's mural was planned and painted between 1957 and 1961. The basic design of Benton's mural, however, had been determined by the end of 1959. In 1995–1996, the area around the Oval Office replica was remodeled in an attempt

to convey more of the ambience of the West Wing, according to former Truman Library director Larry Hackman.

3. This display of "The Buck Stops Here!" was added in 1996.

4. Truman made two versions of this recording, one in 1963 and one in 1964. The Truman Library currently uses an edited version of the 1964 recording. Truman Library curator Clay Bauske, personal communication, 2001.

5. See especially Renée L. Bergland, *The National Uncanny: Indian Ghosts and American Subjects* (Hanover, N.H.: University Press of New England, 2000); also Leslie A. Fiedler, *The Return of the Vanishing Americans* (New York: Stein and Day, 1968); Lucy Maddox, *Removals: Nineteenth Century American Literature and the Politics of Indian Affairs* (Oxford: Oxford University Press, 1991); Brian Dippie, *The Vanishing American: White Attitudes and U.S. Indian Policy* (Lawrence: University Press of Kansas, 1991); Walter Benn Michaels, *Our America: Nativism, Modernism and Pluralism* (Durham, N.C.: Duke University Press, 1995).

6. Bergland, *The National Uncanny*, 5.

7. Thomas Hart Benton detailed the decline of Regionalism that started with World War II in *An Artist in America*, 4th rev. ed., with afterword by Matthew Baigell (Columbia: University of Missouri Press, 1983). By the early 1950s, he wrote, museums "were relegating the pictures of the Regionalists to their basements," and he was considered "outmoded" (325, 330).

8. Benton was trying to achieve a fusion of modern subject matter and techniques with the techniques of the Old Masters. See Erika Doss, *Benton, Pollock, and the Politics of Modernism: From Regionalism to Abstract Expressionism*

(Chicago: University of Chicago Press, 1991), especially 9–16; Benton, *An Artist in America*, especially 39, 61. See also Henry Adams, *Thomas Hart Benton: An American Original* (New York: Knopf, 1989); Matthew Baigell, *Thomas Hart Benton* (New York: Abrams, 1974); Polly Borroughs, *Thomas Hart Benton: A Portrait* (Garden City, N.Y.: Doubleday, 1981). Benton's bright colors were in part inspired by his friend Stanton MacDonald Wright, who developed chromosynchrony.

9. Bruce Robertson, *Representing America: The Ken Trevey Collection of American Prints* (Santa Barbara: University of California at Santa Barbara Art Museum, 1995), 36–38. Robertson notes that Benton, like other artists, tended to look at the countryside that often appeared in their work through a media-driven lens that presented contradictory views of rural life. See also Doss, *Benton, Pollock, and the Politics of Modernism*, especially 1–5; Adams, Thomas Hart Benton; Baigell, *Thomas Hart Benton*; and Borroughs, *Thomas Hart Benton*.

10. Benton, *An Artist in America*, 348.

11. Ibid., 349.

12. Karal Ann Marling makes the brief but perceptive comment that the Truman Library mural may be seen as "a full-blown illustration of the Turner thesis, with the mountain men, the voyageurs, and the Plainsmen surging westward from the right side of the panel and meeting, at the central doorway that interrupts the wall, the vanishing Indian tribes of the West." See her *Tom Benton and His Drawings: A Biographical Essay and a Collection of His Sketches, Studies, and Mural Cartoons* (Columbia: University of Missouri Press, 1985), 68. In 1893, Frederick Jackson Turner (1861–1932)

gave a widely influential address, "The Significance of the Frontier in American History," republished in Frederick Jackson Turner, *The Frontier in American History* (New York: Holt, 1920), which stated that American society had been shaped more by the western frontier than by European influence. Turner wrote (p. 3), "The frontier is the outer edge of the wave—the meeting point between savagery and civilization. . . . [T]he Indian trade pioneered the way for civilization." Although Turner's view became more sophisticated with time, it was inflected with the ideology of Manifest Destiny, as is Benton's painting. For a contemporary analysis and critique of the "frontier thesis," see Patricia Nelson Limerick, Clyde A. Milner, Charles E. Rankin, eds., *Trails: Toward a New Western History* (Lawrence: University Press of Kansas, 1991). In addition, see Benton, *An Artist in America*, 348–349, 351; and Thomas Hart Benton, *Independence and the Opening of the West* (Independence, Mo.: Harry S. Truman Library and Museum, 1974), unnumbered [5, 9, 11–12]: "Symbolic figures [and] symbolic happenings, [represent] a multiplicity of real individuals and real events." See also Doss, *Benton, Pollock, and the Politics of Modernism*, 3–7.

13. The Abbey Fund, which paid $20,000 of Benton's commission, assisted him in using the latest techniques to ensure the painting's longevity. The mural was painted in acrylic polymer latex on a linen surface with a latex gesso and was adhered to the library's wall with a polyester adhesive, ensuring that it would last for many generations. See Benton, *Independence and the Opening of the West*, [10]. Since its completion at the beginning of the

1960s, more than seven million tourists have seen *Independence and the Opening of the West*, making it one of the more widely viewed pieces of American art created since World War II (attendance figures from the Truman Library). The painting received more exposure in 1971 when the mural's center was reproduced as a commemorative postage stamp, the first time a living artist was so honored by the U.S. Postal Service.

14. Benton, *Independence and the Opening of the West*, [3–4].

15. See Roger Cushing Aiken, "Paintings of Manifest Destiny: Mapping the Nation," *American Art* 14, no. 3 (Fall 2000). See also David M. Lubin, *Picturing a Nation: Art and Social Change in Nineteenth-Century America* (New Haven, Conn.: Yale University Press, 1994), 54–105, for an analysis of Manifest Destiny in relation to George Caleb Bingham's *Emigration of Boone*.

16. Robert N. Bellah, "Civil Religion in America," *Daedalus, Journal of the American Academy of Arts and Sciences* 96, no. 1 (Winter 1967): 4. See also Catherine L. Albanese, *America: Religions and Religion*, 3d ed. (New York: Wadsworth Publishing, 1999), 452–453. For a discussion of how Manifest Destiny is used more recently with civil religion, see Roberta L. Coles, "Manifest Destiny Adapted for 1990s' War Discourse: Mission and Destiny Intertwined," *Sociology of Religion* 63, no. 4 (Winter 2002).

17. Theodore S. Jojola, "Public Image," in *Native America in the Twentieth Century: An Encyclopedia*, ed. Mary B. Davis et al. (New York: Garland, 1994), 483–484; Edward Buscombe, ed., *The BFI Companion to the Western* (New York: De Capo Press, 1988), 156–158.

18. Buscombe, *The BFI Companion to the Western*, 157.

19. Benton, *An Artist in America*, 355–359.

20. Ibid., 358.

21. Benton, *Independence and the Opening of the West*, [4–5].

22. George A. Dorsey, *Traditions of the Skidi Pawnee* (New York: Houghton Mifflin, 1904), 8, 330. Dorsey provides important mythological descriptions of Pawnee culture and religion prior to and shortly after the reservation period. See also Gene Weltfish, *The Lost Universe: Pawnee Life and Culture* (Lincoln: University of Nebraska Press, 1965); and James R. Murie, *Ceremonies of the Pawnee*, parts 1 and 2 (Washington, D.C.: Smithsonian Institution Press, 1981).

23. Benton, *Independence and the Opening of the West*, [6].

24. Such pipes usually had a reed or wooden stem and a carved pipe bowl. When put together, the pieces formed a vital object, which transferred energy from the humans who used it to the gods and back. Benton, *Independence and the Opening of the West*, [5–6]; Dorsey, *Traditions of the Skidi Pawnee*, 8, 330.

25. Men wanting to settle in the West would often uproot their wives and take them to an uncertain and uncomfortable future, where they had to shoulder a harsh workload to support their families. See Lillian Schlissel, *Women's Diaries of the Westward Journey* (New York: Schocken, 1982), for vivid firsthand accounts of the trials of western settlement. See also Lubin, *Picturing a Nation*, 72–75. Benton modeled his pioneer woman on a friend, Mrs. Randall S. Jessee, who was ill and had just been released from the hospital, because he thought her demeanor a perfect expression of the exhausted pioneer woman. Oral History Interview

with Mr. And Mrs. Randall S. Jessee, by Dr. Philip C. Brooks, 19 May 1964, HSTL.

26. See Benton, *Independence and the Opening of the West*, [6]; William Treuttner, ed., *The West as America: Reinterpreting Images of the Frontier* (Washington, D.C.: Smithsonian Institution Press, 1991); and Baigell, *Thomas Hart Benton*, 180.

27. See Buscombe, *The BFI Companion to the Western*.

28. Ibid., 53.

29. Stanley Corkin, "Cowboys and Freemarkets: Post–World War II Westerns and U.S. Hegemony," *Cinema Journal* 39, no. 3 (2000): 66.

30. Buscombe, *The BFI Companion to the Western*, 21, 60–63.

31. Cesare Marino, "Reservations," in *Native America in the Twentieth Century: An Encyclopedia*, ed. Mary B. Davis et al. (New York: Garland, 1994), 545, 554.

32. Benton, *Independence and the Opening of the West*, [6]. Although it is a convention for Americans to present themselves as individualistic, Benton shows their "disciplined cooperative action," demonstrating, I believe, the idea that Americans would stand together both on the frontier and in the Cold War.

33. Benton used Josiah Gregg's book as a source. Gregg was an Independence historian. Benton, *Independence and the Opening of the West*, [5].

34. Tanis Thorne, *The Many Hands of My Relations: French and Indians on the Lower Missouri* (Columbia: University of Missouri Press, 1996), 1–7.

35. Benton, *Independence and the Opening of the West*, [6].

36. The building of wagons relied heavily on blacksmithing for the manufacture of the chassis, springs, brakes, wheels, and pieces of harness. Benton, *Independence and the Opening of*

the West, [6]; David McCullough, *Truman* (New York: Simon and Schuster, 1992), 21.

37. See James MacGregor Burns, *Roosevelt: The Soldier of Freedom, 1940–1945* (New York: Harcourt Brace Jovanovich, 1970), 123–124, 265–266, 471–472, 512; and Doris Kearns Goodwin, *No Ordinary Time: Franklin and Eleanor Roosevelt: The Home Front in World War II* (New York: Simon and Schuster, 1994), 163–165, 168–171, 447.

38. McCullough, *Truman*, especially 586–589, 636–644, 645, 651, 675, 710–711.

39. Benton orally described the mural to Truman and sent him a detailed written description of it. Then, in an attempt to finalize the contract, Benton brought a preliminary model to Truman at the library. At each step, it would seem as if Truman had an opportunity to encourage or discourage aspects of the mural's design. Benton, *An Artist in America*, 350–354; Oral History Interview with Thomas Hart Benton by Milton F. Perry, 21 April 1964, HSTL.

40. See also Susan Scheckel, *The Insistence of the Indian: Race and Nationalism in Nineteenth-Century American Culture* (Princeton, N.J.: Princeton University Press, 1998), especially 151.

41. In contrast to the progressive civil rights ideas associated with African Americans that seem reflected in the mural, a set of policies known as "termination" affected Native Americans during the Truman (1945–1953) and Eisenhower (1953–1961) administrations. Termination was at first supported by progressive whites and Native Americans, but soon the damaging effects of the policy saw a loss of support particularly from Native peoples. Termination sought to move Native peoples into American society

by abolishing reservations and treaty obligations. Some of the ideas behind termination, such as the disappearance of the Indians as discrete groups, may, to a degree, be reflected in Benton's mural. See Donald L. Fixico, *Termination and Relocation: Federal Indian Policy, 1945–1960* (Albuquerque: University of New Mexico Press, 1986).

42. Benton, *Independence and the Opening of the West*, [10].

43. Oral History Interview with Thomas Hart Benton by Milton F. Perry, 21 April 1964, HSTL.

44. Transcript of recording for the Oval Office replica, [1], Museum File, HSTL.

45. From many years of visiting the Truman Library and observing the number of visitors and their comments about the Oval Office replica, I believe it is the most popular exhibit at the Truman Library. Some employees of the library agree.

46. Raymond Geselbracht, personal communication, 14 June 1995.

47. William Seale, *The President's House: A History* (Washington, D.C.: National Geographic Society, 1986), 690–691, 758–759.

48. Taft's remodeling of the West Wing—seven years after it was built— was based on contemporary American business design, because the labors of the president were increasingly being likened to those of a business magnate. For the influence of contemporary business design on Taft's Oval Office, see ibid., 759.

49. Ibid., 758–759.

50. Ibid., 757–758, 794. This treaty between France and England was, in fact, negotiated in the Oval Office.

51. Ibid., 941–947.

52. McCullough, *Truman*, 725, 875–886. On the rebuilding of the Oval Office, see Seale, *The President's House*, 1002–1051.

53. This early plan of the Truman Library can be found in the Museum File, HSTL. The Truman Library was designed by Alonzo Gentry of the architectural firm Gentry and Voskamp, and by Edward Neild of Neild-Somdal Associates. David D. Lloyd to Mr. Lauver, 18 February 1953, HSTL.

54. David Lloyd to Alonzo Gentry, 12 February 1957, Museum File, HSTL.

55. Raymond Geselbracht, personal communication, 14 June 1995.

56. Curtis M. Hinsley, "The World as Marketplace: Commodification of the Exotic at the World's Columbian Exposition, Chicago, 1893," in *Exhibiting Cultures: The Poetics and Politics of Museum Display*, ed. Ivan Karp and Steven D. Lavine, pp. 344–365 (Washington, D.C.: Smithsonian Institution Press, 1991).

57. Janet Berlo, *The Early Years of Native American Art History: The Politics of Scholarship and Collecting* (Seattle: University of Washington Press, 1992).

58. Bonnie Young, *A Walk through the Cloisters* (New York: Metropolitan Museum of Art, 1989); and Philippe de Montebello, *The Metropolitan Museum of Art Guide*, 2d ed. (New York: Metropolitan Museum of Art, 1994).

59. See Karal Ann Marling, "Disneyland, 1955: Just Take the Santa Ana Freeway to the American Dream," *American Art* 5, nos. 1–2 (Winter/Spring 1991): 190–201. Reyner Banham, *Los Angeles: The Architecture of Four Ecologies* (London: Penguin, 1971), 127. For a theoretical discussion of simulacra, see Jean Baudrillard, *Simulacra and Simulation*, translated by Sheila Faria Glaser (Ann Arbor: University of Michigan Press, 1994), especially 2–8. For a contrasting

view, see Hillel Schwartz, *The Culture of the Copy: Striking Likenesses, Unreasonable Facsimiles* (New York: Zone Books, 1996), especially 378. For an analysis of positive practices of cultural reuse, see Michel de Certeau, *The Practice of Everyday Life*, trans. Steven Rendall (Berkeley: University of California Press, 1984), especially xii, 25.

60. Executive Order 9646, "Coat of Arms, Seal, and Flag of the President of the United States," 25 October 1945, 3 Code of Federal Regulations, 1943–1948 Comp., 445.

61. Clark Clifford, *Counsel to the President: A Memoir, with Richard Holbrooke* (New York: Random House, 1991), 62–63. The redesign, as Clifford states, was begun under FDR but approved and ordered changed by President Truman.

62. David McCullough, *Truman*, 833.

63. Raymond Geselbracht, personal communication, 14 June 1995.

64. For the idea of the president as common and extraordinary in commemoration, see Kirk Savage, "The Self-Made Monument: George Washington and the Fight to Erect a National Memorial," in *Critical Issues in Public Art: Content, Context, and Controversy*, ed. Harriet Senie and Sally Webster (New York: HarperCollins, 1992), especially 7.

65. See especially Dean MacCannell, *The Tourist: A New Theory of the Leisure Class*, 2d ed. (New York: Shocken Books, 1989), 2–14.

66. Oral History Interview with Thomas Hart Benton by Milton F. Perry, 21 April 1964, HSTL.

Chapter 3. Symbolic Power, Democratic Access, and the Imperial Presidency

1. Robert Dallek, *Lyndon B. Johnson: Portrait of a President* (New York: Oxford University Press, 2004); and Richard Reeves, *President Nixon: Alone in the White House* (New York: Simon and Schuster, 2000).

2. Transcript, Oral History, Gordon Bunshaft, 25 June 1969, LBJL.

3. David R. Jones, "New Presidential Library: Johnson Calls for the Best," *New York Times*, 30 October 1968, 49.

4. "Office of Presidential Libraries Briefing Book" (Washington, D.C.: Office of Presidential Libraries, NARA, 2003).

5. Robert A. Caro, *The Years of Lyndon Johnson: The Path to Power* (New York: Knopf, 1982), 777.

6. Robert Caro has also conducted hundreds of original interviews with people who knew Lyndon Johnson. These interviews have been essential to Caro's biography.

7. Quoted in Irwin Unger and Debi Unger, *LBJ: A Life* (New York: John Wiley and Sons, 1999), 517.

8. Owings recalled how Mrs. Johnson was crucial for plans he had for remodeling the area around the Capitol, including putting in a reflecting pool. "I went up to the Speaker of the House, Mr. McCormick, an old friend of Mrs. Johnson's. I had a roll of drawings a foot thick. I was going to show him the whole thing. . . . He said, 'Does Mrs. Johnson like it?' I said, 'She does. . . . ' He said, 'Never mind those drawings. Where do I sign?'" Transcript, Oral History, Nathaniel Owings, 25 March 1970, 17–18, LBJL.

9. "Office of Presidential Libraries Briefing Book." Architectural historian William Morgan said to me in 2004 that he prefers the Johnson Library to the Kennedy Library, and I agree with his judgment.

10. Ada Louise Huxtable, "Kennedy Family Announces Selection of Pei

to Design Library," *New York Times*, 14
December 1964, 1.

11. Quoted in Carter Wiseman, *I. M.
Pei: A Profile in American Architecture* (New
York: Abrams, 1990), 95, which has an
entire chapter devoted to the Kennedy
Library. See also Michael Cannell, *I. M.
Pei: Mandarin of Modernism* (New York:
Carol Southern Books, 1995), 163–196.

12. Cannell, *I. M. Pei*, 173–174.
Kennedy rejected the larger site because
it was occupied by subway tracks and
repair sheds, and he thought it too
difficult politically to secure.

13. Ibid., 178.

14. The quotes are by, respectively,
Pebble Gifford (whose husband had once
served as an aide to Senator Theodore
Kennedy) and Ada Louise Huxtable.
Quoted in ibid., 180.

15. John Morris Dixon, *Progressive
Architecture*, January 1980, quoted in
Wiseman, *I. M. Pei*, 137.

16. Michael Beschloss, ed., *Reaching
for Glory: Lyndon Johnson's Secret White
House Tapes, 1964–1965* (New York: Simon
and Schuster, 2001), 270.

17. In 1958, Johnson's mother, Rebekah
Baines Johnson, urged him to add his
papers to the Johnson Museum in Johnson
City, Texas, in "Chronology," [1], LBJL;
memo of call from Bunshaft to JR [Mary
Juanita Dugan Roberts], 17 May 1966, LBJL.

18. Anthony Champagne, *Congressman
Sam Rayburn* (New Brunswick, N.J.:
Rutgers University Press, 1984); Anon.,
"Rayburn Praised as Library Opens;
Speaker Hailed by Truman and Others at
Dedication Ceremonies in Texas," *New
York Times*, 10 October 1957, 22.

19. Letter from Arthur C. Perry to
Dorman H. Winfrey, 19 December 1960,
Special File Regarding Design, Exhibits,
Etc., of LBJ Library, LBJL.

20. Marie Smith, "First Lady to
Promote Great Society," *Washington Post*,
17 January 1965, F3, F8.

21. Heath wrote in a letter to Lady
Bird a few months later, "Let me thank
you for sending me the two pictures
autographed by the President to his
goddaughter and my granddaughter,
Julia Baines Ingels." Letter, William
Heath to Mrs. Johnson, 2 July 1965, FE
12, Johnson, L.B., LBJL.

22. As she later remembered, "I fell
in love with Austin the first moment I
laid eyes on it and that love has never
slackened." Lewis L. Gould, *Lady Bird
Johnson: Our Environmental First Lady*
(Lawrence: University Press of Kansas,
1999), 5.

23. Oral History, William W. Heath, 20
May 1970, tape 1, side 2, 16, 19–20, LBJL.

24. Lady Bird Johnson, *A White House
Diary* (New York: Holt, Rinehart, and
Winston, 1970), 243.

25. Memo from Horace Busby to Mrs.
Johnson about the Presidential Library,
21 February 1965, FE 12, Johnson, L.B.,
2, LBJL.

26. Letter, William Heath to the
President, 6 August 1965; letter, Lyndon
Johnson to William Heath, 9 August
1965; letter, Lyndon Johnson to Lawson
B. Knott, 13 August 1965; letter, Knott
to Johnson, 17 August 1965, FE 12,
Johnson, L.B., LBJL.

27. Press conference, 9 August
1965, FE 12, Johnson, L.B., LBJL. From
the time it was announced, it took less
than a month to pass the authorizing
congressional legislation, H.J. Res. 632,
for the Johnson Library.

28. She made three visits to the
Truman Library, one in 1964 and two in
1965. When she first visited the Truman
Library in 1964 she was not actively

planning the Johnson Library, but she must have had in mind that this was something her husband would embark on some day. Lady Bird Johnson, *A White House Diary*, 180–181. One of the visits in 1965 was for the signing of the Medicare legislation.

29. Ibid., 181–182. She also noted: "The most delightful aspect of all, I think, is the fact that in the auditorium President Truman meets and talks to busloads of school children who come all summer long to visit the Library."

30. Ibid., 313.

31. Letter, Thomas J. Watson, Jr., to LBJ, 18 August 1965, Special File Regarding Design, Exhibits, Etc., of LBJ Library, LBJL.

32. Transcript, Lady Bird Johnson's Diary, 20 October 1965, 4, 6, LBJL.

33. Ibid., 2–3.

34. Gould, *Lady Bird Johnson*.

35. Lady Bird Johnson saw other examples of Bunshaft's work during her tours, including the First National Bank of Fort Worth and the Lincoln Center Library and Museum in New York City. Carol Herselle Krinsky, *Gordon Bunshaft of Skidmore, Owings, & Merrill* (New York: MIT Press, 1988), 243–244.

36. Transcript, Lady Bird Johnson's Diary, 20 October 1965, 5, LBJL.

37. Reyner Banham, "The New Brutalism," in *A Critic Writes: Essays by Reyner Banham*, selected by Mary Banham et al. (Berkeley: University of California Press, 1996), 7–15.

38. Transcript, Lady Bird Johnson's Diary, 20 October 1965, 3, LBJL.

39. The most detailed biography of Philip Johnson's extensive career is Franz Schulze's *Philip Johnson: Life and Work* (New York: Knopf, 1994); see also Steven Fox, *The Architecture of Philip Johnson* (New York: Bullfinch, 2002). For Johnson and the Nazis in brief, see William Shirer, *Berlin Diary: The Journal of a Foreign Correspondent, 1934–1941* (New York: Knopf, 1941).

40. Minoru Yamasaki, *A Life in Architecture* (New York: Weatherhill, 1979), 92–95. President Johnson attended the dedication of Yamasaki's Woodrow Wilson School.

41. Architectural historian William Morgan, who was studying at Princeton when the building was erected and observed the various stages of its construction, states: "The columns are not load bearing (how could they be—they're made from spun sugar) because I saw the building under construction, and the columns went up last." E-mail, 1 June 2004.

42. Transcript, Lady Bird Johnson's Diary, 20 October 1965, 8, LBJL.

43. Krinsky, *Gordon Bunshaft*, 243. These projects included the family's radio station in Austin, the Federal Center in Austin, and the Manned Spacecraft Center in Houston.

44. Transcript, Oral History, William Heath, 25 May 1970, tape 2, 3, LBJL.

45. Yamasaki, *A Life in Architecture*, 9.

46. Transcript, Oral History, William Heath, 25 May 1970, tape 2, 3, LBJL.

47. Apparently, in the fall of 1965, President Johnson requested Philip Johnson's FBI file, which was extensive because of his interest in Hitler's fascism. It probably also had references to Philip Johnson's homosexuality. In any case, in 1966 the White House said in a memo that "no further consideration would be given to the appointment of [Philip Johnson] to the [National] Fine Arts Commission." Schulze, *Philip Johnson*, 163; Transcript, Oral History,

J. Roy White, 24 February 1971, 56,
LBJL. As Alice Friedman writes, it was
known in architectural circles that Philip
Johnson was gay: "The fact was well
known to his friends and indeed, to a
broad circle of colleagues and critics he
knew through The Museum of Modern
Art, the New York art scene, and the
East Coast architectural schools. But,
true to the taboos of the time, Johnson's
gayness was never openly acknowledged,
let alone publicly discussed in
connection with his life and work." Alice
T. Friedman, *Women and the Making of
the Modern House: A Social and Architectural
History* (New York: Abrams, 1998), 148.

48. Transcript, Oral History, Gordon
Bunshaft, 25 June 1969, 5–6, LBJL.

49. Nathaniel Owings believed
that Skidmore, Owings, and Merrill
(SOM) got the job "through my work in
Washington [with] Mrs. Johnson. . . .
[T]he way the whole LBJ Library started
was [that] . . . I pulled in Bunshaft [for
the Hirshhorn Museum]. Then, when
the Library came up, Brooks, who is
a Texas architect of great charm and
considerable influence, and lives down
there and knows the Johnsons very well,
and he had been to school with Bun.
So Brooks and I agreed that Bunshaft
could do both. Now in our firm we
delegate work, we delegate it. I might
also say no one tells Bunshaft anything.
We're doing work all over the United
States. . . . My responsibility was overall
planning—Bunshaft's detailed design."
Undoubtedly Owings, through his
contact with Brooks and Mrs. Johnson,
had an influence on the selection of
Bunshaft, but other factors were at work as
well. Transcript, Oral History, Nathaniel
Owings, 25 March 1970, 2–3, LBJL.

50. Transcript, Oral History, J. Roy
White, 24 February 1971, 57, LBJL.

51. Bunshaft pulled out the telegram
and was holding it in his hand at the
beginning of the interview to check the
exact date. Transcript, Oral History,
Gordon Bunshaft, 25 June 1969, 1, LBJL.

52. Krinsky, *Gordon Bunshaft*, 1.

53. Louis Skidmore and Nathaniel
Owings formed their architectural firm
in 1935. In 1939, John Merrill joined the
firm. Ibid., 4–10.

54. Reyner Banham, *Age of the Masters:
A Personal View of Modern Architecture*, 2d ed.
(New York: Harper and Row, 1975), 114.

55. Dell Upton, *Architecture in the United
States* (New York: Oxford University
Press, 1998), 254.

56. Krinsky, *Gordon Bunshaft*, 25.
Bunshaft's work in the 1950s and early
1960s helped SOM grow.

57. Ibid., 51.

58. Brendan Gill, *Many Masks: A Life
of Frank Lloyd Wright* (New York: Putnam,
1987), 444. Wright's attitude toward
SOM was typical of his response to
almost all other architects.

59. Transcript, Oral History, Gordon
Bunshaft, 25 June 1969, 6, LBJL.

60. Ibid., 7.

61. Carol Krinsky, e-mail
communication, 12 May 2004.

62. Transcript, Oral History, Roy
White, 24 February 1971, 58, LBJL.

63. Transcript, Oral History, Gordon
Bunshaft, 25 June 1969, 8, LBJL.

64. Ibid., 10. As Johnson was
making his decision, Lady Bird was
probably contacted by Nathaniel
Owings, who had worked with her on
the National Commission of Fine Arts.
Owings recalled, about his work on
the beautification and remodeling of

Washington, D.C., that "as I always did when I had a problem, I went to Mrs. Johnson. . . . [When] she says 'This is a lovely plan,' . . . that's just like a contract in your file. You can say, 'See? She approves it.'" Transcript, Oral History, Nathaniel Owings, 25 March 1970, 17, LBJL.

65. Memorandum for Mrs. Lyndon B. Johnson, apparently from W. W. Heath, although it is unsigned, 27 January 1966, Special File Regarding Design, Exhibits, Etc., of LBJ Library, LBJL.

66. Summary Notes of Meeting at White House, 12 May 1966, LBJL.

67. Transcript, Oral History, Gordon Bunshaft, 25 June 1969, 12, LBJL. According to the minutes of the meeting, President Johnson was actually in the room for twenty-nine minutes, but it is possible that he was with Bunshaft for only about fifteen minutes, as he remembered.

68. Transcript, telephone conversation, 17 May 1966, Bunshaft to JR and MJDR, Special File Regarding Design, Exhibits, Etc., of LBJ Library, LBJL.

69. Transcript, Oral History, Gordon Bunshaft, 25 June 1969, 10, LBJL.

70. Ibid., 27.

71. Dorothy Territo to Juanita Roberts, information for President's diary, September 1966, 2, LBJL.

72. Sid Richardson Hall houses the Lyndon B. Johnson School of Public Affairs, the Wasserman Public Affairs Library, the Center for American History, the Eugene C. Barker Texas History Collections, the Benson Latin American Collection, and the Texas State Historical Association.

73. This framework evokes, in heavy concrete forms, grids that are similar in style to two of Bunshaft's earlier buildings: the U.S. Consulate in Düsseldorf, Germany, and the Connecticut General Life Insurance Company, with their low, balanced grids.

74. Leon Moed, interview with Benjamin Hufbauer, 15 May 2003.

75. The balustrade around the platform of the plaza ties together the complex.

76. Summary Notes of Meeting at White House, 12 May 1966, Special File Regarding Design, Exhibits, Etc., of LBJ Library, LBJL.

77. Marilyn Stokstad, Art History, 2d ed. (New York: Abrams, 2002), 70.

78. Bunshaft, to my knowledge, never spoke of ziggurats as an influence, but the library offers visual similarities both to ziggurats and to other ancient monuments, such as the ramped stairways at the Audience Hall at Persepolis. He likely would have been dubious about this idea, even if, as he said, he did like to look at photographs of buildings of architecture's rich history, stretching back many thousands of years (see passage below).

79. In a review in the New York Times, Gary Cartwright wrote that "the L.B.J. Library rises like the Great Pyramids above all things." Gary Cartwright, "The L.B.J. Library: The Life and Times of Lyndon Johnson in Eight Full Stories," New York Times, 17 October 1971, XX1. Martin Waldron, also of the New York Times, wrote that the building was called, by some, "Lyndon's pyramid." Martin Waldron, "Nixon Hails Johnson Library at Dedication," New York Times, 23 May 1971, 1, 39.

80. Krinsky, Gordon Bunshaft, 17.

81. Ibid., especially 4–11, 17, 246.

82. A. L. Sadler, *A Short History of Japanese Architecture* (Rutland, Vt.: Tuttle, 1963), 8–11; Christopher Tadgell, *Japan: The Informal Contained* (London: Ellipsis, 2000), 22–23.

83. Krinsky, *Gordon Bunshaft*, 246.

84. Ibid., 246.

85. Transcript, Oral History, Gordon Bunshaft, 25 June 1969, LBJL.

86. Summary Minutes, meeting on LBJ Library, 28 January 1968, Special File Regarding Design, Exhibits, Etc., of LBJ Library, 3, LBJL.

87. Krinsky, *Gordon Bunshaft*, 246.

88. Ibid., 247. Krinsky notes the parallel with Greek temples but indicates that Bunshaft had not deliberately intended this effect.

89. The cases were set at eye level for adults, which meant that children and people who were wheelchair-bound had a difficult time seeing the exhibits. Claudia Anderson, e-mail, 5 June 2004. This was later changed so that display cases could hold larger materials and so that people of all sizes could see the displays, undermining one of Bunshaft's goals, which was to prevent curatorial alterations that would diminish the effect of the internal vistas within the library.

90. Letter, Naomi Savage to Ms. Davidson, volunteer coordinator, 1 April 1997, LBJL; see also Caro, *The Years of Lyndon Johnson: The Path to Power*, for a photo opposite page 358, which illustrates how Johnson had air-brushed out the person between himself and President Roosevelt.

91. Caro, *The Years of Lyndon Johnson: Path to Power.*

92. Summary Minutes, meeting on LBJ Library, 28 January 1968, Special File Regarding Design, Exhibits, Etc., of LBJ Library, LBJL.

93. Ibid.

94. Ibid., 3.

95. Ibid., 4.

96. Ibid.

97. Memo, Horace Busby, 28 February 1968, 3.

98. Summary Minutes, meeting on LBJ Library, 23 June 1968, Special File Regarding Design, Exhibits, Etc., of LBJ Library, LBJL. The transcript of another meeting from 18 August 1968 was ninety-one pages long.

99. Ibid., 47.

100. Ibid., 50.

101. Ibid., 53.

102. Lady Bird Johnson, *A White House Diary*, 315.

103. Summary Minutes, meeting on LBJ Library, 5 May 1968, Special File Regarding Design, Exhibits, Etc., of LBJ Library, 1, LBJL.

104. The addresses of these people were obtained from visitors' books in the libraries. Summary Minutes, meeting on LBJ Library, 23 June 1968, Special File Regarding Design, Exhibits, Etc., of LBJ Library, 2, LBJL.

105. Ibid., 6.

106. Summary Minutes, meeting on LBJ Library, 18 August 1968, Special File Regarding Design, Exhibits, Etc., of LBJ Library, 37, LBJL.

107. Summary Minutes, meeting on LBJ Library, 23 June 1968, Special File Regarding Design, Exhibits, Etc., of LBJ Library, 10, LBJL.

108. Summary Minutes, meeting on LBJ Library, 18 August 1968, Special File Regarding Design, Exhibits, Etc., of LBJ Library, 39, LBJL.

109. Ibid., 14–15.

110. Telephone conversation, LBJ to Gordon Bunshaft, 10 October 1968, 8:57 P.M. http://www.lbjlib.utexasedu

/johnson/AV.hom/dicta_audio.asp (accessed 30 December 2004). I thank the Johnson Library for making this recording available. Transcript, Oral History, Gordon Bunshaft, 25 June 1969, 19, LBJL.

111. Summary Minutes, meeting on LBJ Library, 8 January 1969, Special File Regarding Design, Exhibits, Etc., of LBJ Library, 5–6, LBJL.

112. Transcript, Oral History, Gordon Bunshaft, 25 June 1969, 20–21, LBJL.

113. Seymour Hersch, *The Price of Power: Kissinger in the Nixon White House* (New York: Summit, 1982).

114. Robert Dallek, *Flawed Giant: Lyndon Johnson and His Times, 1961–1973* (New York: Oxford University Press, 1998), 584–588. Johnson uses the word "treason" in relation to Nixon on page 588.

115. It was declassified at my request, and so I was probably the first researcher to see it.

116. Summary Minutes, meeting on LBJ Library, 9 November 1968, Special File Regarding Design, Exhibits, Etc., of LBJ Library, 5–6, LBJL.

117. Ibid., 15–50.

118. Ibid., 20.

119. Ibid., 21.

120. Ibid., 32.

121. Ibid., 33.

122. Ibid., 34.

123. Ibid., 34–35.

124. Ibid., 36. Lyndon Baines Johnson, *The Vantage Point: Perspectives of the Presidency, 1963–1969* (New York: Holt, Rinehart, and Winston, 1971).

125. Summary Minutes, meeting on LBJ Library, 9 November 1968, Special File Regarding Design, Exhibits, Etc., of LBJ Library, 36–37, LBJL.

126. Ibid., 38.

127. Ibid., 41–44.

128. Ibid., 45–46.

129. Ibid., 45.

130. Ibid., 54.

131. Ibid., 47–48.

132. Ibid., 50.

133. Ibid., 52.

134. Ibid., 53.

135. David Halberstam, "The Vantage Point," *New York Times*, 31 October 1971, BR1.

136. Robert Hardesty was the aid who called him "manic-depressive." Quoted in Dallek, *Lyndon B. Johnson: Portrait of a President*.

137. Waldron, "Nixon Hails Johnson Library"; Cartwright, "The LBJ Library."

138. Cartwright, "The LBJ Library."

139. "Remembering LBJ," *Newsweek*, 24 May 1971, 25.

140. Ibid.

141. Ibid.

142. Ada Louise Huxtable, "A Success as Architecture and as Monument," *New York Times*, 23 May 1971, 39.

143. LBJ AV Committee, 8 January 1969, Special File Regarding Design, Exhibits, Etc., of LBJ Library, 9, LBJL.

144. Reeves, *President Nixon: Alone in the White House*, 41.

145. Anonymous personal communication from an employee of the presidential library system, 2002.

146. Dallek, *Flawed Giant*, 623.

147. Brant Bingamon, "The Long Arm of LBJ," *Austin Chronicle*, 17 May 2002, quotes Harry Middleton as saying that Caro's loathing for Johnson was such that "it coats a steamy sheen over his prose."

148. Robert Caro, *The Years of Lyndon Johnson: Master of the Senate* (New York: Knopf, 2002), 1047.

149. The information in the following paragraphs comes from conversations my wife, Dr. Bess Reed, and I had with Claudia Anderson in 2002 and 2003.

Anderson has also e-mailed additional information, including especially an e-mail of 5 June 2004.

150. Claudia Anderson, e-mail, 5 June 2004.

151. Anderson wrote, "Archival stack areas are usually windowless and often have staff stationed in them. The National Archives building in downtown Washington certainly did in the 1960s and 1970s. Prevailing thought would have been that the archivists need to be near the collections (and natural light is not good for documents). The archivists, along with Library administration, made the decision that we would prefer to make trips to the stacks and be on the floor that had windows." Ibid.

152. Insects attracted to decaying matter on the ledges were able to penetrate the sealing around the windows.

153. There have also been some problems with water leaking onto archival material from various sources. A system for routing storm water away from the roof occasionally leaks water onto the seventh floor, dampening several boxes of documents that the archivists successfully recovered. The library also once had a leak from the shower drain in the president's bathroom on the eighth floor that threatened materials on the floor below. Claudia Anderson, e-mail, 5 June 2004. Anderson notes that "several years ago we had a contractor who did extensive repairs and renovations to the roof, and most of the drainage problems were fixed."

154. Ada Louise Huxtable, "Selling the President, Architecturally," *New York Times*, 30 September 1973, 31,148.

155. Leon Moed, interview, 15 May 2003; "Johnson Library in Repair Fight," *New York Times*, 22 July 1973, 45.

156. Claudia Anderson also notes the problems with the library's plaza. There have been "extensive and serious problems with the plaza foundation surrounding the building. There are multiple problems with multiple causes. The different areas of the buildings in the complex expand and contract at different rates along the expansion joints, and this causes cracks and leaks to form in the travertine, which does not have expansion joints. Water can then penetrate the walls. Coal tar was used as a sealant under the plaza, and the coal tar melts in the hot Texas temperature and runs off, filling the storm water drains (which are under-sized to begin with). There is also a problem with calcium from the travertine dissolving in rainwater and then hardening in the same drains. All of this causes water to backup and to get into places where it causes rust, corrosion, rotting, and mildew." Claudia Anderson, e-mail, 4 June 2004.

157. The adjective "brutality" is, of course, subjective and is meant to be distinct from the architectural movement "Brutalism."

158. Michael R. Beschloss, *Taking Charge: The Johnson White House Tapes, 1963–64* (New York: Simon and Schuster, 1997), 568. Beschloss credits director Harry Middleton's "commitment to openness" for allowing the tapes to be opened "as quickly and fully as possible."

Chapter 4. Celebrity and Power

1. Henry James, *Novels, 1881–1886: Washington Square, The Portrait of a Lady, The Bostonians* (New York: Library of

America, 1985), 397–398. There is, of course, a huge literature on Henry James and The Portrait of a Lady. In relation to dress in this particular novel, see Clair Hughes, "The Color of Life: The Significance of Dress in the Portrait of a Lady," Henry James Review 18, no. 1 (1997): 66–80. Hughes analyzes the symbolic use that James makes of dress in the novel as Isabel Archer moves from relative innocence to being trapped in an unhappy marriage. As Hughes argues, "Isabel chooses black [for her dress] out of unhappiness but equally as a positive expression of herself by material means, independent of what others have tried to make of her, with their 'genius for upholstery'" (75).

2. Edith Mayo, interview, 4 September 2003.

3. Carl Sferrazza Anthony, First Ladies: The Saga of the Presidents' Wives and Their Power, 1789–1961 (New York: Quill, 1990), 81–91.

4. Edith Mayo, interview, 4 September 2003.

5. Douglas Cole, Franz Boas: The Early Years, 1858–1906 (Seattle: University of Washington Press, 1999).

6. Ibid. Steven Lubar and Kathleen M. Kendrick, Legacies: Collecting America's History at the Smithsonian (Washington, D.C.: Smithsonian Institution Press, 2001); Curtis M. Hinsley, Jr., Savages and Scientists: The Smithsonian Institution and the Development of American Anthropology, 1846–1910 (Washington, D.C.: Smithsonian Institution Press, 1981); and William Y. Adams, The Philosophical Roots of Anthropology (Stanford, Calif.: CSLI, 1998), 235–242.

7. Webster Prentiss True, The Smithsonian Institution (1929) (reprint, Smithsonian Scientific Series, vol. 1, ed.

Charles Greeley Abbott, New York: Smithsonian Institution Series, 1934). See caption to Plate 8, opposite page 20.

8. Ibid., 103, 25.

9. For the background on social Darwinism, see Mike Hawkins, Social Darwinism in European and American Thought, 1860–1945: Nature as Model and Nature as Threat (Cambridge: Cambridge University Press, 1997); and Pat Shipman, The Evolution of Racism: Human Difference and the Use and Abuse of Science (New York: Simon and Schuster, 1994).

10. Robert W. Rydell, All the World's a Fair (Chicago: University of Chicago Press, 1984), 45.

11. See Robert W. Rydell, John E. Findling, and Kimberly D. Pelle, Fair America: World's Fairs in the United States (Washington, D.C.: Smithsonian Institution Press, 2000), especially 29–40; and Rydell, All the World's a Fair, especially 38–71.

12. Hinsley, Savages and Scientists, 111–112.

13. Anon., "Through the Looking Glass," Chicago Tribune, 1 November 1893, 9.

14. Hinsley, Savages and Scientists, 108.

15. Ibid., 94.

16. Dress was featured prominently at the International Health Exhibition in London in 1884 with an emphasis on national and ethnic styles of dress in relation to civilization. Professor Hodgetts, Anglo-Saxon Dress and Food: A Lecture Delivered in the Lecture Room of the Exhibition, June 27th, 1884 (London: W. Clowes and Sons, 1884); Edward William Godwin, Dress, and Its Relation to Health and Climate (London: W. Clowes and Sons, 1884); Lewis Wingfield, Notes on Civil Costume in England from the Conquest to the Regency, as Exemplified in the International Health Exhibition, South

Kensington (London: W. Clowes and Sons, 1884); Lewis Wingfield, *The History of English Dress: A Lecture Delivered in the Lecture Room of the Exhibition, June 24th, 1884* (London: W. Clowes and Sons, 1884); William Morris, *Textile Fabrics: A Lecture Delivered in the Lecture Room of the Exhibition, July 11th, 1884* (London: printed and published for the Executive Council of the International Health Exhibition, and for the Council of the Society of Arts by William Clowes and Sons, 1884).

17. Mrs. Julian James, Foreword, in Rose Gouverneur Hoes, *Catalog of American Historical Costumes, Including Those of the Mistresses of the White House as Shown in the United States National Museum* (Washington, D.C.: Waverly Press, 1915), [i, ii].

18. Quoted in Winzola McLendon, "First Lady Mannequins Acquire a Lively Look," *Washington Post and Times Herald*, 18 November 1962, F17; Margaret W. Brown, *Dresses of the First Ladies of the White House* (Washington, D.C.: Smithsonian Institution, 1952), v.

19. Rose Gouverneur Hoes, *The Dresses of the Mistresses of the White House as Shown in the United States National Museum* (Washington, D.C.: Historical Publishing Company, 1931), [27].

20. Hoes, *Catalog of American Historical Costumes*, 1, 2, 5.

21. Ibid., 44, 48, 69–71.

22. Ibid., 26; see also Rose Gouverneur Hoes, "When the Apparel Proclaimed the Man in America," *Washington Post*, 8 November 1914, SM1.

23. The items of male dress included a court mantle worn by John Hay when he was part of the American legation to the Spanish court, part of the uniform of Major Adams Stevens, part of the court clothing of General Thomas Pinkney, a pair of silk breeches and two nightcaps

once owned by Moses S. Myers from the turn of the nineteenth century, and miscellaneous men's shoe buckles, beaver hats, handkerchiefs, and other appointments. Hoes, *Catalog of American Historical Costumes*.

24. Ann B. Rossilli, *Interpretative Dioramas as Material Culture of Natural History Museums: A Case Study at the National Museum of Natural History* (master's thesis, University of Maryland, 2000), 21.

25. Rose Gouverneur Hoes's ownership of this family heirloom was one of the triggers for the inclusion of gowns of mistresses of the White House in the original costume collection. Hoes explains: "After a gown of Mrs. Monroe was placed on exhibition, it was decided to allow the costume of Mrs. Gouverneur to remain on account of its being unique in character and an example of the vagaries of fashion now obsolete. It is a fine specimen of the Louis Seize period, and was worn at a time when straw work was all the rage." Hoes, *The Dresses of the Mistresses of the White House*, [12].

26. Garret P. Serviss, *San Antonio Light*, 1917, news service clipping, First Ladies File, Smithsonian Institution archives.

27. Hoes, *Catalog of American Historical Costumes*, 1.

28. Serviss, *San Antonio Light*.

29. Helen Herron Taft gown records, Taft to Hoes, 5 December 1912, Smithsonian Institution archives; and Taft to James, 6 March, Smithsonian Institution archives.

30. Hoes, *The Dresses of the Mistresses of the White House*. The pages are unnumbered—the first quote is from Jackson, case 4, and the second is from Fillmore, case 8.

31. Rose Gouverneur Hoes, "Evolution of Fashions for Women for

More Than a Century Shown by Period Costumes on Exhibition at the National Museum," unpublished lecture, First Ladies File, Smithsonian Institution archives, ca. 1918, 2: "As an illustration, a skirt . . . owned by Mrs. Andrew Jackson Donaldson . . . was loaned by the owner . . . to be used in an artist's studio for drapery, where it was destroyed by fire."

32. Ibid., 1.

33. Ibid., 2–3.

34. Rossilli, "Interpretive Dioramas," 18.

35. Hinsley, *Savages and Scientists*, 95.

36. Administrative Assistant to the Secretary to Mrs. Hoes, 3 August 1916, Smithsonian Institution archives; Ravenel to Hoes, 14 November 1924, Smithsonian Institution archives; memorandum of call of Mrs. R. G. Hoes from the Administrative Assistant to the Secretary, 17 October 1922, Smithsonian Institution archives; and Administrative Assistant to the Secretary to Hoes, 14 October 1920, Smithsonian Institution archives.

37. Holmes to Ravenel, 12 April 1916, Smithsonian Institution archives: "I beg to say that she has done and is doing so much for the Museum, that no reasonable or unharmful request of hers should be denied."

38. Letters in the archive, such as from the Administrative Assistant to the Secretary to Hoes, 12 January 1921, Smithsonian Institution archives, giving Hoes the $22.10 earned by sales of the catalog. This shows that although some staff members were annoyed, the museum was diligent in sending catalog proceeds to Hoes. Another letter, from Olmsted to Graf, 10 August 1932, Smithsonian Institution archives, shows that this practice was continuing just before Hoes's death.

39. Memorandum, Ravenel to Rathbun, 21 December 1914,

Smithsonian Institution archives; letter, Theodore Belote to Professor Holmes, 5 April 1916, Smithsonian Institution archives; letter, Theodore Belote to Professor Holmes, 28 April 1916, Smithsonian Institution archives.

40. Holmes to Ravenel, 19 July 1920, Smithsonian Institution archives.

41. Ravenel to the Secretary, 10 April 1916, Smithsonian Institution archives; Holmes to Ravenel, 12 April 1916, Smithsonian Institution archives.

42. James to Walcott, 22 February 1918, Smithsonian Institution archives.

43. Walcott to James, 1 March 1918, Smithsonian Institution archives; Holmes to Rathbun, 28 September 1917, Smithsonian Institution archives.

44. James to Walcott, 22 February 1918, Smithsonian Institution archives.

45. By 1918 the Smithsonian staff were concerned with the damage caused by the sun and were already taking steps to shield the dresses from further solar damage.

46. Ravenel to Rathbun, 6 January 1916, Smithsonian Institution archives. At this time, more electric lights were installed in the hall.

47. Brown to Frederick Atkins, 26 December 1944, Smithsonian Institution archives. Additional information can be found on the dress in Margaret W. Brown, *Dresses of the First Ladies*, 114–117.

48. Belote to Ravenel, 12 August 1921, Smithsonian Institution archives.

49. Memorandum to Wetmore, 5 May 1945, Smithsonian Institution archives.

50. Sarah Booth Conroy, "First Ladies' Special Lady," *Washington Post*, 10 October 1994, B3. This article has some brief information on Margaret Brown Klapthor's career.

51. Brown to Atkins, 26 December 1944, Smithsonian Institution archives.

52. Cheney to Regan, 4 January 1945, Smithsonian Institution archives.

53. Brown to Wetmore, 13 January 1945, Smithsonian Institution archives; Brown to Wetmore, 5 May 1945, Smithsonian Institution archives; Ryland to Brown, 12 July 1945, Smithsonian Institution archives; Wilde to Ryland, 17 July 1945, Smithsonian Institution archives; requisition, 15 yards of white pure dye silk chiffon at $1.75 per yard, 8 September 1945, Margaret Brown, Smithsonian Institution archives. During this process, the Smithsonian began to obtain some backup gowns as replacements for those damaged beyond repair. Brown to Wetmore, 5 May 1945, Smithsonian Institution archives.

54. Mamie Eisenhower to Margaret Brown, 9 November 1954, Smithsonian Institution archives.

55. Edith Mayo, interview, 4 September 2003.

56. *Annual Report for the Smithsonian Institution for the Year 1955* (Washington, D.C.: Smithsonian, 1955), 4; Rossilli, *Interpretive Dioramas*, 28; and Smithsonian Archives Web page: http://www.si.edu/archivees/ihd/arts/modern. The Division of Civil History, in which Brown worked, had long been in charge of costume, political collections, and furniture—in essence, much the same material that James and Hoes had used in their creation of the first costume displays in 1915 but now greatly expanded. With money and support available for new displays and with the crowded display conditions in the Arts and Industries building, a new means of displaying these popular gowns and accommodating other distinguished pieces in the Civil History collection was called for.

57. William Seale, *The President's House: A History* (Washington, D.C.: National Geographic Society, 1986), 1002–1051.

58. Edwin Bateman Morris, *Report of the Commission on the Renovation of the Executive Mansion* (Washington, D.C.: Government Printing Office, 1952), 104; Margaret Brown Klapthor, *The First Ladies Hall* (Washington, D.C.: Smithsonian Institution Press, 1973), 20.

59. Margaret Brown, *The First Ladies Hall* (Washington, D.C.: Smithsonian, 1955), [1]. (This illustrated ten-page museum catalog on the exhibit for the Smithsonian Institution was revised in 1963 to showcase the expanded display in the new museum building. In 1965 the catalog was revised and expanded—and again in 1980 to include information on china and tableware used at the White House on display in the First Ladies Hall.)

60. Klapthor, *The First Ladies Hall*, 1973), [20]. The piano came to the Smithsonian in the 1930s.

61. Ruth Shumaker, "First Ladies on View at Smithsonian," *Washington Post and Times Herald*, 25 May 1955, 1.

62. Karal Ann Marling, *As Seen on T.V.: The Visual Culture of Everyday Life in the 1950s* (Cambridge: Harvard University Press, 1994), 8–49.

63. Ibid., 37.

64. Anon., "Gowns of History," *Washington Post and Times Herald*, 23 May 1954, S4. The show was sponsored by four of the first ladies then alive.

65. Marling, *As Seen on T.V.*, 8–49.

66. Anthony, *First Ladies*, 90.

67. Ibid., 90–94.

68. Margaret Brown Klapthor, "Benjamin Latrobe and Dolley Madison Decorate the White House," *Contributions from the Museum of History and*

Technology, Paper 49 (Washington, D.C.: Smithsonian Institution Press, 1965).

69. The National Society of the Daughters of the American Revolution Museum was a pioneer in the installation of re-created period rooms in the United States, having installed its first, the New Jersey Room, in 1910. No doubt Margaret Brown and Frank Klapthor's common work interests helped draw them together.

70. McLendon, "First Lady Mannequins Acquire a Lively Look," F17.

71. Anon., "First Lady's Inaugural Ball Gown Is to Join Collection," Washington Post and Times Herald, 11 November 1962, F8.

72. Klapthor, The First Ladies Hall, 1973, [1].

73. Margaret Brown Klapthor, The First Ladies Hall (Washington, D.C.: Smithsonian Institution, 1965), [7].

74. Margaret Brown Klapthor, Official White House China, 1789 to the Present (Washington, D.C.: Smithsonian Institution Press, 1975).

75. Elisabeth L. Cameron, Isn't S/he a Doll?: Play and Ritual in African Sculpture (Los Angeles: UCLA Fowler Museum of Cultural History, 1996), 11.

76. First ladies dolls have been displayed temporarily at the Eisenhower, Carter, and Nixon libraries.

77. Letter to Margaret Klapthor, 20 August 1976, Margaret Klapthor files, Correspondence Files, Smithsonian Institution archives, 1976.

78. Betty Ford and Chris Chase, The Times of My Life (New York: Harper and Row, 1978), 6; Carol Mattingly, Appropriate[ing] Dress: Women's Rhetorical Style in Nineteenth-Century America (Carbondale and Edwardsville, Ill.: Southern Illinois University Press, 2002).

79. Klapthor to model lab, n.d., First Ladies File, Smithsonian Institution archives, 1973–1976.

80. Klapthor, First Ladies Hall, 1973, [1].

81. Carol Mattingly, interview, 11 September 2003.

82. Erika Doss, e-mail, 14 April 2004.

83. Eleanor Boime, a docent and editor of First Ladies Newsletter 9, 7466, Box 2, Margaret B. Klapthor Papers, Docents File.

84. According to Edith Mayo, necessary updates in the heating and air-conditioning systems in the building contributed to the need to revise the displays. Edith Mayo, interview, 17 July 2003.

85. Quoted in Sarah Booth Conroy, "Going, Going, Gown; First Ladies Exhibit May Travel to Dallas," Washington Post, 17 August 1997, 1.

86. Erika Doss, e-mail, 14 April 2004.

87. Conroy, "Going, Going, Gown," 1.

88. Mary A. Becker, Polly Willman, and Noreen C. Tuross, "The U.S. First Ladies Gowns: A Biochemical Study of Silk Preservation," Journal of the American Institute for Conservation 34, no. 2 (1995): 141–152.

89. The first script was by Dr. Karen Mittelman, who for a brief time was curator of the first ladies collection. The second script was by Melinda Fry, who was Margaret Klapthor's protégé. Most of the Smithsonian's internal correspondence and records for this period are closed as of this writing. Most of this account comes from interviews that I conducted with Edith Mayo, 4 September 2003, and from conversations with other Smithsonian employees. I briefly saw but was not allowed to copy the two earlier scripts by Mittelman and Fry, as well as some correspondence

related to the review of these scripts. However, these materials all confirm Mayo's account. In the acknowledgments to the catalog for the exhibit, *First Ladies: Political Role and Public Image,* coauthored with Denise D. Meringolo (Washington, D.C.: Smithsonian, 1994), Mayo credits the first two scripts with helping to inform her own.

90. Edith Mayo, interview, 4 September 2003.

91. Ibid., 17 July 2003.

92. Apparently when these rooms were dismantled, a few of the furnishings were placed in storage, but most of the re-created rooms were lost.

93. Edith Mayo, interview, 4 September 2003.

94. Ibid. These included Denise Meringolo, who helped transform exhibition script into catalog; Kate Henderson, who was in charge of the care and safekeeping of objects, object research, and exhibition installation; Jana Justin, "whose jewel-like colors and gown gallery design greatly enhanced our presentation"; costume conservator Polly Willman; Lynn Chase, project and budget manager; as well as others.

95. Margaret Klapthor, undated memorandum titled "General Thoughts on the First Ladies Script," in First Ladies archive, Smithsonian Institution archives. It was probably written in 1991.

96. In addition, the removal of the gowns from the plaster mannequins provided an opportunity for conservation, and this too required money, provided in part by Belle Dames of Los Angeles.

97. Chubb underwrote the film on the first ladies that played in a small theater at the front of the first gallery after the exhibition itself had opened.

98. Edith Mayo, interview, 4 September 2003.

99. This exhibit was curated by the late Richard Martin of the Metropolitan Museum.

100. Office of Policy and Analysis, Smithsonian Institution, "Study of Visitors at The American Presidency," August 2001, 97.

101. James, *Novels, 1881–1886: The Portrait of a Lady,* 397.

102. Dean MacCannell, *The Tourist: A New Theory of the Leisure Class,* 2d ed. (New York: Schocken Books, 1989), 2–14.

Chapter 5. Reinventing the Presidential Library

1. Larry Hackman, interview, 21 January 2004.

2. The text of the 1995 exhibit appears beneath a photograph of a Japanese American child being processed before being transported to an internment camp. The text reads:

JAPANESE-AMERICAN INTERNMENT

On February 19, 1942, FDR signed Executive Order 9066 authorizing the removal of 120,000 Japanese-Americans from the West Coast to internment camps inland. All internees lost personal liberties; most lost their homes and property as well.

At the time, America was reeling from the attack on Pearl Harbor, followed by a string of Japanese military triumphs in the Pacific. Fear of a Japanese invasion gripped much of the West Coast. And Roosevelt, long persuaded of the dangers posed by citizens sympathetic to the enemy, accepted the War Department's argument that internment was vital to national security.

Yet no case for military necessity was

ever made. The internment was the product of war hysteria and racism, fanned by West Coast politicians, senior military officers, columnists and the public.

Indeed, young Japanese-Americans later recruited from the internment camps fought in Europe with extreme valor as the 442nd Regimental Combat Team, one of the most decorated units in American history.

Japanese-American internment left a bitter legacy to later generations of Americans. Years of searching for legal redress culminated in August 1988 when the United States Congress approved financial restitution and an apology to the surviving Japanese-American internees.

3. See also the *Public Historian* journal.

4. Presidential Libraries Briefing Book; Larry Hackman, interview, 21 January 2004.

5. Raymond Geselbracht, interview, 21 January 2004.

6. The only survey that exists is from the Johnson Library discussed in the previous chapter. Only a summary of the survey exists, not the survey itself.

7. I am heavily indebted in this introductory material to an insightful, unpublished essay by Larry Hackman: "A Presidential Library Partnership: The Harry S. Truman Library and the Harry S. Truman Library Institute for National and International Affairs" (unpublished document, Harry S. Truman Library, February 2002).

8. Jon Wiener, *Professors, Politics, and Pop* (New York: Verso, 1991), 274.

9. The Nixon Library, as of this writing, is in the process of being absorbed into the National Archives system of presidential libraries. One of the priorities of the Office of Presidential Libraries in taking over the

Nixon Library is to revise its Watergate displays. Sharon Fawcett, Meeting on Presidential Libraries, Princeton University, 9 April 2004.

10. Susan Naulty, "Creating an Archives at the Richard Nixon Library and Birthplace," *Government Information Quarterly* 11, no. 1 (1994): 37–45.

11. Frank L. Schick, with Renee Schick and Mark Carroll, *Records of the Presidency* (Phoenix, Ariz.: Oryx Press, 1989). See also the pre-Watergate, post-Watergate, post-1986, respectively, Reagan law, Clinton law, and Bush executive order.

12. Wiener, *Professors, Politics, and Pop*, 274.

13. Larry Hackman, interview, 21 January 2004.

14. Lawrence E. Walsh, *Iran-Contra: The Final Report* (New York: Times Books, 1994), xiv.

15. Ibid., xv.

16. Jennifer Sternaman, e-mail, 13 April 2004.

17. Leslie Rankin, e-mail, 3 May 2004.

18. Larry Hackman also remarked on this display at the Reagan Library. Interview, 21 January 2004.

19. Raymond Geselbracht, interview, 21 January 2004.

20. Ibid. Larry Hackman told me that although he worked on an interactive project at the Kennedy Library, it ultimately was not used in the library's exhibits.

21. Harry Truman gave a speech in April 1959 that described in detail the six roles. See Harry Truman, *Truman Speaks* (New York: Columbia University Press, 1960), especially 4–9.

22. Museum photographs, audiovisual archives, HSTL.

23. One of the problems posed by presidential library museum displays

is a relative lack of visually compelling objects with which to create narratives of presidential accomplishments. Edward T. Linenthal, in his excellent analysis of the founding of the United States Holocaust Museum in Washington, D.C., discusses a similar phenomenon. In this museum, curators did not lack for objects lent or donated by survivors and their families, but they did not have large-scale objects and images to create compelling displays. To solve this problem, the Holocaust Museum curators traveled to Holocaust sites to find relevant materials and to gather material for evocative re-creations. Edward T. Linenthal, *Preserving Memory: The Struggle to Create America's Holocaust Museum* (New York: Viking, 1995), 140–159. Presidential library displays have long used replicas and are increasingly using historic images and objects drawn from popular culture to fill out their displays.

24. Benedict Zobrist, interview, 17 March 2004. In the late 1970s, the National Archives' Office of Presidential Libraries (NARA) made an attempt to support the development of new and updated displays at all presidential libraries. Rather than attempting to direct things from Washington, D.C., NARA funded the construction of an exhibition workshop in the basement of the Truman Library to produce exhibits for several presidential libraries. However, this initiative did not pan out, and after a few years most of the employees at this facility left for positions elsewhere. Around 1980, NARA handed the facility over to the Truman Library for its own use. At this point, each presidential library was thrown back on its own resources. Raymond Geselbracht, interview, 21

January 2004; Clay Bauske, interviews, 17 June 1995, 21 January 2004; Clay Bauske, e-mail, 10 May 2004.

25. Meeting on Presidential Libraries, Princeton University, 10 April 2004.

26. Donald W. Wilson, "Presidential Libraries Developing to Maturity," *Presidential Studies Quarterly* 21, no. 4 (Fall 1991): 771–780.

27. Benedict Zobrist, interview, 17 March 2004.

28. Clay Bauske, interview, 6 June 1995.

29. Greta Kempton Papers, HSTL; Harry S. Truman File, Box 24, HSTL; Financial and Legal Affairs file, Box 32–33, HSTL. Benedict Zobrist, interview, 17 March 2004.

30. Clay Bauske, interviews, 6 June 1995, 21 January 2004.

31. Clay Bauske, interview, 21 January 2004; Clay Bauske, e-mail, 10 May 2004. In retrospect, Larry Hackman regards the film, which was "far too long" for most visitors, as "largely a waste of $$." Larry Hackman, letter, 12 May 2004.

32. Larry Hackman, "The State of the Harry S. Truman Library: A Preliminary Assessment," 5 October 1995, unpublished report. He recalls that he distributed this document to the board but "probably not the staff." Larry Hackman, letter, 12 May 2004.

33. One of Hackman's goals in reforming the archival side of the library was to overhaul the way materials were organized and accessed. Archivists at the Truman Library, as at some other presidential libraries, tended to bend over backwards to help the researcher who was with them at the moment. As a result, the Truman Library had an outstanding reputation among researchers, and the acknowledgments of many books and articles are filled

with praise for the Truman staff. But archivists neglected building systematic finding aids and working toward the systematic organization and preservation of material. Some senior archivists had amazing knowledge in their heads about what was in the collection and where to find it, but not enough of this knowledge was codified in finding aids. The retirement of senior archivists had the potential to become a serious setback for the library. Hackman reoriented the archivists' efforts so that they focused as much on long-range efforts for preservation and cataloging as they spent helping that day's researchers. Edwin Bridges and Michael Fox, "The Truman Presidential Library in a Time of Change: A Report and Recommendations" (unpublished report, Harry S. Truman Library, April 1996), 4–5, 12.

34. Larry Hackman, "The State of the Harry S. Truman Library: A Preliminary Assessment," 5 October 1995, unpublished report, 1.

35. As Hackman noted in his report, "In 1994 alone, the library lost six full time staff (150 years of experience); of these, only the director's position has been filled." Ibid., 6.

36. Hackman, "A Presidential Library Partnership."

37. Ibid., 9.

38. Ibid., 7.

39. Ibid., 17.

40. Ibid., 31.

41. Ibid., 13.

42. Tom Geismar, interview, 30 March 2004; Herman Eberhardt, interview, 21 March 2004. Eberhardt also emphasized the important contributions to the exhibition's content of the outside academic review. It consisted of historians Alonzo Hamby, Richard

Kirkendall, and Dennis Merrill. Clay Bauske, interview, 21 January 2004.

43. Former Senator Thomas Eagleton, serving at that time as the president of the Truman Institute, was very effective at lobbying Congress for this federal appropriation. Hackman, "A Presidential Library Partnership," 35.

44. Ibid., 18.

45. Raymond Geselbracht, interview, 21 January 2004.

46. Larry Hackman, interview, 21 January 2004.

47. Linda Man, "Truman Library Has More Than a New Look," Kansas City Star, 26 February 2001, A1.

48. Ibid., A1.

49. Brian McTavish, "This Truman Campaign Is on Billboards," Kansas City Star, 14 March 2001, F1.

50. Ibid.

51. Raymond Geselbracht, interview, 12 May 2002.

52. Friedrich Nietzsche, "On the Uses and Disadvantages of History for Life," in Untimely Meditations, trans. R. J. Hollingdale (New York: Cambridge University Press, 1983), 57–124. Hayden White, Metahistory: The Historical Imagination in Nineteenth Century Europe (Baltimore: Johns Hopkins University Press, 1975); and Hayden White, The Content of the Form: Narrative Discourse and Historical Representation (Baltimore: Johns Hopkins University Press, 1987).

53. Clay Bauske, e-mail, 10 May 2004.

54. Herman Eberhardt, interview, 21 March 2004.

55. See Steven C. Dubin, Displays of Power: Controversy in the American Museum from the Enola Gay to Sensation (New York: New York University Press, 2000); and Tom Engelhardt and Edward Linethal, eds., History Wars: The Enola Gay and Other

Battles for the American Past (New York: Henry Holt, 1996).

56. For instance, in the Nixon Library, President Nixon is credited with landing a man on the moon. This just happened to occur during his first year of office, and greater credit should go to presidents Kennedy (for first proposing the idea and getting it under way) and Johnson (for strongly supporting the space program during the 1960s). See Robert Dallek, *Flawed Giant: Lyndon Johnson and His Times: 1961–1973* (New York: Oxford University Press, 1998), 22–23, 418–425. Another example is the lack of serious discussion of the budget deficits of the 1980s and 1990s in the Reagan and Bush libraries.

57. Clay Bauske, e-mail, 26 April 2004.

58. Ibid., 21 January 2004.

59. Raymond Geselbracht, interview, 21 January 2004.

60. Clay Bauske, interview, 21 January 2004.

61. Larry Hackman, interview, 21 January 2004.

62. "The Year of the Woman: Candidates, Voters, and the 1992 Elections," *Political Science Quarterly* 108, no. 1 (Spring 1993): 29–37; Steven Stark, "Gap Politics," *Atlantic Monthly*, July 1996, 71–80.

63. Arthur M. Schlesinger, Jr., *The Imperial Presidency*, with a new epilogue by the author (Boston: Houghton Mifflin, 1989), 135; see also Clark Clifford with Richard Holbrooke, *Counsel to the President: A Memoir* (New York: Random House, 1991), 274–275; Alexander DeConde, *Presidential Machismo: Executive Authority, Military Intervention, and Foreign Relations* (Boston: Northeastern University Press, 2000), 145–147.

64. Clay Bauske, e-mail, 10 May 2004. According to Tom Geismar, the designers did not set out to create the reflection effect; but when they noticed how evocative this framing of the visitors was during the testing of the Decision Theaters, they decided to heighten the effect for the exhibit. Tom Geismar, interview, 30 March 2004.

65. Henry Luce, "The American Century," *Life* magazine, 1941 (reprinted as a booklet, New York: Time, 1941); Erika Doss, "Introduction: Looking at Life: Rethinking America's Favorite Magazine, 1936–1972," in *Looking at Life Magazine*, ed. Erika Doss (Washington, D.C.: Smithsonian Institution Press, 2001).

66. Doss, "Introduction," 16.

67. Benedict Zobrist, interview, 17 March 2004.

68. Larry Hackman, interview, 10 April 2004.

Conclusion

1. Historian Doris Kearns Goodwin, one of the assistants who worked with Johnson on his memoirs, recalled in 1985 that the Johnson Library staff, "half-jokingly and half-seriously, started clicking themselves in and out to raise the count a little." Dudley Clendinen, "Ex-Presidents Compete for History's Attention with Libraries," *New York Times*, 13 October 1985, 30; Robert Dallek, *Flawed Giant: Lyndon Johnson and His Times, 1961–1973* (New York: Oxford University Press, 1998), 623. Claudia Anderson said to me that Johnson was quite interested in admission figures. Personal communication, 29 December 2003.

2. Johnson staff member, interview, 31 December 2002. This longtime and highly reliable staff member's story appears to be confirmed by photos of the event.

This staff member did not ask for his or her identity to remain anonymous, but because of possible sensitivity regarding the identities and actions of the people involved, I decided it would be advisable.

3. Robert A. Caro, *The Years of Lyndon Johnson: The Path to Power* (New York: Knopf, 1982), xvii.

4. Johnson staff member, interview, 31 December 2002.

5. Lewis L. Gould, *The Modern American Presidency* (Lawrence: University Press of Kansas, 2003), 236, 237.

6. Additions have substantially increased the Roosevelt Library, including an 11,000-square-foot Eleanor Roosevelt wing completed in 1972 and a new visitors center completed in 2004.

7. Brian Skoloff, "Clinton Library Gains Big Steel Structure," *Associated Press*, 27 January 2003.

8. Bill Clinton, "Speech by President at WJC Presidential Center," 9 December 2000, www.clintonpresidentialcenter .org/legacy/120900.

9. www.clintonpresidentialcenter .org/faq.htm.

10. Anon., "Gallup Poll: Clinton popularity at an All Time Low," 9 March 2001, www.cnn.com/2001/ ALLPOLITICS/03/09/clinton.popularity; Anon., "Improving Impressions: Time Tempers Take on Bill Clinton," 22 June 2004, abcnews.go.com/sections/us/ Polls/clinton_poll_040622.html.

11. Bill Clinton, *My Life* (New York: Alfred A. Knopf, 2004), 876. See also Thomas F. Schaller and Thomas W. Williams, "The Contemporary Presidency: Postpresidential Influence in the Postmodern Era," *Presidential Studies Quarterly* 33, no. 1 (March 2003): 188–201.

12. William E. Schmidt, "Reshaped Carter Image Tied to Library Opening,"

New York Times, 21 September 1986, 24. See also Peter Applebome, "Carter Center: More Than the Past," *New York Times*, 30 May 1993, XX9.

13. The library was designed by the Atlanta architectural firm Jova/Daniels/ Busby, in cooperation with Lawton/ Umemura/Yamamoto of Hawaii.

14. For a detailed study of Carter's postpresidential career, see Douglas Brinkley, *The Unfinished Presidency: Jimmy Carter's Journey beyond the White House* (New York: Penguin Books, 1999).

15. The archives of both Stanford and the University of California at Irvine have substantial documents about the controversial proposals to locate the Reagan Library at those campuses.

16. The affiliated private foundations at presidential libraries, for both Democratic and Republican presidents, sponsor symposia, public lectures, and other programs that help advance causes associated with each party. The Johnson Library's building was paid for by the University of Texas, which allowed the Johnson foundation to begin gathering funds for such programs immediately without embarking on fund-raising for the building itself. This meant that the Johnson Library had and continues to have particularly robust programs—ones that are sometimes coordinated with the Johnson School of Public Affairs.

17. Ronald Reagan, *Ronald Reagan: An American Life* (New York: Pocket Books, 1999), 226–227.

18. Lou Cannon, *Governor Reagan: His Rise to Power* (New York: Public Affairs, 2003), 400.

19. For a description and analysis of the *Presidential Libraries Act of 1986* (Public Law 99-323), as well as of other laws and regulations pertaining to presidential

libraries, see Frank L. Schick, with Renee Schick and Mark Carroll, *Records of the Presidency* (Phoenix, Ariz.: Oryx Press, 1989), 13–19. See also the occasional pamphlet produced by the National Archives, entitled "Office of Presidential Libraries Briefing Book" (Washington, D.C.: Office of Presidential Libraries, NARA, 2002). Anon., "Aid to Ex-Presidents: How Much Is Too Much?" *New York Times*, 29 April 1986, A18.

20. Anon., "Reagan Asked to Support Presidential Library Bill," *New York Times*, 30 March 1985, 8.

21. Fred A. Bernstein, "Who Should Pay for Presidential Posterity," *New York Times*, 10 June 2004, D1. Sharon Fawcett indicated that recent legislation has boosted the required endowment to 40 percent for libraries built after the projected George W. Bush Library.

22. Presidential Libraries Act of 1986, sec. 5a.

23. Richard A. Jacobs, personal interview, August 1995.

24. Raymond Geselbracht, interview, 12 May 2002.

25. Clinton, *My Life*, 940; Paula Span, "Monumental Ambition: Presidential Libraries Are History and Hagiography, Archival Mother Lodes and Gift Shops Pushing Star-Spangled Dish Towels and 'Gippergear'—Are They Worth the $55 Million Taxpayers Spent Last Year to Maintain Them?" *Washington Post*, 17 February 2002, W24.

26. "Bill Clinton Says He Regrets Rich Pardon, Denies Wrongdoing," *Washington Post*, 1 April 2002, A4.

27. Clinton, *My Life*, 941.

28. Schick, Schick, and Carroll, *Records of the Presidency*, 243.

29. Robert M. Warner, *Diary of a Dream: A History of the National Archives Independence Movement, 1980–1985* (Metuchen, N.J.: Scarecrow Press, 1995), 117.

30. Schick, Schick, and Carroll, *Records of the Presidency*, 17–19.

31. Steve Henson, president of the Society of American Archivists, to Representative Stephen Horn, 6 November 2001, www.archivists.org/statements/stephenhorn.asp.

32. Richard Reeves, "Hiding History," *American Heritage* 53, no. 4 (August/September 2002): 64–67.

33. Sharon Fawcett, National Public Radio, "The Connection," 28 May 2004.

34. "Transcript of Debate," *New York Times*, 9 October 2004.

35. Tom Heuertz, e-mail correspondence, 22 July 2004. By 2004, a few hundred adults were also using the White House Decision Center each year, including groups of retirees, National Guard groups, and private business groups.

36. Anon., "Teacher's Guide to the White House Decision Center," White House Decision Center, Harry S. Truman Library, 2001.

37. Larry Hackman and Kay Geselbracht, "The White House Decision Center at the Truman Presidential Museum and Library: Learning through the Experience of Making History," *AASLH History News* 59, no. 2 (Spring 2004): 7–10.

38. White House Decision Center video, Truman Library, 2002.

39. Teacher Testimonials, White House Decision Center, Truman Library, 2001.

40. Tom Heuertz, e-mail correspondence, 20 July 2004.

41. Ibid.

42. Tom Heuertz indicated that sometimes civic groups and private

philanthropists would sponsor students within a school. Personal communication, 22 July 2004.

43. Judi O'Neill, interview, May 2002.

44. Fred A. Bernstein, "Archive Architecture: Setting the Spin in Stone," *New York Times*, 10 June 2004, F1, F9.

45. Ibid.

46. Andrew Demillo, "Study: Clinton Library Impact at Least $8.65 Million a Year," *Arkansas Democrat-Gazette*, 4 June 2004, 1.

47. Span, "Monumental Ambition"; Bernstein, "Archive Architecture."

48. The following presidents and first ladies are buried at the sites of their presidential libraries: Herbert and Lou Hoover, Franklin and Eleanor Roosevelt, Harry and Bess Truman, Dwight and Mamie Eisenhower, Richard and Patricia Nixon. A grave site has been consecrated for Nancy Reagan to rest beside Ronald.

49. Susan Naulty, an archivist at the Nixon Library, stated that "the actual Nixon burial site is sanctified ground. It was deeded to the Friends Church when Patricia Nixon died, because the State of California requires that land be sanctified for all cemeteries. Although the Friends Church officially owns the land, it is maintained by the Nixon Library." Susan Naulty, personal communication, 22 January 1996.

50. Reagan to Fellow Americans, 5 November 1994, Reagan.webteamone.com/alz.cfm.

51. Press Release, Reagan Library, 6 June 2004.

52. Press Release, "President Reagan to Lie in Repose at the Ronald Reagan Presidential Library; Reagan Library and Foundation to Produce Official CD and DVD of Funeral for 40th President," Reagan Library, 13 June 2004.

53. Erika Doss, *Elvis Culture: Fans, Faith, and Image* (Lawrence: University Press of Kansas, 1999).

54. Dennis Medina, personal communication, 17 June 1995.

55. The Place of Meditation was completed in 1966. The Eisenhower's firstborn child, Doud Dwight Eisenhower, is also interred there. Three-year-old Doud died of scarlet fever on 2 January 1921, leaving his parents grief stricken. For fifty years afterward on "Icky's" birthday, Eisenhower sent flowers to Mamie. Steven E. Ambrose, *Soldier, General of the Army, President-Elect, 1890–1952*, vol. 1 of *Eisenhower* (New York: Simon and Schuster, 1983), 75.

56. Robert Caro, quoted in Span, "Monumental Ambition."

57. See Werner Forman and Stephen Quirke, *Hieroglyphs and the Afterlife in Ancient Egypt* (Norman: University of Oklahoma Press, 1996).

58. For a discussion of the life cycles of presidential libraries, see Donald W. Wilson, "Presidential Libraries: Developing to Maturity," *Presidential Studies Quarterly* 21, no. 4 (Fall 1991): 771–780.

59. David McCullough, *Truman* (New York: Simon and Schuster, 1992). This book was a best seller during the 1992 presidential campaign between Republican incumbent George Bush and Democratic challenger Bill Clinton. Bush's advisors suggested that the president read the portion of McCullough's book dealing with Truman's come-from-behind incumbent victory. Bush's campaign then attempted to re-create Truman's whistle-stop campaign, even using part of the train Truman used. According to Raymond Geselbracht, "the simulation was unsuccessful because in America in the 1990s almost no one knows where

the train station is—so few people travel that way today. In 1948, almost everyone traveled by train, and in Truman's campaign he was able to talk to almost 10% of Americans by train. The Clinton campaign, on the other hand, read the book as a metaphorical rather than literal model, and used a bus that could stop anywhere to meet people, which was more successful." Raymond Geselbracht, personal communication, 14 June 1995.

60. Raymond Geselbracht, personal communication, 14 June 1995.

61. Ibid.

62. Maurice Halbwachs, *On Collective Memory*, ed. and trans. Lewis A. Coser (Chicago: University of Chicago Press, 1992), 176, 182.

63. Catherine L. Albanese, *America: Religions and Religion*, 3d ed. (New York: Wadsworth Publishing, 1999), 449.

64. Penelope J. E. Davies, *Death and the Emperor: Roman Imperial Funerary Monuments from Augustus to Marcus Aurelius* (Cambridge: Cambridge University Press, 2000), 15.

BIBLIOGRAPHY

Abbott, Philip. *Strong Presidents: A Theory of Leadership.* Knoxville: University of Tennessee Press, 1996.

Adams, Henry. *Thomas Hart Benton: An American Original.* New York: Knopf, 1989.

Adams, William Y. *The Philosophical Roots of Anthropology.* Stanford, Calif.: CSLI, 1998.

Aiken, Roger Cushing. "Paintings of Manifest Destiny: Mapping the Nation." *American Art* 14, no. 3 (Fall 2000): 78–90.

Albanese, Catherine L. *America: Religions and Religion.* 3d ed. New York: Wadsworth Publishing, 1999.

———. *Sons of the Fathers: Civil Religion of the American Revolution.* Philadelphia: Temple University Press, 1976.

Alsobrook, David E. "The Birth of the Tenth Presidential Library: The Bush Presidential Materials Project, 1993–1994." *Government Information Quarterly* 12, no. 1 (1995): 33–41.

Alter, Stephen G. *Darwinism and the Linguistic Image: Language, Race, and Natural Theology in the Nineteenth Century.* Baltimore: Johns Hopkins University Press, 1999.

Ambrose, Steven E. *Soldier, General of the Army, President-Elect, 1890–1952.* Vol. 1 of *Eisenhower.* New York: Simon and Schuster, 1983.

Anderson, Patricia. *Promoted to Glory: The Apotheosis of George Washington.* Northhampton, Mass.: Smith College Museum of Art, 1980.

Annual Report for the Smithsonian Institution for the Year 1955. Washington, D.C.: Smithsonian Institution, 1955.

Anon. "Aid to Ex-Presidents: How Much Is Too Much?" *New York Times,* 29 April 1986, A18.

———. "Dedication of the Hayes Memorial Library." *Ohio Archaeological and Historical Quarterly* 25, no. 4 (October 1916): 401–484.

———. "First Lady's Inaugural Ball Gown Is to Join Collection." *Washington Post, Times Herald,* 11 November 1962, F8.

———. "Gallup Poll: Clinton Popularity at an All Time Low." 9 March 2001, www.cnn.com/2001/ALLPOLITICS/03/09/clinton/popularity.

———. "Gowns of History." *Washington Post, Times Herald,* 23 May 1954, S4.

———. "Improving Impressions: Time Tempers Take on Bill Clinton." 22 June 2004, abcnews.go.com/sections/us/Polls/clinton_poll_040622.html.

———. "Jefferson's 200th." *Time Magazine,* 12 April 1943.

———. "Johnson Library in Repair Fight." *New York Times,* 22 July 1973, 45.

———. "Plan for Jefferson Memorial Is under Attack." *New York Times,* 8 April 1937, 2.

———. "Rayburn Praised as Library Opens; Speaker Hailed by Truman and Others at Dedication Ceremonies in Texas." *New York Times,* 10 October 1957, 22.

———. "Reagan Asked to Support Presidential Library Bill." *New York Times,* 30 March 1985, 8.

———. "Remembering LBJ." *Newsweek,* 24 May 1971, 25.

———. "Roosevelt Estate to House Archives, Go to Public Later." New York Times, 11 December 1938, 1.

———. [Sam Rayburn's library]. Washington Post, 17 January 1965, F10.

———. "Teacher's Guide to the White House Decision Center." White House Decision Center, Harry S. Truman Library, 2001.

———. "Through the Looking Glass." Chicago Tribune, 1 November 1893, 9.

———. White House Decision Center video, Harry S. Truman Library, 2002.

Anthony, Carl Sferrazza. First Ladies: The Saga of the Presidents' Wives and Their Power, 1789–1961. New York: Quill, 1990.

Applebome, Peter. "Carter Center: More Than the Past." New York Times, 30 May 1993, XX9.

———. "Could the Old South Be Resurrected? Cherished Ideas of the Confederacy (Not Slavery) Find New Backers. Revisiting the Ideas of the Confederate South." New York Times, 7 March 1998, B9.

Ariès, Philippe. Western Attitudes towards Death. Translated by Patricia Ranum. Baltimore: Johns Hopkins University Press, 1974.

Arnebeck, Bob. Through a Fiery Trial: Building Washington, 1790–1800. New York: Madison Books, 1991.

Asbell, Bernard. When FDR Died. New York: Holt, Rinehart, and Winston, 1961.

Ashabranner, Brent. No Better Hope: What the Lincoln Memorial Means to America. Brookfield, Conn.: Twenty-first Century Books, 2001.

Ashcroft, Bill, Gareth Griffiths, and Helen Tiffin, eds. The Post-Colonial Studies Reader. London: Routledge, 1995.

Badinter, Elisabeth. On Masculine Identity. Translated by Lydia Davis. New York: Columbia University Press, 1995.

Baigell, Matthew. Thomas Hart Benton. New York: Abrams, 1974.

Bailey, F. G. Stratagems and Spoils: A Social Anthropology of Politics. 1969. Reprint with postscript, Boulder, Colo.: Westview, 2001.

Bailyn, Bernard. The Ideological Origins of the American Revolution. Cambridge, Mass.: Belknap, 1971.

Bailyn, Bernard, ed. The Debate on the Constitution: Federalist and Antifederalist Speeches, Articles, and Letters during the Struggle over Ratification. Parts 1–2. New York: Library of America, 1993.

Bal, Mieke, Jonathan Crewe, and Leo Spitzer, eds. Acts of Memory: Cultural Recall in the Present. Hanover, N.H.: Dartmouth College, 1999.

Baldwin, Lewis V., with Rufus Burrow, Jr., Barbara A. Holmes, and Susan Holmes Winfield. The Legacy of Martin Luther King, Jr.: The Boundaries of Law, Politics, and Religion. Notre Dame, Ind.: University of Notre Dame Press, 2002.

Balibar, Etienne, and Immanuel Wallerstein. Race, Nation and Class: Ambiguous Identities. Translated by Chris Turner. London: Verso, 1991.

Banham, Reyner. Age of the Masters: A Personal View of Modern Architecture. 2d ed. New York: Harper and Row, 1975.

———. Los Angeles: The Architecture of Four Ecologies. London: Penguin, 1971.

———. "The New Brutalism." In A Critic Writes: Essays by Reyner Banham, selected by Mary Banham et al., pp. 7–15. Berkeley: University of California Press, 1996.

Barnes, Ruth, and Joanne B. Eichner, eds. *Dress and Gender: Making and Meaning of Cultural Contexts.* Oxford: Berg, 1992.

Barry, Joseph. *Passions and Politics: A Biography of Versailles.* Garden City, N.Y.: Doubleday, 1972.

Barthes, Roland. *Camera Lucida: Reflections on Photography.* Translated by Richard Howard. New York: Noonday Press, 1981.

Bassanese, Lynn. "The Franklin D. Roosevelt Library: Looking to the Future." *Government Information Quarterly* 12, no. 3 (1995): 103–112.

Baudrillard, Jean. *Simulacra and Simulation.* Translated by Sheila Faria Glaser. Ann Arbor: University of Michigan Press, 1994.

———. *The System of Objects.* Translated by James Benedict. New York: Verso, 1996.

Becker, Mary A., Polly Willman, and Noreen C. Tuross. "The U.S. First Ladies Gowns: A Biochemical Study of Silk Preservation." *Journal of the American Institute for Conservation* 34, no. 2 (1995): 141–152.

Bederman, Gail. *Manliness and Civilization: A Cultural History of Gender and Race in the United States, 1880–1917.* Chicago: University of Chicago Press, 1995.

Belair, Felix, Jr. "Roosevelt Mocks Third-Term Talk, Dedicates Library." *New York Times,* 20 November 1939, 1.

Belk, Russell W. *Collecting in a Consumer Society.* London: Routledge, 1995.

Bellah, Robert N. "Civil Religion in America." *Daedalus, Journal of the American Academy of Arts and Sciences* 96, no. 1 (Winter 1967): 1–21.

Benjamin, Walter. *Illuminations.* Edited by Hannah Arendt and translated by Harry Zohn. New York: Schocken, 1969.

Benton, Thomas Hart. *An Artist in America.* 4th rev. ed., with afterword by Matthew Baigell. Columbia: University of Missouri Press, 1983.

———. *Independence and the Opening of the West.* Independence, Mo.: Harry S. Truman Library and Museum, 1974.

Berger, Maurice, Brian Wells, and Simon Watson, eds. *Constructing Masculinities.* London: Routledge, 1995.

Berger, Robert W. *In the Garden of the Sun King: Studies on the Park of Versailles under Louis XIV.* Washington, D.C.: Dumbarton Oaks Research, 1985.

Bergland, Renée L. *The National Uncanny: Indian Ghosts and American Subjects.* Hanover, N.H.: University Press of New England, 2000.

Berkhofer, Robert F., Jr. *The White Man's Indian: Images of the American Indian from Columbus to the Present.* New York: Knopf, 1978.

Berlo, Janet. *The Early Years of Native American Art History: The Politics of Scholarship and Collecting.* Seattle: University of Washington Press, 1992.

Bernstein, Fred A. "Archive Architecture: Setting the Spin in Stone." *New York Times,* 10 June 2004, F1, F9.

———. "Who Should Pay for Presidential Posterity." *New York Times,* 10 June 2004, D1.

Bernstein, Irving. *Guns or Butter: The Presidency of Lyndon Johnson.* Oxford: Oxford University Press, 1996.

Beschloss, Michael. *Taking Charge: The Johnson White House Tapes, 1963–64.* New York: Simon and Schuster, 1997.

Beschloss, Michael, ed. *Reaching for Glory: Lyndon Johnson's Secret White House Tapes,
    1964–1965.* New York: Simon and Schuster, 2001.

Betsky, Aaron. *Building Sex: Men, Women, Architecture, and the Construction of Sexuality.*
    New York: Morrow, 1995.

Bishop, Carl Whiting, C. G. Abbot, and Ales Hrdlicka. *Man from the Farthest Past.* 1930.
    Reprint, Smithsonian Scientific Series, vol. 7, edited by Charles Greeley Abbott.
    New York: Smithsonian Institution Series, 1934.

Blanchard, Pascal, Nicolas Bancel, and Sandrine Lemaine. "From Human Zoos to
    Colonial Apotheoses: The Era of Exhibiting the Other." www.africultures.com/
    anglais/ articles_anglais/43blanchard.htm. Accessed 14 May 2005.

Blaser, Roy P., ed. *The Collected Works of Abraham Lincoln.* New Brunswick, N.J.: Rutgers
    University Press, 1953.

Bloch, Ruth H. "The Gendered Meanings of Virtue in Revolutionary America." *Signs:
    Journal of Women in Culture and Society* 13, no. 1 (1987): 37–58.

Bloomer, Dexter C. *Life and Writings of Amelia Bloomer.* 1895. Reprint, with new
    introduction by Susan J. Kleinberg, New York: Shocken, 1975.

Bodnar, John. *Remaking America: Public Memory, Commemoration, and Patriotism in the
    Twentieth Century.* Princeton, N.J.: Princeton University Press, 1992.

Borroughs, Polly. *Thomas Hart Benton: A Portrait.* Garden City, N.Y.: Doubleday, 1981.

Bowen, Catherine Drinker. *Miracle at Philadelphia: The Story of the Constitution, May to
    September 1787.* New York: Little, Brown, 1966.

Bowles, Hamish, ed. *Jacqueline Kennedy: The White House Years: Selections from the John F.
    Kennedy Library and Museum.* New York: Metropolitan Museum of Art, 2001.

Bowling, Kenneth R. *The Creation of Washington, D.C.: The Idea and Location of the National
    Capital.* Fairfax, Va.: George Mason University Press, 1991.

Boylan, Timothy S. "War Powers, Constitutional Balance, and The Imperial
    Presidency Idea at Century's End." *Presidential Studies Quarterly* 29, no. 2 (June 1999):
    232–249.

Brigham, David R. *Public Culture in the Early Republic: Peale's Museum and Its Audience.*
    Washington, D.C.: Smithsonian Institution Press, 1995.

Brinkley, Douglas. *The Unfinished Presidency: Jimmy Carter's Journey beyond the White House.*
    New York: Penguin Books, 1999.

Brookhiser, Richard. *Founding Father: Rediscovering George Washington.* New York: Free
    Press, 1996.

Brown, Glenn. "The Lincoln Memorial in Washington, D.C., Part II: The Design."
    American Architect 118 (27 October 1920): 522–539.

Brown, Kathleen M. *Good Wives, Nasty Wenches, and Anxious Patriarchs: Gender, Race, and
    Power in Colonial Virginia.* Chapel Hill: University of North Carolina Press, 1996.

Brown, Margaret W. *Dresses of the First Ladies of the White House.* Washington, D.C.:
    Smithsonian Institution, 1952.

———. *The First Ladies Hall.* Washington, D.C.: Smithsonian Institution, 1955. See
    also Klapthor, Margaret Brown.

Buck, Elizabeth H. "General Legislation for Presidential Libraries." *American Archivist*
    18, no. 4 [1955]: 337.

Bullock, Steven C. *Revolutionary Brotherhood: Freemasonry and the Transformation of the American Social Order, 1730–1840*. Chapel Hill: University of North Carolina Press, 1996.

Burcaw, G. Ellis. *Introduction to Museum Work*. 3d ed. Walnut Creek, Calif.: AltaMira Press, 1997.

Burns, James MacGregor. *Roosevelt: The Soldier of Freedom, 1940–1945*. New York: Harcourt Brace Jovanovich, 1970.

Buscombe, Edward, ed. *The BFI Companion to the Western*. New York: De Capo Press, 1988.

Bush, George. *Heartbeat: George Bush in His Own Words*. Compiled and edited by Jim McGrath. New York: Scribners, 2001.

Bush, George, and Brent Scowcroft. *A World Transformed*. New York: Knopf, 1998.

Butler, Judith. *Bodies That Matter: On the Discursive Limits of Sex*. London: Routledge, 1993.

Butterfield, L. H., Marc Friedlaender, and Richard Alan Ryerson, eds. *Adams Family Correspondence*. Cambridge, Mass.: Harvard University Press, 1963–1973.

Caemmerer, H. Paul. *The Life of Pierre Charles L'Enfant, Planner of the City Beautiful, the City of Washington*. Washington, D.C.: National Republic Publishing, 1950.

Calloway-Thomas, Carolyn, and John Louis Lucaites, eds. *Martin Luther King, Jr., and the Sermonic Power of Public Discourse*. Tuscaloosa: University of Alabama Press, 1993.

Cameron, Elisabeth L. *Isn't S/he a Doll?: Play and Ritual in African Sculpture*. Los Angeles: UCLA Fowler Museum of Cultural History, 1996.

Cannell, Michael. *I. M. Pei: Mandarin of Modernism*. New York: Carol Southern Books, 1995.

Cannon, Lou. *Governor Reagan: His Rise to Power*. New York: Public Affairs, 2003.

Cappon, Lester J. "The National Archives and the Historical Profession." *Journal of Southern History* 35 (November 1964): 491.

Carey, James W. *Communication as Culture: Essays on Media and Society*. Boston: Unwin Hyman, 1988.

Carmichael, Leonard, and J. C. Long. *James Smithson and the Smithsonian Story*. New York: Putnam's Sons, 1965.

Carnes, Mark C., and Clyde Griffen, eds. *Constructions of Manhood in Victorian America*. Chicago: University of Chicago Press, 1990.

Caro, Robert A. *The Years of Lyndon Johnson*. 4 vols. New York: Knopf, 1982–2002.

Carroll, J. A., and M. W. Ashworth. *First in Peace*. Vol. 7 of *George Washington: A Biography*, originally begun by D. S. Freeman. New York: Scribners, 1951–1957.

Carter, Edward C., II, ed. *Journals of Benjamin Henry Latrobe*. New Haven, Conn.: Yale University Press, 1977.

Carter, Rosalynn. *First Lady from Plains*. Boston: Houghton Mifflin, 1984.

Cartwright, Gary. "The L.B.J. Library: The Life and Times of Lyndon Johnson in Eight Full Stories." *New York Times*, 17 October 1971, XXI.

Castronovo, Russ. *Fathering the Nation: American Genealogies of Slavery and Freedom*. Berkeley: University of California Press, 1995.

Certeau, Michel de. *The Practice of Everyday Life*. Translated by Steven Rendall. Berkeley: University of California Press, 1984.

Champagne, Anthony. *Congressman Sam Rayburn*. New Brunswick, N.J.: Rutgers University Press, 1984.

Cherniavska, Eva. *That Pale Mother Rising: Sentimental Discourses and the Imitation of Mothering in Nineteenth Century America*. Bloomington: Indiana University Press, 1995.

Cladis, Mark S. *Public Vision, Private Lives: Rousseau, Religion, and 21st-Century Democracy*. Oxford: Oxford University Press, 2003.

Clawson, Mary Ann. *Constructing Brotherhood: Class, Gender and Fraternalism*. Princeton, N.J.: Princeton University Press, 1989.

Clendinen, Dudley. "Ex-Presidents Compete for History's Attention with Libraries." *New York Times*, 13 October 1985, 30.

Clifford, Clark. *Counsel to the President: A Memoir, with Richard Holbrooke*. New York: Random House, 1991.

Clifford, James, George E. Marcus, and Sidney E. Mead, eds. *Writing Culture: The Poetics and Politics of Ethnography*. Berkeley: University of California Press, 1986.

Clinton, Bill. *My Life*. New York: Alfred A. Knopf, 2004.

———. "Speech by President at WJC Presidential Center." 9 December 2000, www.clintonpresidentialcenter.org/legacy/120900.

Clotworthy, William G. *Homes and Libraries of the Presidents: An Interpretive Guide*. 2d ed. Blacksburg, Va.: McDonald and Woodward, 2003.

Cochrane, Lynn Scott. "The Presidential Library System: A Quiescent Policy Subsystem." Ph.D. diss., Virginia Polytech Institute and State University, 1998.

Cole, Douglas. *Franz Boas: The Early Years, 1858–1906*. Seattle: University of Washington Press, 1999.

Coles, Roberta L. "Manifest Destiny Adapted for 1990s' War Discourse: Mission and Destiny Intertwined." *Sociology of Religion* 63, no. 4 (Winter 2002): 403–426.

Collier, Christopher, and James Lincoln Collier. *Decision in Philadelphia: The Constitutional Convention of 1787*. New York: Ballantine Books, 1986.

Conroy, Sarah Booth. "First Ladies' Special Lady." *Washington Post*, 10 October 1994, B3.

———. "Going, Going, Gown; First Ladies Exhibit May Travel to Dallas." *Washington Post*, 17 August 1997, 1.

Cooper, James Fenimore. *The Last of the Mohicans: A Narrative of 1757*. 1826. Reprint, edited by James F. Beard, Albany: SUNY Press, 1980.

Corkin, Stanley. "Cowboys and Freemarkets: Post–World War II Westerns and U.S. Hegemony." *Cinema Journal* 39, no. 3 (2000): 66–91.

Cowan, Tyler. *What Price Fame?* Cambridge, Mass.: Harvard University Press, 2000.

Crane, Sylvia E. *White Silence: Greenough, Powers, and Crawford, American Sculptors in Nineteenth-Century Italy*. Coral Gables, Fla.: University of Miami Press, 1972.

Cresson, Margaret French. *Journey into Fame: The Life of Daniel Chester French*. Cambridge, Mass.: Harvard University Press, 1947.

Crimp, Douglas. *On the Museum's Ruins*. With photographs by Louise Lawler. Cambridge, Mass.: MIT Press, 1993.

Cristi, Marcela. *From Civil to Political Religion: The Intersection of Culture, Religion and Politics*. Waterloo, Ontario: Wilfred Laurier University Press, 2001.

Curl, James Stevens. *Egyptomania: The Egyptian Revival: A Recurring Theme in the History of Taste*. New York: Manchester University Press, 1994.

Daellenbach, Dennis A. "The Ronald Reagan Presidential Library." *Government Information Quarterly* 11, no. 4 (1994): 23–36.

Dallek, Robert. *Flawed Giant: Lyndon Johnson and His Times, 1961–1973.* New York: Oxford University Press, 1998.

———. *Lyndon B. Johnson: Portrait of a President.* New York: Oxford University Press, 2004.

Dalzell, Robert E., and Lee Baldwin Dalzell. *George Washington's Mount Vernon: At Home in Revolutionary America.* New York: Oxford University Press, 1998.

Davidson, James West. *To 1877.* Vol. 1 of *Nation of Nations: A Concise Narrative of the American Republic.* 3d ed. Boston: McGraw-Hill, 2002.

Davies, Penelope J. E. *Death and the Emperor: Roman Imperial Funerary Monuments from Augustus to Marcus Aurelius.* Cambridge: Cambridge University Press, 2000.

Davis, Mary B., ed. *Native America in the Twentieth Century: An Encyclopedia.* New York: Garland Publishing, 1994.

Dean, David. *Museum Exhibition: Theory and Practice.* London: Routledge, 1994.

DeConde, Alexander. *Presidential Machismo: Executive Authority, Military Intervention, and Foreign Relations.* Boston: Northeastern University Press, 2000.

The Dedication of Washington National Monument. Washington, D.C.: Government Printing Office, 1885.

De la Haye, Amy, and Elizabeth Wilson, eds. *Defining Dress: Dress as Object, Meaning and Identity.* Manchester, Eng.: Manchester University Press, 1999.

Demillo, Andrew. "Donations to Clinton Library up 78% in '03." *Arkansas Democrat-Gazette,* 14 July 2004.

———. "New Library to Pave Way for Tourism, Officials Say Clinton Site to Offer LR 'Untapped Market.'" *Arkansas Democrat-Gazette,* 25 July 2003.

———. "Study: Clinton Library Impact at Least $8.65 Million a Year." *Arkansas Democrat-Gazette,* 4 June 2004.

Derrida, Jacques. *Archive Fever: A Freudian Impression.* Translated by Eric Prenowitz. Chicago: University of Chicago Press, 1996.

Dippie, Brian. *The Vanishing American: White Attitudes and U.S. Indian Policy.* Lawrence: University Press of Kansas, 1991.

Divine, Robert A. *America: Past and Present.* 3d ed. New York: HarperCollins, 1991.

Donald, David Herbert. *Lincoln.* New York: Simon and Schuster, 1995.

Dorsey, George A. *Traditions of the Skidi Pawnee.* New York: Houghton Mifflin, 1904.

Doss, Erika. *Benton, Pollock, and the Politics of Modernism: From Regionalism to Abstract Expressionism.* Chicago: University of Chicago Press, 1991.

———. *Elvis Culture: Fans, Faith, and Image.* Lawrence: University Press of Kansas, 1999.

———. "Introduction: Looking at *Life*: Rethinking America's Favorite Magazine, 1936–1972." In *Looking at Life Magazine,* edited by Erika Doss, 1–21. Washington, D.C.: Smithsonian Institution Press, 2001.

———. *Spirit Poles and Flying Pigs: Public Art and Cultural Democracy in American Communities.* Washington, D.C.: Smithsonian Institution Press, 1995.

Douglass, Frederick. *Life and Times.* Edited by Henry Louis Gates. New York: Library of America, 1994.

Dumenil, Lynn. *Freemasonry and American Culture, 1880–1930.* Princeton, N.J.: Princeton University Press, 1984.

Elsner, John, and Roger Cardinal. *The Cultures of Collecting.* Cambridge, Mass.: Harvard University Press, 1994.

Etlin, Richard A. *The Architecture of Death: The Transformation of the Cemetery in Eighteenth-Century Paris.* Cambridge, Mass.: MIT Press, 1984.

Euing, Charles. *Yesterday's Washington, D.C.* Miami: Seemann, 1976.

Fabian, Johannes. *Time and the Other: How Anthropology Makes Its Objects.* New York: Columbia University Press, 1983.

Fairclough, Adam. *Martin Luther King, Jr.* Athens: University of Georgia Press, 1995.

Falassi, Alessandro. "Festival: Definition and Morphology." In *Time Out of Time: Essays on the Festival,* edited by Alessandro Falassi, pp. 1–7. Albuquerque: University of New Mexico Press, 1987.

Fenn, Richard K. *Beyond Idols: The Shape of a Secular Society.* Oxford: Oxford University Press, 2001.

Ferrand, Max, ed. *Records of the Federal Convention of 1787.* 2d ed. 3 vols. New Haven, Conn.: Yale University Press, 1937.

Ferris, John C. "Access to the Opening Salvos of Franklin D. Roosevelt: The Opening Salvo." Manuscript, Franklin D. Roosevelt Library, [1989].

Fiedler, Leslie A. *The Return of the Vanishing Americans.* New York: Stein and Day, 1968.

Finkelstein, Joanne. *The Fashioned Self.* Philadelphia: Temple University Press, 1991.

Finley, David Edward. *A Standard of Excellence: Andrew W. Mellon Founds the National Gallery of Art in Washington.* Washington, D.C.: Smithsonian Institution, 1973.

Fitzpatrick, John C., ed. *The Writings of George Washington.* Washington, D.C.: Government Printing Office, 1931–1944.

Fixico, Donald L. *Termination and Relocation: Federal Indian Policy, 1945–1960.* Albuquerque: University of New Mexico Press, 1986.

Fletcher, George P. *Our Secret Constitution: How Lincoln Redefined American Democracy.* New York: Oxford University Press, 2001.

Flexner, James Thomas. *George Washington.* Vols. 1–4. Boston: Little, Brown, 1965–1972.

Fliegelman, Jay. *Prodigals and Pilgrims: The American Revolution against Patriarchal Authority, 1750–1800.* Cambridge: Cambridge University Press, 1982.

Foote, Kenneth. *Shadowed Ground: America's Landscapes of Violence and Tragedy.* Austin, University of Texas Press, 2003.

Ford, Betty, and Chris Chase. *The Times of My Life.* New York: Harper and Row, 1978.

Forgie, George B. *Patricide in the House Divided: A Psychological Interpretation of Lincoln and His Age.* New York: Norton, 1979.

Forman, Werner, and Stephen Quirke. *Hieroglyphs and the Afterlife in Ancient Egypt.* Norman: University of Oklahoma Press, 1996.

Forrest, Elizabeth Kellam de. *The Gardens and Grounds at Mount Vernon.* Mount Vernon, N.Y.: Mount Vernon Ladies Association of the Union, 1982.

Foster, Hal. *Recodings: Art, Spectacle, Cultural Politics.* Port Townsend, Wash.: Bay Press, 1985.

Foucault, Michel. *Madness and Civilization.* Translated by Richard Howard. New York: Pantheon, 1965.

———. *The Order of Things: An Archaeology of the Human Sciences.* New York: Pantheon, 1970.

Fowler, Robert Booth. *Dance with Community: The Contemporary Debate in American Political Thought.* Lawrence: University Press of Kansas, 1991.

Fox, Steven. *The Architecture of Philip Johnson.* New York: Bullfinch, 2002.

Frady, Marshall. *Martin Luther King, Jr.* New York: Viking, 2002.

Frank, Stephen M. *Life with Father: Parenthood and Masculinity in the Nineteenth Century American North.* Baltimore: Johns Hopkins University Press, 1998.

Fraser, Douglas, and H. M. Cole, eds. *African Art and Leadership.* Madison: University of Wisconsin Press, 1972.

Freeman, D. S. *George Washington: A Biography.* New York: Scribners, 1951–1957.

Freidel, Frank. *Franklin D. Roosevelt: A Rendezvous with Destiny.* New York: Little, Brown, 1990.

———. "Roosevelt to Reagan: The Birth and Growth of Presidential Libraries." *Prologue: Quarterly of the National Archives* 21 (Summer 1989): 106.

Freud, Sigmund. *Totem and Taboo.* Translated by James Strachey. New York: Norton, 1950.

Fryd, Vivien Green. *Art and Empire: The Politics of Ethnicity in the U.S. Capitol, 1815–1860.* New Haven, Conn.: Yale University Press, 1992.

Furst, Peter T., and Jill L. Furst. *North American Indian Art.* New York: Rizzoli, 1982.

Gabor, Andrea. "Even Our Most Loved Monuments Had a Trial by Fire." *Smithsonian* 28, no. 2 (May 1997): 96–109.

Garber, Daniel. *Descartes' Metaphysical Physics.* Chicago: University of Chicago Press, 1992.

Garrett, Wendell. *George Washington's Mount Vernon.* New York: Monacelli Press, 1998.

Gaukroger, Stephen. *Descartes: An Intellectual Biography.* Oxford: Clarendon Press, 1995.

Geer, Emily Apt. *First Lady: The Life of Lucy Webb Hayes.* Kent, Ohio: Kent State University Press, 1983.

Gelles, Edith B. *Portia: The World of Abigail Adams.* Bloomington: Indiana University Press, 1992.

Giles, David. *Illusions of Immortality: A Psychology of Fame and Celebrity.* New York: St. Martin's, 2000.

Gill, Brendan. *Many Masks: A Life of Frank Lloyd Wright.* New York: Putnam, 1987.

Gillette, Howard, Jr. *Between Justice and Beauty: Race, Planning, and the Failure of Urban Policy in Washington, D.C.* Baltimore: Johns Hopkins University Press, 1995.

Gillis, John R., ed. *Commemorations: The Politics of National Identity.* Princeton, N.J.: Princeton University Press, 1994.

Godwin, Edward William. *Dress, and Its Relation to Health and Climate.* London: W. Clowes and Sons, 1884.

Gondos, Victor, Jr. *J. Franklin Jameson and the Birth of the National Archives, 1906–1926.* Philadelphia: University of Pennsylvania Press, 1981.

Goodwin, Doris Kearns. *No Ordinary Time: Franklin and Eleanor Roosevelt: The Home Front in World War II.* New York: Simon and Schuster, 1994.

Gould, Lewis L. *Lady Bird Johnson: Our Environmental First Lady.* Lawrence: University Press of Kansas, 1999.

———. *The Modern American Presidency.* Lawrence: University Press of Kansas, 2003.

Gould, Lewis L., ed. *American First Ladies: Their Lives and Their Legacy.* 2d ed. London: Routledge, 2001.

Green, Constancy M. *Washington: Village and Capital*. Princeton, N.J.: Princeton University Press, 1962.

Gregg, Gary L., II. *The Presidential Republic: Executive Representation and Deliberative Democracy*. Lanham, Md.: Rowman and Littlefield, 1997.

Grubin, David. FDR, PBS documentary, 1994.

Hackman, Lawrence. "Presidential Libraries: A Background Paper on Their Museums and Their Public Programs." Princeton: Princeton University Center for Arts and Cultural Policy Studies, December 2004.

———. "A Presidential Library Partnership: The Harry S. Truman Library and the Harry S. Truman Library Institute for National and International Affairs." Unpublished document, Harry S. Truman Library, February 2002.

Halberstam, David. "The Vantage Point." *New York Times*, 31 October 1971, BR1.

Halbwachs, Maurice. *On Collective Memory*. Edited and translated by Lewis A. Coser. Chicago: University of Chicago Press, 1992.

———. *The Collective Memory*. Translated by Francis J. Ditter, Jr., and Vina Yadzi Ditter. New York: Harper and Row, 1980.

Halio, Jay L., ed. *Critical Essays on Shakespeare's* King Lear. New York: Hall, 1996.

Hamilton, Alexander. The Papers of Alexander Hamilton. Edited by Harold C. Syrett et al. 27 vols. New York: Columbia University Press, 1961–1987.

Harvey, Frederick L. *History of the Washington National Monument and of the Washington National Monument Society*. Washington, D.C.: Norman Elliot Printing, 1902.

Hass, Kristin Ann. *Carried to the Wall: American Memory and the Vietnam Veterans Memorial*. Berkeley: University of California Press, 1998.

Hawkins, Mike. *Social Darwinism in European and American Thought, 1860–1945: Nature as Model and Nature as Threat*. Cambridge: Cambridge University Press, 1997.

Hayes, Rutherford B. *The Diary of a President, 1875–1881*. Edited by T. Harry Williams. New York: McKay, 1964.

Henderson, Amy, and Adrienne L. Kaeppler, eds. *Exhibiting Dilemmas: Issues of Representation at the Smithsonian*. Washington, D.C.: Smithsonian Institution Press, 1997.

Henretta, James A. *America's History*. New York: Worth Publishers, 1993.

Hersch, Seymour. *The Price of Power: Kissinger in the Nixon White House*. New York: Summit, 1982.

Hersh, Burton. *The Mellon Family: A Fortune in History*. New York: William Morrow, 1978.

Hinsley, Curtis M., Jr. *Savages and Scientists: The Smithsonian Institution and the Development of American Anthropology, 1846–1910*. Washington, D.C.: Smithsonian Institution Press, 1981.

———. "The World as Marketplace: Commodification of the Exotic at the World's Columbian Exposition, Chicago, 1893." In *Exhibiting Cultures: The Poetics and Politics of Museum Display*, edited by Ivan Karp and Steven D. Lavine, pp. 344–365. Washington, D.C.: Smithsonian Institution Press, 1991.

Hodge, Jonathan, and Gregory Radick, eds. *The Cambridge Companion to Darwin*. Cambridge: Cambridge University Press, 2003.

Hodgetts, Professor. *Anglo-Saxon Dress and Food: A Lecture Delivered in the Lecture Room of the Exhibition, June 27th, 1884.* London: W. Clowes and Sons, 1884.

Hoes, Rose Gouverneur. *Catalog of American Historical Costumes, Including Those of the Mistresses of the White House as Shown in the United States National Museum.* Washington, D.C.: Waverly Press, 1915.

———. *The Dresses of the Mistresses of the White House as Shown in the United States National Museum.* Washington, D.C.: Historical Publishing Company, 1931.

———. "When the Apparel Proclaimed the Man in America." *Washington Post,* 8 November 1914, SM1.

Holliday, Peter J. *The Origins of Roman Historical Commemoration in the Visual Arts.* Cambridge: Cambridge University Press, 2002.

Hoogenboom, Ari. *Rutherford B. Hayes: Warrior and President.* Lawrence: University Press of Kansas, 1995.

Hooper-Greenhill, Eilean. *Museums and the Shaping of Knowledge.* London: Routledge, 1992.

Horrocks, David A. "Access and Accessibility at the Gerald R. Ford Library." *Government Information Quarterly* 11, no. 4 (1994): 47–66.

Hosmer, Charles B., Jr. *Presence of the Past: A History of the Preservation Movement in the United States before Williamsburg.* New York: Putnam's Sons, 1965.

Hudnut, Joseph. "Twilight of the Gods." *Magazine of Art* (August 1937): 480–484.

Hughes, Clair. "The Color of Life: The Significance of Dress in The Portrait of a Lady." *Henry James Review* 18, no. 1 (1997): 66–80.

Hughes, Robert. *American Visions: The Epic History of Art in America.* New York: Knopf, 1997.

Hutton, Patrick H. *History as an Art of Memory.* Hanover, N.H.: University Press of New England, 1993.

Huxtable, Ada Louise. "Kennedy Family Announces Selection of Pei to Design Library." *New York Times,* 14 December 1964, 1.

———. "Selling the President, Architecturally." *New York Times,* 30 September 1973, 31,148.

———. "A Success as Architecture and as Monument." *New York Times,* 23 May 1971, 39.

Hyland, Pat. *Presidential Libraries and Museums: An Illustrated Guide.* Washington, D.C.: Congressional Quarterly, 1995.

Inglis, Fred. *Clifford Geertz: Culture, Custom and Ethics.* Cambridge, Eng.: Polity Press, 2000.

Jabour, Anya. *Marriage in the Early Republic: Elizabeth and William Wirt and the Compassionate Ideal.* Baltimore: Johns Hopkins University Press, 1998.

Jaffa, Harry V. *Crisis of the House Divided: An Interpretation of the Issues in the Lincoln-Douglas Debates.* Garden City, N.Y.: Doubleday, 1959.

———. *A New Birth of Freedom: Abraham Lincoln and the Coming of the Civil War.* Lanham, Md.: Rowman and Littlefield, 2000.

James, Henry. *Novels, 1881–1886: Washington Square, The Portrait of a Lady, The Bostonians.* New York: Library of America, 1985.

James, Mrs. Julian. Foreword, in Rose Gouverneur Hoes, *Catalog of American Historical Costumes, Including Those of the Mistresses of the White House as Shown in the United States National Museum.* Washington, D.C.: Waverly Press, 1915.

Jefferson, Thomas. *Writings*. Selected and edited by Merrill D. Peterson. New York: Library of America, 1984.

Jenkins, David. "Object Lessons and Ethnographic Displays: Museum Exhibitions and the Making of American Anthropology." *Comparative Studies in Society and History* 36 (1994): 242–270.

Johnson, Gerald W., and Charles Cecil Wall. *Mount Vernon: The Story of a Shrine*. New York: Random House, 1953.

Johnson, Lady Bird. *A White House Diary*. New York: Holt, Rinehart, and Winston, 1970.

Johnson, Lyndon Baines. *The Vantage Point: Perspectives of the Presidency, 1963–1969*. New York: Holt, Rinehart, and Winston, 1971.

Johnson, Paul E., and Sean Wilentz. *The Kingdom of Matthias: The Story of Sex and Salvation in 19th-Century America*. Oxford: Oxford University Press, 1994.

Jojola, Theodore S. "Public Image." In *Native America in the Twentieth Century: An Encyclopedia*, edited by Mary B. Davis. New York: Garland, 1994.

Jones, David R. "New Presidential Library: Johnson Calls for the Best." *New York Times*, 30 October 1968, 49.

Jules Guerin: Master Delineator. Exhibition catalog. Houston: Rice University School of Architecture, 1983.

Kammen, Michael. *In the Past Lane: Historical Perspectives on American Culture*. New York: Oxford University Press, 1997.

———. *A Machine That Would Go of Itself: The Constitution in American Culture*. New York: Knopf, 1986.

———. *Mystic Chords of Memory: The Transformation of Tradition in American Culture*. New York: Vintage, 1991.

Karin, Marcy Lynn. "Out of Sight But Not Out of Mind: How Executive Order 13,233 Expands Executive Privilege While Simultaneously Preventing Access to Presidential Records." *Stanford Law Review* 55 (2002–2003): 529–570.

Karp, Ivan, Christine Mullen Kreamer, and Steven D. Lavine. *Museums and Communities: The Politics of Public Culture*. Washington, D.C.: Smithsonian Institution Press, 1992.

Karp, Ivan, and Steven D. Lavine, eds. *Exhibiting Cultures: The Poetics and Politics of Museum Display*. Washington, D.C.: Smithsonian Institution Press, 1991.

Katz, Stanley. "Museums in Presidential Libraries: A First Report on Policies, Practices and Performance." Princeton: Princeton University Center for Arts and Cultural Policy Studies, December 2004.

Keenan, William J. F., ed. *Dressed to Impress: Looking the Part*. Oxford: Berg, 2001.

Keller, Ulrich. *Highway as Habitat*. Santa Barbara, Calif.: University Art Museum, 1986.

Kemp, Gérald van der. *Versailles*. London: Sotheby Publications, 1978.

Kertzer, David I. *Ritual, Politics, and Power*. New Haven, Conn.: Yale University Press, 1988.

Kidwell, Claudia Brush, and Valerie Steele, eds. *Men and Women: Dressing the Part*. Washington, D.C.: Smithsonian Institution Press, 1989.

Kimbrell, Andrew. *Masculine Mystique: The Politics of Masculinity*. New York: Ballantine, 1995.

King, J. C. H. *Smoking Pipes of the North American Indian*. London: British Museum Publications, 1977.

King, Martin Luther, Jr. *I Have a Dream: Writings and Speeches That Changed the World.*
Edited by James Melvin Washington. San Francisco: Harper, 1992.
————. *A Testament to Hope: The Essential Writings and Speeches of Martin Luther King, Jr.*
Edited by James Melvin Washington. 1986. Reprint, San Francisco: Harper, 1991.
King, Wayne. "Carter Redux." *New York Times,* 10 December 1989, SM38.
Kite, Elizabeth S. *L'Enfant and Washington.* Baltimore: Johns Hopkins University Press,
1929.
Klapthor, Margaret Brown. "Benjamin Latrobe and Dolley Madison Decorate the
White House." *Contributions from the Museum of History and Technology,* Paper 49.
Washington, D.C: Smithsonian Institution Press, 1965.
————. *The First Ladies Hall.* Washington, D.C.: Smithsonian Institution, 1965.
————. *The First Ladies Hall.* Washington, D.C.: Smithsonian Institution Press, 1973.
————. *Official White House China, 1789 to the Present.* Washington, D.C.: Smithsonian
Institution Press, 1975. *See also,* Brown, Margaret.
Knowlton, John D. "Properly Arranged and So Correctly Recorded." *American Archivist*
(July 1969).
Koch, Cynthia M., and Lynn A. Bassanese. "Roosevelt and His Library." *Prologue:*
Quarterly of the National Archives and Records Administration 33 (Summer 2001): 75–84.
Kochmann, Rachel M. *Presidents: A Pictorial Guide to the Presidents' Birthplaces, Homes, and*
Burial Sites. 9th ed. Osage, Minn.: Osage Publications, 1994.
Koonz, Claudia. "Between Memory and Oblivion: Concentration Camps in German
Memory." In *Commemorations: The Politics of a National Identity,* edited by John R.
Gillis, pp. 258–280. Princeton, N.J.: Princeton University Press, 1994.
Kopper, Philip. *America's National Gallery: A Gift to the Nation.* New York: Abrams, 1991.
Koshar, Rudy J. "Building Pasts: Historic Preservation and Identity in Twentieth-
Century Germany." In *Commemorations: The Politics of National Identity,* edited by John
R. Gillis, pp. 215–238. Princeton, N.J.: Princeton University Press, 1994.
————. *Germany's Transient Pasts: Preservation and National Memory in the Twentieth*
Century. Chapel Hill: University of North Carolina Press, 1998.
Kostof, Spiro. *A History of Architecture: Settings and Rituals.* New York: Oxford University
Press, 1995.
Krinsky, Carol Herselle. *Gordon Bunshaft of Skidmore, Owings & Merrill.* New York: MIT
Press, 1988.
Kronenfeld, Judy. *King Lear and the Naked Truth: Rethinking the Language of Religion and*
Resistance. Durham, N.C.: Duke University Press, 1998.
Kurin, Richard. *Reflections of a Culture Broker.* Washington, D.C.: Smithsonian
Institution Press, 1997.
Kurtz, Donald V. *Political Anthropology: Power and Paradigms.* Boulder, Colo.: Westview, 2001.
Lablaude, Pierre-André. *The Gardens of Versailles.* London: Zwemmer Publishers, 1995.
Laderman, Gary. "Managing and Imagining the Dead: A Cultural History of Death
in Nineteenth-Century America." Ph.D. diss., University of California at Santa
Barbara, 1994.
Lantzer, Jason S. "The Public History of Presidential Libraries: How the Presidency Is
Presented to the People." *Journal of the Association for History and Computing* 6, no. 1 (April

2003). http://mcel.pacificu.edu/JAHC/JAHCVl1/ARTICLES/lantzer/lantzer.html. Accessed 21 May 2003.

Laqueur, Thomas W. "Memory and Naming in the Great War." In *Commemorations: The Politics of a National Identity*, edited by John R. Gillis, pp. 150–167. Princeton, N.J.: Princeton University Press, 1994.

Leopold, Richard W. "The Historian and the Federal Government." *Journal of American History* 64 (June 1977): 11–14.

Lescaze, William. "America Is Outgrowing Imitation Greek Architecture." *Magazine of Art* 37 (June 1937): 366–369.

Lessoff, Alan. *The Nation and Its City: Politics, "Corruption," and Progress in Washington, D.C., 1861–1902*. Baltimore: Johns Hopkins University Press, 1994.

Leuchtenburg, William E. *Franklin D. Roosevelt and the New Deal, 1932–1940*. New York: Harper Colophon Books, 1963.

Levinson, Nancy, and William S. Saunders, eds. "Constructions of Memory." *Harvard Design Magazine* (Fall 1999): 2–83.

Lévi-Strauss, Claude. *Tristes tropiques*. Translated by John Weightman and Doreen Weightman. New York: Viking Penguin, 1992.

Limerick, Patricia Nelson, Clyde A. Milner, and Charles E. Rankin, eds. *Trails: Toward a New Western History*. Lawrence: University Press of Kansas, 1991.

Lincoln, Abraham. *Selected Speeches and Writings*. Selected and edited by Don F. Fehrenbacher, with introduction by Gore Vidal. New York: Vintage Books, 1992.
——— . *Speeches and Writings, 1859–1865*. Selected and edited by Don F. Fehrenbacher. New York: Library of America, 1989.

Linenthal, Edward T. *Preserving Memory: The Struggle to Create America's Holocaust Museum*. New York: Viking, 1995.

Liscombe, Rhordri. *Altogether American*. New York: Oxford University Press, 1994.

Loewen, James W. *Lies My Teacher Told Me: Everything Your American History Textbook Got Wrong*. New York: Touchstone, 1995.

Lowe, Donald M. *History of Bourgeois Perception*. Chicago: University of Chicago Press, 1982.

Lubar, Steven, and Kathleen M. Kendrick. *Legacies: Collecting America's History at the Smithsonian*. Washington, D.C.: Smithsonian Institution Press, 2001.

Lubin, David M. *Picturing a Nation: Art and Social Change in Nineteenth-Century America*. New Haven, Conn.: Yale University Press, 1994.

Luce, Henry. "The American Century." *Life Magazine*, 1941. Reprinted as a booklet, New York: Time, 1941.

Luke, Timothy W. "Museum Pieces: The Politics of Aesthetics and Knowledge at the Museum." Third Annual Arlington Humanities Colloquium, University of Texas–Arlington, April 12, 1997, www.edde.vt.edu/tim/tims/Tim530.htm.

MacCannell, Dean. *The Tourist: A New Theory of the Leisure Class*. 2d ed. New York: Schocken Books, 1989.

MacDonald, Sharon, ed. *The Politics of Display: Museums, Science, Culture*. London: Routledge, 1998.

Mackaman, Frank H. "Human Drama: Presidential Museums Tell the Story." *Prologue: Quarterly of the National Archives* 21 (Summer 1989): 134.

Maddox, Lucy. *Removals: Nineteenth Century American Literature and the Politics of Indian Affairs*. Oxford: Oxford University Press, 1991.

Madison, James. "Federalist Paper 17." *Federalist Papers*. New York: New American Library, 1961.

Malone, Dumas. *Jefferson and His Time*. 6 vols. Boston: Little, Brown, 1948–1981.

Man, Linda. "Truman Library Has More Than a New Look." *Kansas City Star*, 26 February 2001, A1.

Marcus, George E. "Law in the Development of Dynastic Families among American Business Elites: The Domestication of Capital and the Capitalization of Family." *Law and Society Review* 14 (1980): 859–903.

Marcus, George E., and Michael M. J. Fischer. *Anthropology as Cultural Critique: An Experimental Movement in the Social Sciences*. Chicago: University of Chicago Press, 1986.

Marin, Louis. *Portrait of the King*. Translated by Martha M. Houle. Minneapolis: University of Minnesota Press, 1988.

Marino, Cesare. "Reservations." In *Native America in the Twentieth Century: An Encyclopedia*. Edited by Mary B. Davis. New York: Garland, 1994.

Marling, Karal Ann. *As Seen on T.V.: The Visual Culture of Everyday Life in the 1950s*. Cambridge, Mass.: Harvard University Press, 1994.

———. "Disneyland, 1955: Just Take the Santa Ana Freeway to the American Dream." *American Art* 5, nos. 1–2 (Winter/Spring 1991): 190–201.

———. *Tom Benton and His Drawings: A Biographical Essay and a Collection of His Sketches, Studies, and Mural Cartoons*. Columbia: University of Missouri Press, 1985.

Marshall, P. David. *Celebrity and Power: Fame in Contemporary Culture*. Minneapolis: University of Minnesota Press, 1997.

Marton, Kati. *Hidden Power: Presidential Marriages That Shaped Our Recent History*. New York: Pantheon, 2001.

Mattingly, Carol. *Appropriate[ing] Dress: Women's Rhetorical Style in Nineteenth-Century America*. Carbondale and Edwardsville, Ill.: Southern Illinois University Press, 2002.

Mayo, Edith P., ed. *The Smithsonian Book of the First Ladies: Their Lives, Times, and Issues*. New York: Henry Holt, 1996.

Mayo, Edith, and Denise D. Meringolo. *First Ladies: Political Role and Public Image*. Washington, D.C.: Smithsonian Institution, 1994.

Mayr, Otto. *Authority, Liberty and Automatic Machinery in Early Modern Europe*. Baltimore: Johns Hopkins University Press, 1986.

McClellan, Andrew. *Inventing the Louvre: Art, Politics, and the Origins of the Modern Museum in Eighteenth Century Paris*. Cambridge: Cambridge University Press, 1994.

McCoy, Donald R. "The Beginnings of the Franklin D. Roosevelt Library." *Prologue* (Fall 1975): 137–150.

———. *The National Archives: America's Ministry of Documents, 1934–1968*. Chapel Hill: University of North Carolina Press, 1978.

McCullough, David. *John Adams*. New York: Simon and Schuster, 2001.

———. *Truman*. New York: Simon and Schuster, 1992.

McDannell, Colleen. *Material Christianity: Religion and Popular Culture in America*. New Haven, Conn.: Yale University Press, 1995.

McLaughlin, Jack. *Jefferson and Monticello: The Biography of a Builder*. New York: Holt, 1990.

McLendon, Winzola. "First Lady Mannequins Acquire a Lively Look." *Washington Post, Times Herald*, 18 November 1962, F17.

McLuhan, Marshall. *Understanding Media: The Extensions of Man*. Cambridge, Mass.: MIT Press, 1994.

McNamara, Robert S., and Brian VanDeMark. *In Retrospect: The Tragedy and Lessons of Vietnam*. New York: Times Books, 1995.

McPherson, James M. *"We Cannot Escape History": Lincoln and the Last Best Hope of Earth*. Urbana: University of Illinois Press, 1995.

McTavish, Brian. "This Truman Campaign Is on Billboards." *Kansas City Star*, 14 March 2001, F1.

Mead, Sidney E. *The Nation with the Soul of a Church*. New York: Harper and Row, 1975.

—————. *The Old Religion in the Brave New World*. Berkeley: University of California Press, 1977.

Melder, Keith. *Beginnings of Sisterhood: The American Women's Rights Movement*. New York: Schocken Books, 1977.

Meyer, Jeffrey J. *Myths in Stone: Religious Dimensions of Washington, D.C.* Berkeley: University of California Press, 2001.

Michaels, Walter Benn. *Our America: Nativism, Modernism and Pluralism*. Durham, N.C.: Duke University Press, 1995.

Middleton, Harry. *LBJ: The White House Years*. New York: Abrams, 1990.

Miller, Keith D. *Voice of Deliverance: The Language of Martin Luther King, Jr., and Its Sources*. New York: Free Press, 1992.

Miller, Nathan. *FDR: An Intimate History*. New York: Doubleday, 1983.

Miller, William Lee. *Lincoln's Virtues: An Ethical Biography*. New York: Knopf, 2002.

Miroff, Bruce. "The Presidency and the Public: Leadership as Spectacle." In *The Presidency and the Political System*, edited by Michael Nelson. 6th ed. Washington, D.C.: Congressional Quarterly Press, 2000.

Montebello, Philippe de. *The Metropolitan Museum of Art Guide*. 2d ed. New York: Metropolitan Museum of Art, 1994.

Montgomery, Bruce P. "Nixon's Ghost Haunts the Presidential Records Act: The Reagan and George W. Bush Administrations." *Presidential Studies Quarterly* 32, no. 4 (December 2002): 789–809.

Morgan, Ted. *FDR: A Biography*. New York: Simon and Schuster, 1985.

Morris, Edwin Bateman. *Report of the Commission on the Renovation of the Executive Mansion*. Washington, D.C.: Government Printing Office, 1952.

Morris, Richard. *Sinners, Lovers, and Heroes: An Essay on Memorializing in Three American Cultures*. New York: SUNY Press, 1997.

Morris, William. *Textile Fabrics: A Lecture Delivered in the Lecture Room of the Exhibition, July 11th, 1884*. London: printed and published for the Executive Council of the International Health Exhibition, and for the Council of the Society of Arts by William Clowes and Sons, 1884.

Morse, Jedidiah. *American Geography; or, A View of the Present Situation of the United States of America*. Elizabethtown, N.J., 1789. Printed by Shepard Kollock for the author.

Mosier, Richard D. *The American Temper: Patterns of Our Intellectual Heritage*. Berkeley: University of California Press, 1952.

Mount Vernon Ladies' Association of the Union. *Mount Vernon and Its Preservation: 1858–1919*. New York: Knickerbocker Press, 1932.

Muensterberger, Werner. *Collecting, an Unruly Passion: Psychological Perspectives*. Princeton, N.J.: Princeton University Press, 1994.

Murie, James R. *Ceremonies of the Pawnee*, parts 1 and 2. Washington, D.C.: Smithsonian Institution Press, 1981.

Naulty, Susan. "Creating an Archives at the Richard Nixon Library and Birthplace." *Government Information Quarterly* 11, no. 1 (1994): 37–46.

Neely, Mark E., Jr. *The Fate of Liberty: Abraham Lincoln and Civil Liberties*. Oxford: Oxford University Press, 1991.

Nelson, Dana D. *National Manhood: Capitalist Citizenship and the Imagined Fraternity of White Men*. Durham, N.C.: Duke University Press, 1998.

Nelson, Michael, ed. *The Presidency and the Political System*. 6th ed. Washington, D.C.: CQ Press, 2000.

Neustadt, Richard E. *Presidential Power and the Modern Presidents: The Politics of Leadership from Roosevelt to Reagan*. New York: Free Press, 1990.

Newton, Joseph Fort. *The Builders: A Story and Study of Freemasonry*. New York: Macoy Publishing, 1930.

Newton, Stella Mary. *Health, Art and Reason: Dress Reformers of the 19th Century*. London: Murray, 1974.

Nietzsche, Friedrich. *The Use and Abuse of History*. Translated by Adrian Collins, with an introduction by Julius Kraft. Indianapolis: Bobbs-Merrill, 1957.

Nieuwnhuijze, C. A. O. van. *The Nation and the Ideal City: Three Studies in Social Identity*. The Hague: Mouton, 1966.

Nora, Pierre. "Between Memory and History: Les Lieux de Mémoire." *Representations* 26 (Spring 1989): 7–24.

Nora, Pierre, ed. *Realms of Memory: The Construction of the French Past*. Translated by Arthur Goldhammer. Vol. 1, *Conflicts and Divisions*, vol. 2, *Traditions*, vol. 3, *Symbols*. New York: Columbia University Press, 1996–1998.

"Office of Presidential Libraries Briefing Book." Washington, D.C.: Office of Presidential Libraries, National Archives and Records Administration, 2003.

Ong, Walter J. *Orality and Literacy: The Technologizing of the Word*. London: Methuen, 1982.

Onuf, Peter S. *Jefferson's Empire: The Language of American Nationhood*. Charlottesville: University Press of Virginia, 2000.

O'Reilly, Kenneth. *Nixon's Piano: Presidents and Radical Politics from Washington to Clinton*. New York: Free Press, 1995.

Owings, Nathaniel Alexander. *The Spaces in Between: An Architect's Journey*. Boston: Houghton Mifflin, 1973.

Padover, Saul K., ed. *Thomas Jefferson and the National Capital: 1783–1818*. Washington, D.C.: Government Printing Office, 1946.

Page, Thomas Nelson. *Mount Vernon and Its Preservation, 1858–1910*. New York: Knickerbocker, 1932.

Paludan, Phillip Shaw. *The Presidency of Abraham Lincoln*. Lawrence: University Press of Kansas, 1994.

Parkins, Wendy. *Fashioning the Body Politic: Dress, Gender, Citizenship*. Oxford: Berg, 2002.

Parmentier, Richard J. *Signs in Society: Studies in Semiotic Anthropology*. Bloomington: Indiana University Press, 1994.

Parry, Benita. "Problems in Current Theories of Colonial Discourse." In *Post-Colonial Studies Reader*, edited by Bill Ashcroft, Gareth Griffiths, and Helen Tiffin, pp. 36–44. London: Routledge, 1995.

Parsons, Gerald. *Perspectives on Civil Religion*. Aldershot, Eng., and Burlington, Vt.: Ashgate, in association with the Open University, 2002.

Peets, Elbert. *On the Art of Designing Cities: Selected Essays of Elbert Peets*. Edited by Paul D. Spreiregen. Cambridge, Mass.: MIT Press, 1968.

Penley, Constance. *NasaTrek: Popular Science and Popular Sex in America*. New York: Verso, 1997.

Peterson, Merrill D. *Lincoln in American Memory*. New York: Oxford University Press, 1994.

Peterson, Merrill D., ed. *Thomas Jefferson: Writings*. New York: Library of America, 1984.

Pierard, Richard V., and Robert D. Linder. *Civil Religion and the Presidency*. Grand Rapids, Mich.: Academy Books, 1988.

Pika, Joseph A., John Anthony Maltese, and Norman C. Thomas. *The Politics of the Presidency*. 5th ed. Washington, D.C.: Congressional Quarterly Press, 2002.

Plante, Ellen M. *Women at Home in Victorian America: A Social History*. New York: Facts on File, 1997.

Pommier, Édouard. "Versailles: The Image of the Sovereign." In *Realms of Memory*, edited by Pierre Nora, vol. 3, pp. 293–324. New York: Columbia University Press, 1998.

Powers of the Presidency. 2d ed. Washington, D.C.: *Congressional Quarterly*, 1997.

Price, S. R. F. *Rituals and Power: The Roman Imperial Cult in Asia Minor*. Cambridge: Cambridge University Press, 1984.

Reagan, Ronald. *Ronald Reagan: An American Life*. New York: Pocket Books, 1999.

Reeves, Richard. "Hiding History." *American Heritage* 53, no. 4 (August/September 2002): 64–67.

———. *President Nixon: Alone in the White House*. New York: Simon and Schuster, 2000.

Reilly, Michael F. *Reilly of the White House*. New York: Simon and Schuster, 1947.

Relyea, Harold C. "The Federal Presidential Library System." *Government Information Quarterly* 11, no. 4 (1994): 7–22.

Reps, John W. *Monumental Washington: The Planning and Development of a Capital Center*. Princeton, N.J.: Princeton University Press, 1967.

Richey, Russell E., and Donald G. Jones, eds. *American Civil Religion*. San Francisco: American Research University Press, 1990.

Richman, Michael. *Daniel Chester French: An American Sculptor*. New York: National Trust for Historic Preservation, 1976.

Riley, Russell L. *The Presidency and the Politics of Racial Inequality: Nation-Keeping from 1831 to 1965*. New York: Columbia University Press, 1999.

Robertson, Bruce. *Representing America: The Ken Trevey Collection of American Prints.* Santa Barbara, Calif.: University Art Museum, 1995.

Rogers, Everett M. *A History of Communication Study: A Biographical Approach.* New York: Free Press, 1994.

Rollins, Peter C., and John E. O'Connor, eds. *Hollywood's White House: The American Presidency in Film and History.* Lexington: University Press of Kentucky, 2003.

Rosenberg, Marvin. *The Masks of King Lear.* Berkeley: University of California Press, 1972.

Ross, Rodney A. "The National Archives of the United States: The Formative Years, 1934–1949." *Prologue* (Summer 1984): 106–123.

Rossilli, Ann B. "Interpretative Dioramas as Material Culture of Natural History Museums: A Case Study at the National Museum of Natural History." Master's thesis, University of Maryland, 2000.

Roth, William V., Jr. "Ex-Presidential Perks Are Way Out of Hand." *USA Today,* 28 March 1984.

Rouner, Leroy S., ed. *Civil Religion and Political Theology.* Notre Dame, Ind.: University of Notre Dame Press, 1986.

Rousseau, Jean-Jacques. *The Social Contract and the First and Second Discourses.* Edited and with an Introduction by Susan Dunn, with essays by Gita May, Robert N. Bellah, David Bromwich, and Conor Cruise O'Brian. New Haven: Yale University Press, 2002.

Ryan, Susan M. *The Grammar of Good Intentions: Race and the Antebellum Culture of Benevolence.* Ithaca, N.Y.: Cornell University Press, 2003.

Rydell, Robert W. *All the World's a Fair.* Chicago: University of Chicago Press, 1984.

Rydell, Robert W., John E. Findling, and Kimberly D. Pelle. *Fair America: World's Fairs in the United States.* Washington, D.C.: Smithsonian Institution Press, 2000.

Sadler, A. L. *A Short History of Japanese Architecture.* Rutland, Vt.: Tuttle, 1963.

Safire, William, ed. *Lend Me Your Ears: Great Speeches in History.* New York: Norton, 1992.

Sandage, Scott A. "A Marble House Divided: The Lincoln Memorial, the Civil Rights Movement, and the Politics of Memory, 1939–1963." *Journal of American History* 80 (June 1993): 135–187.

Savage, Kirk. "The Politics of Memory: Black Emancipation and the Civil War Monument." In *Commemorations: The Politics of National Identity,* edited by John R. Gillis. Princeton, N.J.: Princeton University Press, 1994, 127–149.

———. "The Self-Made Monument: George Washington and the Fight to Erect a National Memorial." In *Critical Issues in Public Art: Content, Context, and Controversy,* edited by Harriet Senie and Sally Webster, pp. 5–32. New York: HarperCollins, 1992.

———. *Standing Soldiers, Kneeling Slaves: Race, War, and Monument in Nineteenth-Century America.* Princeton, N.J.: Princeton University Press, 1997.

Schaefer, Peggy. *Presidential Homes and Libraries.* Nashville, Tenn.: Ideals Press, 2002.

Schaller, Thomas F., and Thomas W. Williams. "The Contemporary Presidency: Postpresidential Influence in the Postmodern Era." *Presidential Studies Quarterly* 33, no. 1 (March 2003): 188–201.

Scheckel, Susan. *The Insistence of the Indian: Race and Nationalism in Nineteenth-Century American Culture.* Princeton, N.J.: Princeton University Press, 1998.

Schewe, Donald B. "The Jimmy Carter Library." *Government Information Quarterly* 6, no. 3 (1989): 237–246.

———. "The Jimmy Carter Library: An Update." *Government Information Quarterly* 11, no. 4 (1994): 67–72.

Schick, Frank L., with Renee Schick and Mark Carroll. *Records of the Presidency: Presidential Papers and Libraries from Washington to Reagan.* Phoenix, Ariz.: Oryx Press, 1989.

Schlesinger, Arthur M., Jr. *The Age of Roosevelt: The Crisis of the Old Order.* Boston: Houghton Mifflin, 1957.

———. *The Age of Roosevelt: The Politics of Upheaval.* Boston: Houghton Mifflin, 1960.

———. *The Coming of the New Deal.* Boston: Houghton Mifflin, 1958.

———. *The Imperial Presidency.* With a new epilogue by the author. Boston: Houghton Mifflin, 1989.

Schlissel, Lillian. *Women's Diaries of the Westward Journey.* New York: Schocken, 1982.

Schmidt, William E. "Reshaped Carter Image Tied to Library Opening." *New York Times,* 21 September 1986, 24.

Schulze, Franz. *Philip Johnson: Life and Work.* New York: Knopf, 1994.

Schwartz, Barry. *Abraham Lincoln and the Forge of National Memory.* Chicago: University of Chicago Press, 2000.

Schwartz, Hillel. *The Culture of the Copy: Striking Likenesses, Unreasonable Facsimiles.* New York: Zone Books, 1996.

Seale, William. *The President's House: A History.* Washington, D.C.: National Geographic Society, 1986.

Sellers, Charles Coleman. *Charles Willson Peale: A Biography.* New York: Charles Scribners, 1969.

Serviss, Garret P. *San Antonio Light.* 1917. News service clipping, First Ladies Files, Smithsonian Archives.

Shackel, Paul A., ed. *Myth, Memory, and the Making of the American Landscape.* Gainesville: University Press of Florida, 2001.

Shapiro, Robert Y., Martha Joyntkumar, and Lawrence R. Jacobs, eds. *Presidential Power: Forging the Presidency for the Twenty-first Century.* New York: Columbia University Press, 2000.

Sharp, James Roger. *American Politics in the Early Republic: The New Nation in Crisis.* New Haven, Conn.: Yale University Press, 1993.

Shelley, Percy Bysshe. *Shelley's Poetry and Prose: Authoritative Texts,* Criticism. 2d ed. Selected and edited by Donald H. Reiman and Neil Fraistat. New York: W. W. Norton, 2002.

Sherman, Daniel J. "Art, Commerce, and the Production of Memory in France after World War I." In *Commemorations: The Politics of a National Identity,* edited by John R. Gillis, pp. 186–211. Princeton, N.J.: Princeton University Press, 1994.

Sherman, Daniel, and Irit Rogoff. *Museum Culture: Histories, Discourses, Spectacles.* Minneapolis: University of Minnesota Press, 1994.

Sherwood, Robert E. *Roosevelt and Hopkins: An Intimate History.* New York: Harper, 1948.

Shipman, Pat. *The Evolution of Racism: Human Difference and the Use and Abuse of Science.* New York: Simon and Schuster, 1994.

Short, Martin. *Inside the Brotherhood*. London: Grafton Books, 1989.

Shumaker, Ruth. "First Ladies on View at Smithsonian." *Washington Post, Times Herald*, 25 May 1955, 1.

Skoloff, Brian. "Clinton Library Gains Big Steel Structure." *Associated Press*, 27 January 2003.

Small, Alastair, and Duncan Fishwick, ed. "Subject and Ruler: The Cult of the Ruling Power in Classical Antiquity, Papers presented at the University of Alberta on April 13–15, 1994." *Journal of Roman Archaeology* 17 (supp. series) (1996).

Smith, Curt. *Windows on the White House: The Story of Presidential Libraries*. South Bend, Ind.: Diamond Communications, 1997.

Smith, Marie. "First Lady to Promote Great Society." *Washington Post*, 17 January 1965, F3, F8.

Smith, Richard Norton. "A Presidential Revival: How the Hoover Library Overcame a Mid-Life Crisis." *Prologue: Quarterly of the National Archives* 21 (Summer 1989): 115–116.

Smith, Shawn Michelle. *American Archives: Gender, Race, and Class in Visual Culture*. Princeton, N.J.: Princeton University Press, 1999.

Smith-Rosenberg, Carroll. *Disorderly Conduct: Visions of Gender in Victorian America*. Oxford: Oxford University Press, 1985.

Solnit, Rebecca. "The Struggle of Dawning Intelligence: On Monuments and Native Americans." *Harvard Design Magazine* (Fall 1999): 52–57.

Span, Paula. "Monumental Ambition: Presidential Libraries Are History and Hagiography, Archival Mother Lodes and Gift Shops Pushing Star-Spangled Dish Towels and 'Gippergear'—Are They Worth the $55 Million Taxpayers Spent Last Year to Maintain Them?" *Washington Post*, 17 February 2002, W24.

Stark, Steven. "Gap Politics." *Atlantic Monthly*, July 1996, 71–80.

Stein, Nathaniel E. "The Discarded Inaugural Address of George Washington." *Manuscripts* 10, no. 2 (Spring 1958).

Stevenson, David. *The Origins of Freemasonry: Scotland's Century, 1590–1710*. Cambridge: Cambridge University Press, 1988.

Stewart, Susan. *On Longing: Narratives of the Miniature, the Gigantic, the Souvenir, the Collection*. Baltimore: Johns Hopkins University Press, 1984.

Stokstad, Marilyn. *Art History*. 2d ed. New York: Abrams, 2002.

"Symposium on Presidential Libraries." *Government Information Quarterly* 11, no. 1 (1994): 7–72.

Tadgell, Christopher. *Japan: The Informal Contained*. London: Ellipsis, 2000.

Taliaferro, John. *Great White Fathers: The Story of the Obsessive Quest to Create Mount Rushmore*. New York: Public Affairs, 2002.

Teasley, Martin M. "No Signs of Mid-Life Crisis: The Eisenhower Library at Thirty-Something." *Government Information Quarterly* 12, no. 1 (1995): 83–92.

Thomas, Christopher Alexander. *The Lincoln Memorial and American Life*. Princeton, N.J.: Princeton University Press, 2002.

———. "The Lincoln Memorial and Its Architect, Henry Bacon (1866–1924)." Ph.D. diss., Yale University, 1990.

Thompson, Brian Chandler. "Making History: The Sitting Modern President and the National Archives." *Government Information Quarterly* 12, no. 1 (1995): 17–32.

Thorne, Tanis. *The Many Hands of My Relations: French and Indians on the Lower Missouri.* Columbia: University of Missouri Press, 1996.

Tocqueville, Alexis de. *Democracy in America.* 1840. Translated by George Lawrence. New York: Harper and Row, 1966.

Tort, Patrick. *Darwin and the Science of Evolution.* New York: Abrams, 2001.

Trefousse, Hans L. *Rutherford B. Hayes.* New York: Times Books, 2002.

Treuttner, William, ed. *The West as America: Reinterpreting Images of the Frontier.* Washington, D.C.: Smithsonian Institution Press, 1991.

True, Webster Prentiss. *The Smithsonian Institution.* 1929. Reprint, *Smithsonian Scientific Series,* vol. 1, edited by Charles Greeley Abbott. New York: Smithsonian Institution Series, 1934.

Truman, Harry. *Truman Speaks.* New York: Columbia University Press, 1960.

Truman, Margaret. *First Ladies.* New York: Random House, 1995.

Tucker, Robert C., ed. *The Marx-Engels Reader.* 2d ed. New York: Norton, 1978.

Turner, Frederick Jackson. "The Significance of the Frontier in American History." 1893. Republished in Frederick Jackson Turner, *The Frontier in American History.* New York: Holt, 1920.

Turner, Victor. *The Anthropology of Performance.* New York: PAJ, 1988.

Unger, Irwin, and Debi Unger. *LBJ: A Life.* New York: Wiley and Sons, 1999.

Upton, Dell. *Architecture in the United States.* New York: Oxford University Press, 1998.

Vale, Lawrence J. *Architecture, Power, and National Identity.* New Haven, Conn.: Yale University Press, 1992.

Vidal, Gore. *Inventing a Nation: Washington, Adams, Jefferson.* New Haven, Conn.: Yale University Press, 2003.

Walch, Timothy. "Reinventing the Herbert Hoover Presidential Library." *Government Information Quarterly* 12, no. 1 (1995): 113–125.

Waldron, Martin. "Nixon Hails Johnson Library at Dedication." *New York Times,* 23 May 1971, 1, 39.

Walker, John. *Self-Portrait with Donors: Confessions of a Collector.* Boston: Little, Brown, 1974.

Walpole, Horace. *Memoirs of the Reign of King George II.* London: Henry Colbert, 1847.

Walsh, Lawrence E. *Iran-Contra: The Final Report.* New York: Times Books, 1994.

Walton, Guy. *Louis XIV's Versailles.* New York: Viking, 1986.

Ward, Geoffrey C. *Before the Trumpet: Young Franklin Roosevelt, 1882–1905.* New York: Harper and Row, 1988.

———. *A First-Class Temperament: The Emergence of Franklin Roosevelt.* New York: Harper and Row, 1989.

———. "Future Historians Will Curse as Well as Praise Me." *Smithsonian* 20, no. 9 (December 1989): 58–69.

Warner, Robert M. *Diary of a Dream: A History of the National Archives Independence Movement, 1980–1985.* Metuchen, N.J.: Scarecrow Press, 1995.

Washington, George. *The Papers of George Washington.* Edited by W. W. Abbott et al. 11 vols. Charlottesville: University of Virginia Press, 1983–.

Washington, George. *Writings*. New York: Library of America, 1996.

Washington's Home and the Story of the Mount Vernon Ladies' Association of the Union. Washington, D.C.: Mount Vernon Ladies' Association, 1915.

Watson, Robert P. *First Ladies of the United States: A Biographical Dictionary*. Boulder, Colo.: Lynne Rienner, 2001.

Weems, Mason. *A History of the Life and Death, Virtues and Exploits of General George Washington*. 1809. Reprint, New York: Macy-Masius, 1927.

———. *The Life of Washington*. 1809. Edited by Peter S. Onuf. Armonk, N.Y.: Sharpe, 1996.

Weltfish, Gene. *The Lost Universe: Pawnee Life and Culture*. Lincoln: University of Nebraska Press, 1965.

West, Patricia. *Domesticating History: The Political Origins of America's House Museums*. Washington, D.C.: Smithsonian Institution Press, 1999.

The West Wing: The Official Companion. New York: Warner Brothers Worldwide Publishing and Pocket Books, 2002.

White, Hayden. *The Content of the Form: Narrative Discourse and Historical Representation*. Baltimore: Johns Hopkins University Press, 1987.

———. *Metahistory: The Historical Imagination in Nineteenth Century Europe*. Baltimore: Johns Hopkins University Press, 1975.

White, Ronald C., Jr. *Lincoln's Greatest Speech: The Second Inaugural*. New York: Simon and Schuster, 2002.

Wiber, Melanie G. *Erect Men, Undulating Women: The Visual Imagery of Gender, "Race" and Progress in Reconstructive Illustrations of Human Evolution*. Waterloo, Ontario: Wilfrid Laurier University Press, 1997.

Wick, Wendy C. *George Washington, An American Icon: The Eighteenth-Century Graphic Portraits*. Washington, D.C.: Barra Foundation, 1982.

Wieck, Carl F. *Lincoln's Quest for Equality: The Road to Gettysburg*. DeKalb: Northern Illinois University Press, 2002.

Wiener, Jon. *Professors, Politics, and Pop*. New York: Verso, 1991.

Williams, Charles R. *The Life of Rutherford Birchard Hayes: Nineteenth President of the United States*. 1914. Reprint, New York: Da Capo, 1971.

Williams, T. Harry. *Lincoln and His Generals*. New York: Knopf, 1952.

Wills, Gary. *Cincinnatus: George Washington and the Enlightenment*. Garden City, N.Y.: Doubleday, 1984.

———. *Lincoln at Gettysburg: The Words That Remade America*. New York: Simon and Schuster, 1992.

Wilson, Donald W. "Culture and Conflict: Defining the National Archives." *Government Information Quarterly* 13, no. 2 (1996): 187–194.

———. "Presidential Libraries: Developing to Maturity." *Presidential Studies Quarterly* 21, no. 4 (Fall 1991): 771–780.

———. "Presidential Records: Evidence for Historians or Ammunition for Prosecutors." *Government Information Quarterly* 14, no. 4 (1997): 339–349.

Wilson, John F. *Public Religion in American Culture*. Philadelphia: Temple University Press, 1979.

Wingfield, Lewis. *The History of English Dress: A Lecture Delivered in the Lecture Room of the Exhibition, June 24th, 1884*. London: W. Clowes and Sons, 1884.

————. *Notes on Civil Costume in England from the Conquest to the Regency, as Exemplified in the International Health Exhibition, South Kensington*. London: W. Clowes and Sons, 1884.

Winn, Kenneth H. *Exiles in a Land of Liberty: Mormons in America, 1830–1846*. Chapel Hill: University of North Carolina Press, 1989.

Winthrop, Robert C., and John W. Daniel. *The Dedication of the Washington National Monument*. Washington, D.C.: Government Printing Office, 1885.

Wiseman, Carter. *I. M. Pei: A Profile in American Architecture*. New York: Abrams, 1990.

Woestman, Kelly Alicia. "Mr. Citizen: Harry S. Truman and the Institutionalization of the Ex-Presidency." Ph.D. diss., University of North Texas, 1993.

Wonders, Karen. *Habitat Dioramas: Illusions of Wilderness in Museums of Natural History*. Uppsala, Sweden: Almqvist and Wiksell, 1993.

Wood, Gordon S. *The Radicalism of the American Revolution*. New York: Knopf, 1992.

Woodward, C. Vann. *Reunion and Reaction: The Compromise of 1877 and the End of Reconstruction*. Boston: Little, Brown, 1951.

Wright, Nathalia, ed. *Letters of Horatio Greenough*. Madison: University of Wisconsin Press, 1972.

Yamasaki, Minoru. *A Life in Architecture*. New York: Weatherhill, 1979.

Yates, Frances A. *The Art of Memory*. Chicago: University of Chicago Press, 1966.

Young, Bonnie. *A Walk through the Cloisters*. New York: Metropolitan Museum of Art, 1989.

INDEX